MW00992613

WOODSMITH CUSTOM WOODWORKING

Shop-Built Machines

SHOP SAFETY IS YOUR RESPONSIBILITY
Using hand or power tools improperly can result in
serious injury or death. Do not operate any tool until
you read the manual and understand how to operate
the tool safely. Always use all appropriate safety
equipment as well as the guards that come with your
tools and equipment and read the manuals that
accompany them. In some of the illustrations in this
book, the guards and safety equipment have been
removed only to provide a better view of the operation.
Do not attempt any procedure without using all
appropriate safety equipment or without ensuring that
all guards are in place. Neither August Home Publishing
Company nor Time-Life Books assume any responsibility
for any injury, damage or loss suffered as a result of
your use of the material, plans or illustrations
contained in this book.

WOODSMITH CUSTOM WOODWORKING

Shop-Built Machines

By the editors of *Woodsmith* magazine

CONTENTS

WOODSMITH CUSTOM WOODWORKING

Shop-Built Machines

Jig Saw Table

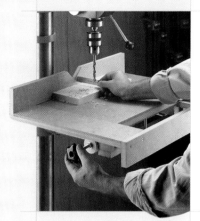

Drill Press Table

SHOP-BUILT MACHINES 74

Edge Sander

BENCHTOP MACHINES

ach machine in this section has a hand-held tool at its core. But that doesn't turn your tool into a "one-trick pony." You can still remove it from the project and use it handheld when needed. The machine just makes each tool more versatile so you can work more efficiently.

The first project lets you mount a jig saw upside-down under a sturdy table. With both hands free to hold and move the workpiece, you have greater control during complicated cuts. A ball-bearing guide system keeps the blade from flexing and wandering when working with thick stock.

Likewise, the plate joiner table takes a hand-held tool and mounts it in a table to free up your hands. Doing this eliminates the time-consuming process of clamping workpieces to a benchtop. Instead, just position the workpiece on the table, then step down on a foot pedal to cut a slot for a biscuit. The end result is that you can work faster.

And the next time you have a project that requires a lot of mortises, you will appreciate the convenience of our mortising machine. It eliminates all of the tedious drilling and chopping. Instead, mount your router in this shop-built machine, and you'll make quick work of cutting uniform mortises with smooth cheeks.

Jig Saw Table

A simple table and a unique adjustable arm convert your jig saw into a precision cutting tool. The key to that precision is a pair of rollers that keep the blade from wandering, even when cutting thick stock.

Take a good tool and make it better. That's the idea behind this Jig Saw Table. This shop-built table allows you to mount a portable jig saw upside down under the table. Reversing the saw like this has a number of advantages over using it in a hand-held position.

First, it provides a much more stable, controlled cut. That's because you push the workpiece through the blade on a large table instead of guiding the saw on a small base. And second, since the blade now cuts on the downstroke instead of the upstroke, the top side of the workpiece won't splinter and obscure the cut line. So it's easier to stay accurate when cutting.

GUIDE SYSTEM. But there's more to this table than just inverting your jig saw. It also has a unique guide system to prevent the blade from moving side to side. So even when making a curved cut, you end up with an edge that's perfectly square to the face. And adjusting the guide system can be done in just three simple steps. I'll show you how in the Setup box on page 13.

HOLD-DOWN. In addition to the guide system, there's a hold-down that keeps the workpiece flat against the table as you make a cut. And for safety, an acrylic plastic guard is attached to the hold-down to cover the blade, but keep it visible.

ADJUSTABLE ARM. To make both the guide system and hold-down work with pieces of different thicknesses, they're supported by an adjustable arm. This arm can be raised (or lowered) so you can cut workpieces up to 1" thick.

BASIC DESIGN. The Jig Saw Table works well because it's loaded with features. But if you don't use your jig saw quite as often, a simpler design might be called for. You'll find plans for a Basic Jig Saw Table in the Woodworker's Notebook starting on page 14. Its easy-to-build design still works great. But what's really great is that with fewer parts, you'll be able to build it in an afternoon.

EXPLODED VIEW

OVERALL DIMENSIONS:
18W x 27 1/4D x 16H

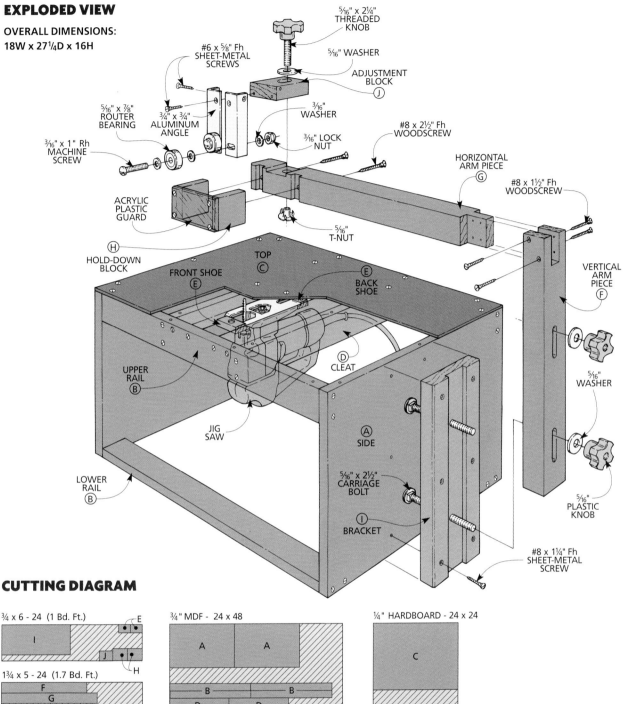

CUTTING DIAGRAM

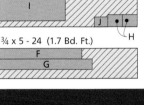

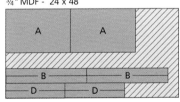

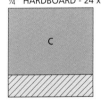

MATERIALS LIST

WOOD

A	Sides (2)	3/4 MDF - 11 3/4 x 18
B	Upper/Lower Rails (4)	3/4 MDF - 2 x 22 1/2
C	Top (1)	1/4 hdbd. - 18 x 24
D	Cleats (4)	3/4 MDF - 2 x 16 1/2
E	Front/Back Shoes (2)	3/4 x 1 3/8 - 2
F	Vertical Arm Piece (1)	1 3/4 x 1 3/4 - 14 1/2
G	Horizontal Arm Piece (1)	1 3/4 x 1 3/4 - 16 5/16
H	Hold-Down Blocks (2)	3/4 x 2 - 2 1/2
I	Bracket (1)	3/4 x 5 - 11 3/4
J	Adjustment Block (1)	3/4 x 1 5/8 - 2 3/8

HARDWARE SUPPLIES
- (2) No. 8 x 2 1/2" Fh woodscrews
- (4) No. 8 x 1 1/2" Fh woodscrews
- (2) No. 8 x 3/4" Fh woodscrews
- (32) No. 8 x 2" Fh sheet-metal screws
- (6) No. 8 x 1 1/4" Fh sheet-metal screws
- (28) No. 6 x 5/8" Fh sheet-metal screws
- (1) 5/16" x 1" Fh machine screw
- (2) 3/16" x 1" Rh machine screws
- (2) 5/16" x 2 1/2" carriage bolts
- (2) 5/16" T-nuts
- (2) 5/16" plastic knobs
- (1) 5/16" x 2 1/4" threaded knob
- (3) 5/16" washers
- (2) 3/4" x 3/4" - 3" aluminum angle
- (2) 5/16" x 7/8" router bearings
- (6) 3/16" flat washers
- (2) 3/16" lock nuts
- (1) 1/4"-thick acrylic plastic (2 1/2" x 3 5/8")

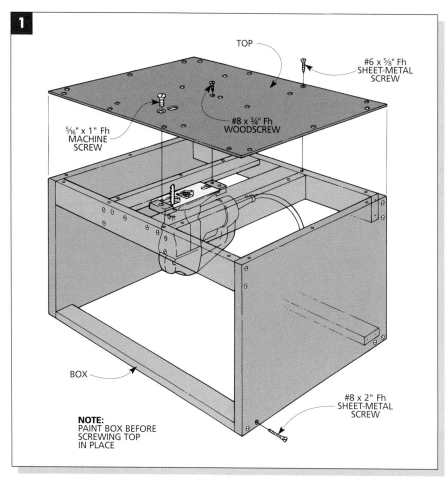

1

TOP

#6 x ⅝" Fh
SHEET-METAL
SCREW

#8 x ¾" Fh
WOODSCREW

⁵⁄₁₆" x 1" Fh
MACHINE
SCREW

BOX

#8 x 2" Fh
SHEET-METAL
SCREW

NOTE:
PAINT BOX BEFORE
SCREWING TOP
IN PLACE

BASE

I started on the Jig Saw Table by making the base. It consists of two parts: a box that's open at the front and back to house the jig saw, and a ¼" hardboard top that serves as a work surface *(Fig. 1)*.

BOX. Since I planned on painting the Jig Saw Table box, I made it from a material that has a durable, smooth surface —

medium-density fiberboard (MDF). But you could just as easily use plywood.

The ¾" MDF sides (A) of the box are held together with two lower and two upper rails (B) *(Fig. 2)*. The rails are also made with ¾" MDF. And although they are the exact same width and length, they're oriented differently.

To provide a solid clamping surface, each lower rail is screwed in place so its face will rest on the bench. And for strength, the upper rails are attached so the edges will support the top.

Note: To avoid splitting MDF when screwing into it, I like to use a sheet-metal screw with a straight shank (see the Shop Tip on the facing page).

TOP. With the box complete, the next step is to add the top (C) *(Fig. 3)*. It's just a piece of ¼" hardboard that's cut to fit flush with the outside edges of the box.

To create an opening for the saw blade, there's a short slot cut in the top *(Fig. 3a)*. Although this slot is centered on the length of the top, it's located closer to the front edge. This way, the body of the saw won't stick out the back of the box.

CLEATS. After screwing the top in place, the next step is to add two cleats. Besides providing additional support for the tabletop, these cleats form a pocket that accepts the metal base of the jig saw. Each cleat (D) is made by gluing up two pieces of ¾"-thick MDF into an L-shape *(Fig. 4)*. Once the glue dries, you'll need to use your jig saw to determine the location of the cleats.

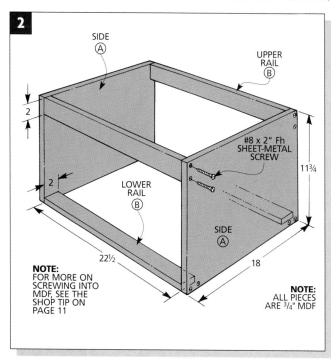

2

SIDE
Ⓐ

UPPER
RAIL
Ⓑ

2

#8 x 2" Fh
SHEET-METAL
SCREW

11¾

2

LOWER
RAIL
Ⓑ

SIDE
Ⓐ

22½

18

NOTE:
FOR MORE ON
SCREWING INTO
MDF, SEE THE
SHOP TIP ON
PAGE 11

NOTE:
ALL PIECES
ARE ¾" MDF

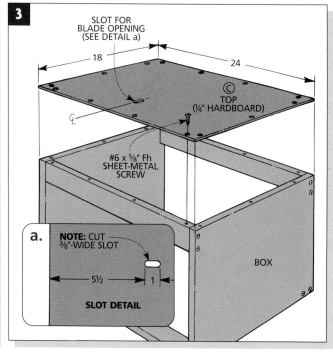

3

SLOT FOR
BLADE OPENING
(SEE DETAIL a)

18

24

Ⓒ
TOP
(¼" HARDBOARD)

₵

#6 x ⅝" Fh
SHEET-METAL
SCREW

BOX

a.

NOTE: CUT
⅜"-WIDE SLOT

5½

1

SLOT DETAIL

This is just a matter of flipping the table upside down and putting the jig saw in place with the blade centered in the slot. Then you can position the cleats so they fit tight against the saw base and simply screw them in place *(Fig. 4a)*.

PAINT. At this point, if you're planning to paint the box, it's easiest to remove the top. I sprayed on two coats of paint and reattached the top by screwing it to the box as well as the cleats *(Fig. 4)*.

MOUNTING THE SAW

With the base complete, you're ready to mount the saw. While the cleats keep the saw from moving side to side, you still need a way to secure the front and back of the metal base.

To lock the saw in place (yet still make it easy to take out and use as a hand-held), the base is secured with two "shoes" — a back shoe that's permanently attached and a front shoe that's removable (see photo at right).

BACK SHOE. The back shoe (E) is a $3/4$"-thick hardwood block with a rabbet cut in one edge so it fits tight over the base of the saw *(Fig. 5)*.

Note: Depending on the size of your saw's base, you may need to customize the length of the blocks and the height (depth) of the rabbets.

To attach the back shoe, the process is basically the same as with the cleats. Fit the saw between the cleats so the blade is centered in the slot, slip the shoe over the base, and screw it in place *(Fig. 5a)*.

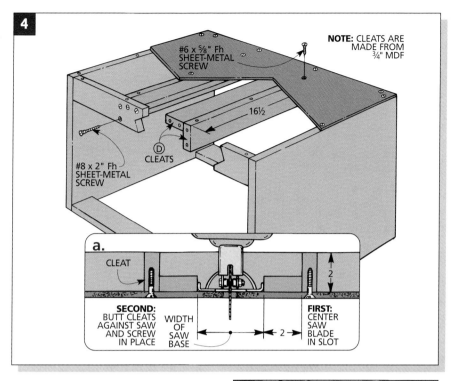

FRONT SHOE. The front shoe (E) is identical to the one in the back. If you have more than one jig saw, you could make the installation permanent and screw down the front shoe, but to make it easy to remove the saw, it's held in place with a machine screw that threads into a T-nut installed in the shoe.

MOUNT SAW. Now all that's left is to mount the saw to the table. This is just a matter of sliding the saw base under the back shoe and tightening down the front shoe to lock the saw to the table.

In addition to cleats that keep the saw from moving side to side, two blocks (or shoes) lock it in place.

SHOP TIP

Screws for MDF

To avoid splitting medium-density fiberboard (MDF), first drill pilot holes and use a sheet-metal screw with a straight shank. Now the shank is less likely to push out the sides of the MDF.

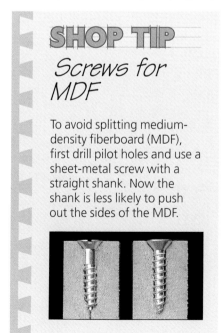

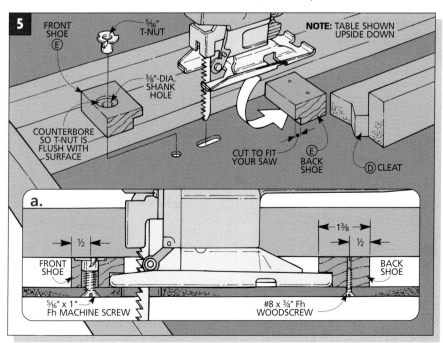

The unique thing about this Jig Saw Table is an adjustable wood arm that extends over the table. It consists of two parts: a vertical arm piece that slides up and down in a bracket, and a horizontal arm piece to support the hold-down and the blade guide system *(Fig. 6)*.

VERTICAL ARM. For strength, the vertical arm piece (F) is made from a 1¾" square hardwood block (I used maple) *(Fig. 6)*. A pair of slots cut in this piece make the arm adjustable. And an open mortise in the top end accepts the horizontal arm *(Fig. 6a)*.

HORIZONTAL ARM. Here again, the horizontal arm piece (G) is made from a 1¾"-square block (maple). The horizontal arm has a tenon cut on the end so it fits in the open mortise. But before assembling the two pieces, there are a couple of things to do.

NOTCH. First of all, there's a notch cut in the top side of the horizontal arm for the guide system added later *(Fig. 6b)*. A counterbored shank hole drilled in the center of this notch is used to attach the guide system (refer to *Fig. 9b*).

HOLD-DOWN. The second thing is to add the hold-down. In addition to keeping the workpiece from bouncing up and down as you make a cut, the hold-down has an acrylic plastic guard attached to it that covers the exposed blade.

The hold-down assembly consists of two ¾"-thick hardwood hold-down blocks (H) that fit in dadoes cut near the end of the horizontal arm *(Figs. 6 and 7)*. It's easiest to glue and screw the blocks in place first *(Fig. 7a)*. Then screw the acrylic plastic to the blocks.

ASSEMBLY. Now assemble the two arm pieces with glue and screws *(Fig. 6a)*.

Note: To prevent the screws from hitting each other, they're offset from one side to the other.

BRACKET. Once the arm is assembled, the next step is to add a bracket to the side of the table *(Fig. 6)*. In addition to holding the arm in place, the bracket tracks it straight up and down. This way, you won't have to readjust the guide system every time you reposition the arm.

The bracket (I) is a piece of ¾"-thick hardwood with a centered groove cut in it to fit the arm *(Fig. 8)*. Two carriage bolts pass through counterbored shank holes in the bracket (and slots cut in arm) to hold the arm *(Fig. 8b)*.

An easy way to locate these holes is to fit the arm into the bracket so the ends are

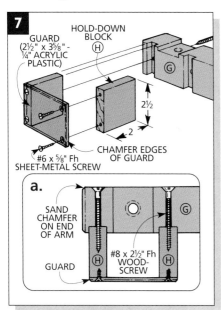

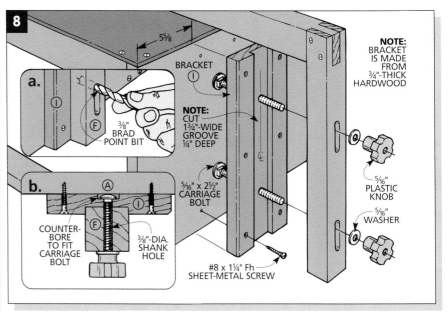

flush at the bottom *(Fig. 8a)*. Then just use a brad point bit to mark through the top end of each slot.

After drilling the holes, you can install the bolts and fasten the arm to the bracket with washers and plastic knobs (or wing nuts). Then simply screw this assembly to the side of the table *(Figs. 8 and 8b)*.

GUIDE SYSTEM. Once the arm is in place, you can add the blade guide system. To ensure a square cut, the blade guide system keeps the blade from deflecting to the side.

What makes this work is a pair of router bearings that track the blade straight up and down *(Fig. 9)*. (Bearings are available through woodworking suppliers, see Sources on page 126.) Each bearing is attached to a bracket cut from a piece of aluminum angle *(Fig. 9a)*.

To make the bearings adjustable from side to side, there's a slot cut in each bracket. And an ordinary wood block allows you to adjust them front to back.

This adjustment block (J) is a scrap of $3/4$"-thick hardwood with a slot cut in it. After screwing a bracket to each corner of the block, it's attached to the arm with a threaded knob and T-nut.

ASSEMBLY. The guide system is almost complete. All that's left is to install the bearings. To allow them to spin freely, they're held in place with a machine screw, three washers, and a lock nut *(Fig. 9b)*. ■

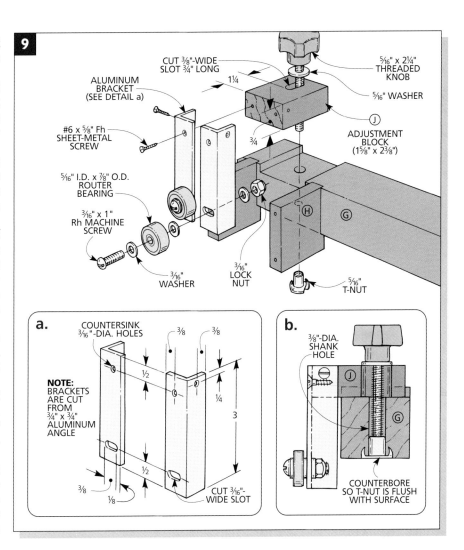

Before you can use the Jig Saw Table, you'll have to spend a few minutes setting up the guide system. The set-up isn't difficult but it will be necessary to make these changes each time you switch to a different style jig saw blade.

The first thing you'll do is align the bearings with the blade. To do this, slide the adjustment block so that the bearings line up just behind the teeth of the blade *(Step 1)*. Once the block is aligned, tighten the knob to hold it in place.

Next, remove the guard and move the bearings close to the saw blade *(Step 2)*. Make sure they're not touching the blade.

Finally, adjust the arm so the hold-down is just above the workpiece ($1/32$") and lock the arm in place *(Step 3)*.

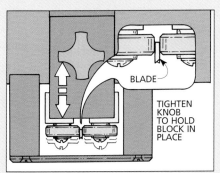

1 *Slide the adjustment block forward (or back) so the bearings line up right behind the teeth on the saw blade.*

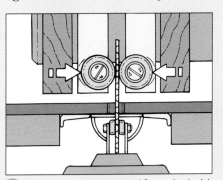

2 *Now remove the guard from the hold-down and position the bearings close to (but not touching) the saw blade.*

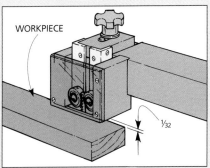

3 *Finally, adjust the arm assembly so the hold-down is raised about $1/32$" above the workpiece and lock it in place.*

WOODWORKER'S NOTEBOOK

Build this table with basic materials in just a few hours. Turnbuttons underneath the table hold the jig saw securely in place and a blade guard can be easily made from wood, acrylic plastic, and a plastic bottle.

CONSTRUCTION NOTES:

■ One of the problems with using portable power tools is that they can be awkward to control, especially with small workpieces. I find it's much easier to move the piece rather than the jig saw. But what if you don't use a jig saw table that much? After building the Jig Saw Table shown on page 8, I decided that there might be a need for a simpler design that can be built in a few hours. This basic table holds the jig saw safely beneath a sturdy, plywood table, while letting you use it like a band saw or scroll saw.

■ To make the Basic Jig Saw Table, start with a quarter sheet (24" x 48") of ³/₄" plywood. Cut one 18"-square piece for the top (A) and two 11"-wide, 18"-long pieces for the sides (B) *(Fig. 1)*.

■ Then the sides are strengthened by adding crossbraces in front and back. I cut the crossbraces (C) from the same quarter-sheet of ³/₄" plywood.

■ To cut a slot in the top for the blade, I first drilled a series of overlapping ¹/₁₆" holes centered on the width for the top *(Fig. 2)*. Then I cleaned up the holes using a fine blade in my hand-held jig saw and some sandpaper.

■ The jig saw mounts in a recess *(Fig. 2)*. To mark the recess, hold the jig saw on the underside of the table top with the blade sticking through the slot. Then trace the outline of the saw base.

■ Next, use a ¹/₂" straight bit mounted in a hand-held router to rout the recess slightly larger than the base of the portable jig saw *(Fig. 2)*. The recess should also be deep enough so the edge of the base protrudes just above the surface of the top itself. This way the jig saw can be secured with four turnbuttons that hold the base tightly in its recess *(Fig. 3)*. Rout as close as possible to the layout lines, then you can use a chisel to clean up to the lines and square up the corners.

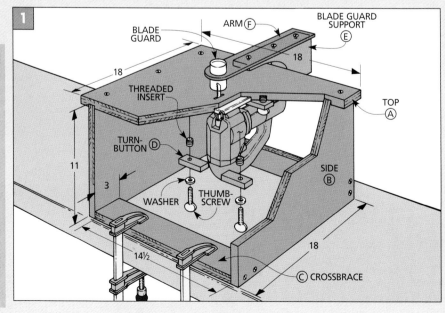

BASIC JIG SAW TABLE

MATERIALS LIST

WOOD
A	Top (1)	³/₄ ply - 18 x 18
B	Sides (2)	³/₄ ply - 11 x 18
C	Crossbraces (2)	³/₄ ply - 3 x 14¹/₂
D	Turnbuttons (2)	¹/₂ x 1 - 3
E	Blade Guard Spprt. (1)	1¹/₂ x 3¹/₂ - 10
F	Arm (1)	¹/₄ acrylic plastic - 2 x 15

Note: Can also make arm from hardboard.

HARDWARE SUPPLIES
(16) No. 8 x 1¹/₄" Fh woodscrews
(3) No. 8 x ¹/₂" Fh woodscrews
(2) ¹/₄"-20 threaded inserts
(2) ¹/₄" washers
(2) ¹/₄" x 1¹/₂" thumbscrews
(1) 1¹/₂"-dia. plastic canister

■ Once the recess is complete, rip an extra long piece of ½"-thick hardwood to width (1") and then crosscut a pair of turnbuttons (D) to length (3") *(Fig. 3a)*.

■ The turnbuttons clamp "down" on the base of the jig saw to hold it in place. And to make it easier to remove the jig saw, I added threaded inserts to the underside of the table. Then I drilled a shank hole in one end of the turnbutton for a thumb-screw and washer *(Fig. 3a)*.

■ To keep this table safe as well as useful, I made a guard that covers the exposed teeth of the moving blade. The guard consists of a simple arm support (E) made from a scrap piece of 2x4 (1½" x 3½") and an arm made of acrylic plastic (hardboard would also do). At the end of the arm is a plastic canister (a brad container or pill bottle, flipped upside-down) which acts as a blade guard *(Fig. 4)*.

■ To attach the support piece to the table, you'll need to cut a notch out of one end *(Fig. 4a)*. Size the notch so there is about 1½" of clearance beneath the top and the end of the arm. (This should be plenty of clearance for most workpieces.) Then center the support arm on the base before attaching it with screws from below.

■ Drill a hole in one end of the arm to hold the blade guard (see the Shop Tip below), then cut and sand a radius at the same end of the arm. Finally, attach the arm to the support with screws.

■ The trick to using the Jig Saw Table is keeping the workpiece from jumping up and down while you're sawing.

There are a few things you can do to keep that from happening. First, hold the workpiece tightly and use a sharp blade. Also, don't try to saw workpieces that are too thick (over about 1"). They may "catch" on the tip of the blade, causing the workpiece to bounce up and down.

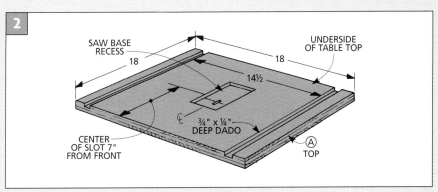

2
SAW BASE RECESS
18
UNDERSIDE OF TABLE TOP
18
14½
CENTER OF SLOT 7" FROM FRONT
¾" x ¼"- DEEP DADO
(A) TOP

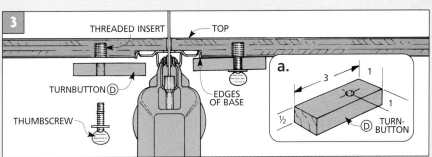

3
THREADED INSERT
TOP
TURNBUTTON (D)
THUMBSCREW
EDGES OF BASE

a.
3
1
1
½
TURN-BUTTON (D)

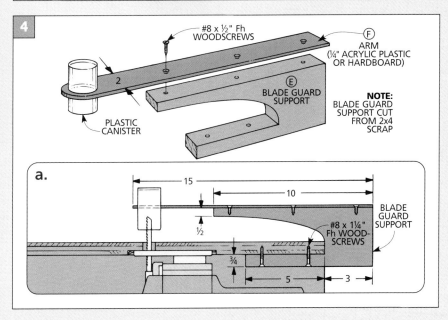

4
#8 x ½" Fh WOODSCREWS
(F) ARM (¼" ACRYLIC PLASTIC OR HARDBOARD)
(E) BLADE GUARD SUPPORT
2
PLASTIC CANISTER
NOTE: BLADE GUARD SUPPORT CUT FROM 2x4 SCRAP

a.
15
10
½
¾
5
3
BLADE GUARD SUPPORT
#8 x 1¼" Fh WOOD-SCREWS

SHOP TIP . . . . *Working with Plastic*

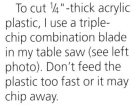

To cut ¼"-thick acrylic plastic, I use a triple-chip combination blade in my table saw (see left photo). Don't feed the plastic too fast or it may chip away.

Although there are special bits available for drilling into acrylic plastic, a sharp Forstner bit is all you need. It cuts cleanly.

Also important is the the drill press speed. If the bit's spinning too fast, it melts the plastic. So set it to turn at around 500 RPM. Apply only light pressure as you drill. Let the bit do the work (right photo).

Plate Joiner Table

Tired of constantly clamping and unclamping workpieces when cutting biscuit joints? Speed up your work with this shop-built table that converts your hand-held plate joiner into a benchtop tool.

It's hard to imagine a quicker way to join two workpieces together than using a plate joiner. In fact, cutting the slots for the wood plate (biscuit) actually takes less time than clamping and unclamping the workpieces.

The constant fiddling with clamps gets to be a nuisance. Especially if I need to cut slots in a number of workpieces. To make it easy to cut a slot without having to first secure the piece, I mounted my plate joiner to a table that clamps to my bench.

The biggest advantage to doing this is that it frees up both hands to hold the workpiece. But that presents another little problem — how do you plunge the blade into the workpiece to cut a slot?

PLUNGE SYSTEM. The solution is an easy to build plunge system that consists of a foot pedal and a wood arm.

When you step on the foot pedal, a wire cable pulls on an arm that's located on the Plate Joiner Table (inset photos). As a result, the arm pivots against the body of the plate joiner and pushes it forward. This plunges the blade of the plate joiner into the workpiece, which cuts a slot for the biscuit.

SLIDING TABLE. The exact location of the biscuit slot on the edge of the workpiece is determined by the position of a sliding table. Depending on the thickness of the workpiece, you just raise or lower the table so the blade will cut at the desired height. With the table locked in place, it provides a large, stable work surface.

SETUP. After you've built the table, you'll need to set it up. Doing this and using the Plate Joiner Table is explained in detail on page 25.

QUICK RELEASE. One last thing. If you're working with an extremely large piece that's awkward to handle on the sliding table, it's easy to remove the plate joiner and use it in the regular hand-held position.

EXPLODED VIEW

OVERALL DIMENSIONS:
20W x 25¾D x 20¾H

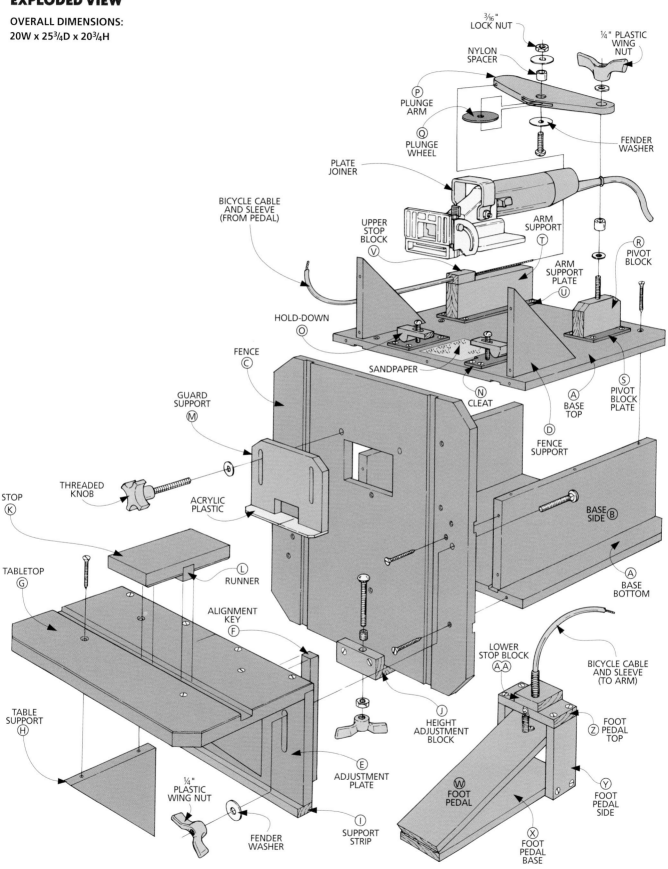

³⁄₁₆" LOCK NUT

NYLON SPACER

¼" PLASTIC WING NUT

PLUNGE ARM Ⓟ

PLUNGE WHEEL Ⓠ

FENDER WASHER

PLATE JOINER

BICYCLE CABLE AND SLEEVE (FROM PEDAL)

UPPER STOP BLOCK Ⓥ

ARM SUPPORT Ⓣ

PIVOT BLOCK Ⓡ

ARM SUPPORT PLATE Ⓤ

HOLD-DOWN Ⓞ

FENCE Ⓒ

SANDPAPER

GUARD SUPPORT Ⓜ

CLEAT Ⓝ

BASE TOP Ⓐ

PIVOT BLOCK PLATE Ⓢ

FENCE SUPPORT Ⓓ

THREADED KNOB

ACRYLIC PLASTIC

STOP Ⓚ

TABLETOP Ⓖ

RUNNER Ⓛ

ALIGNMENT KEY Ⓕ

BASE SIDE Ⓑ

BASE BOTTOM Ⓐ

TABLE SUPPORT Ⓗ

HEIGHT ADJUSTMENT BLOCK Ⓙ

LOWER STOP BLOCK Ⓐ Ⓐ

BICYCLE CABLE AND SLEEVE (TO ARM)

¼" PLASTIC WING NUT

FENDER WASHER

ADJUSTMENT PLATE Ⓔ

SUPPORT STRIP Ⓘ

FOOT PEDAL Ⓦ

FOOT PEDAL TOP Ⓩ

FOOT PEDAL SIDE Ⓨ

FOOT PEDAL BASE Ⓧ

MATERIALS LIST

WOOD

A	Base Top/Bottom (2)	¾ MDF - 15¼ x 20
B	Base Sides (2)	¾ MDF - 6½ x 15
C	Fence (1)	¾ MDF - 20 x 20
D	Fence Supports (2)	¾ MDF - 6 x 6
E	Adjustment Plate (1)	¾ MDF - 7⅞ x 20
F	Alignment Keys (2)	¾ MDF - 7/16 x 7⅞
G	Tabletop (1)	¾ MDF - 10 x 20
H	Table Supports (2)	¾ MDF - 7 x 7
I	Support Strip (1)	½ x 1 - 20
J	Height Adj. Block (1)	1½ x 2⅜ - 4
K	Stop (1)	¾ MDF - 4 x 9
L	Runner (1)	¾ MDF - ¾ x 4
M	Guard Support (1)	½ x 5 - 7½
N	Cleats (2)	¼ hdbd. - 2½ x 4⅛
O	Hold-downs (2)	¾ x ¾ - 2¾
P	Plunge Arm (1)	½ x 2½ - 13½
Q	Plunge Wheel (1)	¼ hdbd. - 2 dia.
R	Pivot Block (1)	1½ x 2½ - 3¾
S	Pivot Block Plate (1)	¼ hdbd. - 3¾ x 4
T	Arm Support (1)	1½ x 2½ - 7¾
U	Arm Support Plate (1)	¼ hdbd. - 4 x 7¾
V	Upper Stop Block (1)	¾ x 1½ - 1½
W	Foot Pedal (1)	¾ x 3⅞ - 14
X	Foot Pedal Base (1)	¾ x 4 - 14
Y	Foot Pedal Sides (2)	¾ x 2½ - 6
Z	Foot Pedal Top (1)	¾ x 2½ - 5½
AA	Lower Stop Block (1)	¾ x 2½ - 2½

HARDWARE SUPPLIES

- (2) No. 8 x 2¼" Fh sheet-metal screws
- (58) No. 8 x 1¼" Fh sheet-metal screws
- (18) No. 8 x ¾" Fh sheet-metal screws
- (2) No. 8 x 2" Rh sheet-metal screws
- (6) No. 8 x ½" Fh woodscrews
- (2) ¼" x 2" Rh machine screws
- (1) 3/16" x ¾" Rh machine screw
- (3) No. 6 x ½" Ph sheet-metal screws
- (1) ¼" x 3½" carriage bolt
- (2) ¼" x 2" carriage bolts
- (1) ¼" x 5" carriage bolt
- (4) ¼" plastic wing nuts
- (2) 1½"-long threaded knobs
- (1) ¼" hex nut
- (1) ¼" threaded insert
- (4) ¼" T-nuts
- (1) 3/16" nylon lock nut
- (6) ¼" flat washers
- (2) ¼" x 1½" fender washers
- (2) 3/16" x 1¼" fender washers
- (3) No. 6 flat washers
- (1) No. 6 external lock washer
- (1) .257" x ½" nylon spacer (9/16" long)
- (1) .194" x ½" nylon spacer (9/16" long)
- (1) 1/16"-dia. wire cable (7 feet)
- (1) Flexible sleeve (7 feet)
- (1) 1/16" crimp-on stop
- (1) ⅜" x 1 15/32" tension spring
- (1) 5/16" x 2 13/16" tension spring
- (1) 1⅞" x 3" hinge
- (1) ¼" acrylic plastic (2" x 7½")

CUTTING DIAGRAM

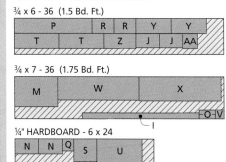

¾ x 6 - 36 (1.5 Bd. Ft.)
P R R Y Y
T T Z J J AA
¾ x 7 - 36 (1.75 Bd. Ft.)
M W X
O V
I
¼" HARDBOARD - 6 x 24
N N Q S U
¾" MDF - 48 x 48
A A H
B B D
K L
G C
E F

BASE

I began work on the table by building a base and fence. The base provides a sturdy platform for the plate joiner. And a tall fence supports the workpiece. The base is a simple box made from ¾"-thick medium-density fiberboard (MDF). And I left an opening in the back of the base to provide a place to store the foot pedal when the table is not being used.

TOP AND BOTTOM. The base consists of a top and bottom that are held together by two sides. To create a clamping surface for securing the base to the bench, the sides fit in grooves that are set in from the edges of the top and bottom.

To ensure these grooves align, I started with a large blank that's cut to final width, but oversize in length *(Fig. 1)*. Then I used a table saw with a ¾" dado blade to cut the grooves.

Once the grooves are cut in the blank, you can cut the base top and bottom (A) to final length. While I was at it, I used the table saw (a jig saw would also work) to cut an angled notch (for clearance) in each back corner of both pieces *(Fig. 1)*.

SIDES. All that's left to complete the base is to add the two base sides (B) *(Fig. 2)*. One thing to be aware of here is the sides are set in ¼" from the front edge of the top and bottom. That's because later on, the top and bottom will fit into dadoes in the back of the fence *(Fig. 5)*. And this offset allows the sides to fit tight against the back of the fence.

After cutting the sides to size, they're placed in the grooves in the top and bottom. Then the base is simply glued and screwed together *(Fig. 2)*.

Note: To prevent the MDF from splitting, I used sheet-metal screws with straight shanks instead of woodscrews (refer to the Shop Tip on page 11).

FENCE

With the base complete, you can turn your attention to the fence. In addition to providing support for the workpiece as you make a cut, the fence guides the sliding table up and down.

GROOVES. The way this works is simple. There are two grooves in the front of the fence that align with grooves

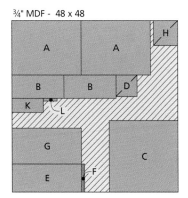

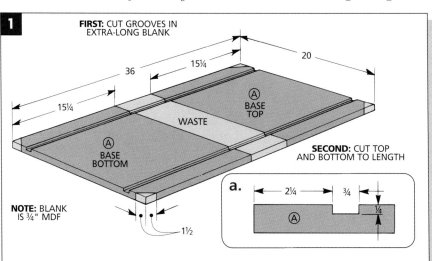

1
FIRST: CUT GROOVES IN EXTRA-LONG BLANK
36
15¼
15¼
20
A BASE TOP
WASTE
A BASE BOTTOM
SECOND: CUT TOP AND BOTTOM TO LENGTH
NOTE: BLANK IS ¾" MDF
1½
a.
2¼
¾
¼
A

in the back of the sliding table. A pair of keys (added later) that fit into these grooves will "track" the sliding table up and down the fence.

In order to get the table to slide back and forth in the grooves smoothly (and evenly), it's important that they are properly aligned. So once again, it's best to start with a single MDF blank and cut the grooves in the fence (C) and the adjustment plate (E) for the sliding table assembly at the same time *(Fig. 3)*.

Now it's just a matter of cutting the fence and the adjustment plate to final length. After setting aside the adjustment plate, I cut an angled notch on each corner of the fence as before *(Fig. 4)*.

DADOES. The next step is to cut a pair of shallow dadoes in the back of the fence *(Fig. 4)*. These dadoes accept the top and bottom of the base.

OPENING. But before you attach the base, there's one last thing to do. That's to cut an opening in the fence for your plate joiner that allows the blade to plunge into the workpiece *(Fig. 4)*.

When determining the size of the opening, the goal is to make it large enough so the face of the plate joiner will sit flush with the front of the fence. So you want to check that there's enough clearance for any knobs or levers on the tool. (I sized it to provide $\frac{1}{8}$" clearance all around for my plate joiner.)

Once you've established the size, you're ready to lay out the opening. I centered it on the width of the fence and located it so the bottom of the opening is flush with the top dado *(Fig. 4)*.

An easy way to cut the opening is to drill a hole in each corner and remove the waste with a jig saw.

ATTACH FENCE TO BASE. At this point, the fence is complete. Now you're ready to attach it to the base. To help strengthen the large fence and more importantly keep it square to the base, I added two triangular fence supports (D) *(Fig. 5)*. As with all the other parts, fence supports are also made with $\frac{3}{4}$" MDF.

These triangular fence supports are screwed to the fence from the front. But to attach them to the base, you'll need to drill a counterbored shank hole in the angled edge of each support *(Fig. 5)*.

Once you've drilled all the shank holes, the only thing left to do is glue and screw the pieces together.

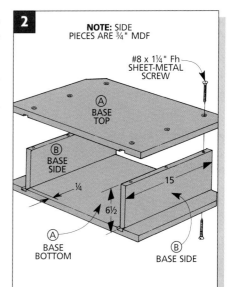

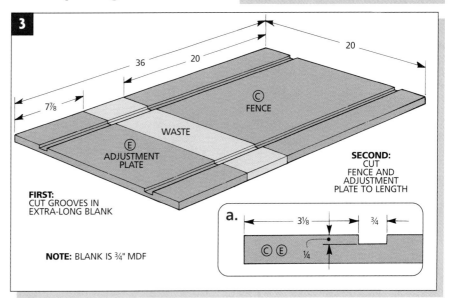

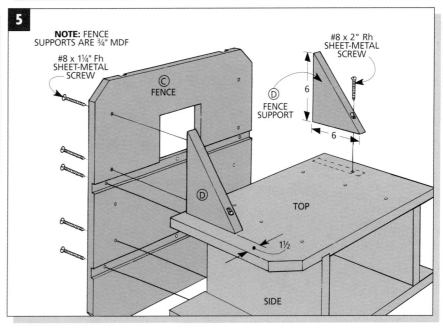

With the base and fence complete, I added the sliding table. This is an L-shaped assembly that supports the workpiece as you cut the slot for a biscuit.

There are a few things to consider before starting on the sliding table. First, the height of the table determines the location of this slot on the thickness of the workpiece, so it has to be adjustable up and down. Also, to ensure that the matching slots in the two workpieces align, the table has to remain parallel to the blade of the plate joiner.

ADJUSTMENT PLATE. That's where the adjustment plate (E) comes in *(Fig. 7)*. (It's the remaining piece of the blank cut earlier when making the fence.)

To guide the table up and down, a pair of alignment keys (F) fit in grooves in the back of the adjustment plate. Since these grooves were cut earlier, completing the adjustment plate is just a matter of cutting a pair of slots *(Fig. 7a)* and gluing in the keys (F).

TABLETOP. At this point, you can set aside the adjustment plate and start on the tabletop (G) *(Fig. 8)*. It's just a piece of ¾" MDF that's rabbeted along the back edge to fit the adjustment plate.

To accept a stop that's added later, you'll need to cut a centered groove in the tabletop. Now trim the front corners of the tabletop at an angle *(Fig. 8)*. And to avoid chipping the edges with a workpiece, I routed a slight (⅛") chamfer around the top edges *(Fig. 9)*. (The

chamfer along the back edge of the tabletop also acts as a dust relief.)

ATTACH TABLETOP. Next, attach the tabletop to the adjustment plate. Here again, a pair of large triangular supports (H) add rigidity to the table *(Fig. 9)*.

SUPPORT STRIP. Now you can mount the sliding table to the fence. To provide a solid bearing surface for a height adjustment bolt (added later), glue and screw a hardwood support strip (I) to the bottom edge of the adjustment plate *(Fig. 9)*.

MOUNT TABLE. Now it's time to mount the table to the fence. It's held in place by two carriage bolts that pass through holes drilled in the fence and the slots cut earlier in the adjustment plate *(Fig. 6)*. Tightening a wing nut on the end of each bolt locks the table in place.

When determining the location of the holes for these bolts, there's one thing to keep in mind. To avoid cutting into the table, you want to establish the maximum height that it can be raised to.

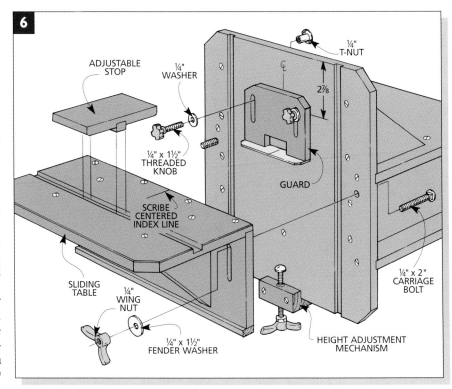

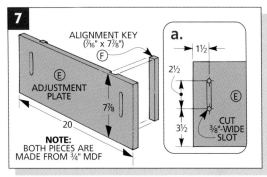

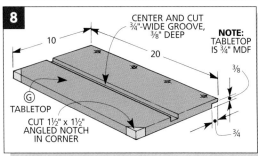

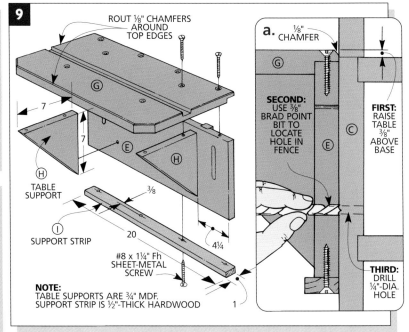

An easy way to do this is to temporarily clamp the table in place so it's $3/8$" above the top of the base (*Fig. 9a*). Then, all that's needed is to mark the location of the bottom of the adjustment slots.

ADJUSTING TABLE HEIGHT. With the sliding table in place, you still need a way to move it up and down. That's the job of a simple height adjustment mechanism.

What makes it work is a carriage bolt. It threads into an insert that's installed in a height adjustment block (J) attached to the fence (*Fig. 10*). The head of the bolt rests against the support strip (I) on the adjustment plate (*Fig. 10a*). When you turn a wing nut that's tightened against a nut on the end of the bolt, the head raises (or lowers) the table.

Since the wood block that holds the height adjustment mechanism is kind of small, it's best to start with a long blank (*Figs. 11 and 11a*). (I glued up two hardwood pieces.) After cutting a groove to fit the fence and drilling holes for the threaded insert and bolt, install the insert. Then just screw the height adjustment block (J) in place, attaching it to the bottom edge of the fence (*Fig. 10a*).

ACCESSORIES

To make it easier and safer to use the Plate Joiner Table, I added two easy-to-build accessories to the joiner table: an adjustable stop with a runner and a see-through blade guard (*Fig. 6*).

STOP. If you're cutting a slot in end grain, the rotation of the blade will have a tendency to kick the workpiece to the side. To prevent this, a simple stop is clamped to the table (see photo below).

The stop (K) is a piece of MDF with a runner (L) that fits the groove in the tabletop (*Fig. 12*). The runner keeps the stop aligned and is simply glued into a dado that's cut in the stop.

BLADE GUARD. The second accessory you can build is a blade guard that protects your fingers when cutting a slot in the end or edge of a workpiece. The guard is an L-shaped assembly that consists of a hardwood guard support (M) and a piece of acrylic plastic (*Fig. 13*).

Before screwing the pieces together, you'll need to cut two vertical slots to make the guard adjustable (*Fig. 13a*). And a square notch in the support helps with visibility. Also, scribing a centered index line on the acrylic plastic will make it easy to position a workpiece when cutting a slot. (To make the index line more visible, I filled it with ink.)

After attaching the guard to the fence with T-nuts and threaded knobs, I scribed another index line in the tabletop (*Fig. 6*). This line helps to position vertical pieces (see bottom right photo on page 25).

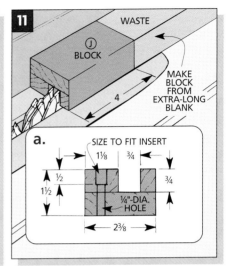

Table accessories like an adjustable stop and a blade guard provide safer cuts — especially when cutting a slot in end grain.

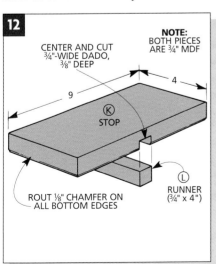

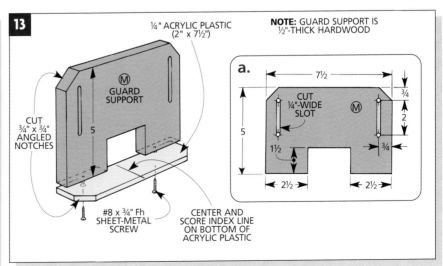

The heart of the Plate Joiner Table is a system that plunges the blade of the plate joiner through the opening in the fence.

This requires two things: a way to secure the plate joiner to the base, and an arm that applies pressure against the back of the joiner *(Fig. 14)*.

CLEATS. To keep the plate joiner from moving from side to side during use, a pair of hardboard cleats (N) fit against the base of the tool *(Fig. 15)*.

Note: Depending on your plate joiner, you may be able to screw it directly to the base (see photo below).

HOLD-DOWNS. In addition to the cleats, I added two whistle-shaped hold-downs (O) to apply downward pressure on the plate joiner *(Fig. 15b)*.

The curved end of each hold-down rests on a hardboard cleat *(Fig. 15a)*. And the opposite end sits flat on top of the base of the plate joiner. When you apply pressure on the hold-down, it rocks on its curved end and pinches the flat end tight against the plate joiner.

This clamping pressure is produced by a machine screw that passes through a slot in the hold-down and into a T-nut installed in the base. (See the Shop Tip on page 24 for a tip on installing a T-nut.)

ARM. Once the plate joiner is mounted to the base, you can start on the plunge arm (P) *(Fig. 16)*. It's a piece of hardwood that's shaped like a boomerang. This shape provides a single point of contact so the arm can push the body of the plate joiner forward and plunge the blade out of the opening in the fence.

A hole drilled in one end of the arm serves as a pivot point. And a counterbored shank hole in the opposite end accepts a cable that connects the arm to the foot pedal *(Figs. 14 and 16a)*.

WHEEL. To reduce wear on the plastic housing of the plate joiner, I added a ¼" hardboard plunge wheel (Q) that spins as the arm pivots *(Fig. 16)*. It fits into a deep mortise in the arm. The wheel is held in place with a nylon spacer and a lock nut that tightens on a machine screw.

SUPPORT BLOCKS. Before you attach the arm, you'll need to add two supports that position it at the proper height. The first support is a pivot block. The second is an arm support.

PIVOT BLOCK. The arm is secured to the base using a thick hardwood pivot block (R) and a short pivot block plate (S) made of ¼" hardboard *(Fig. 17)*.

What's important here is the combined height of these two pieces. The idea is to make the pivot block tall (wide)

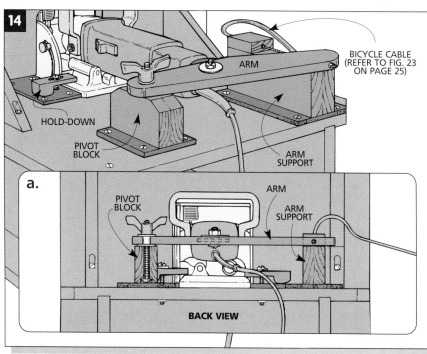

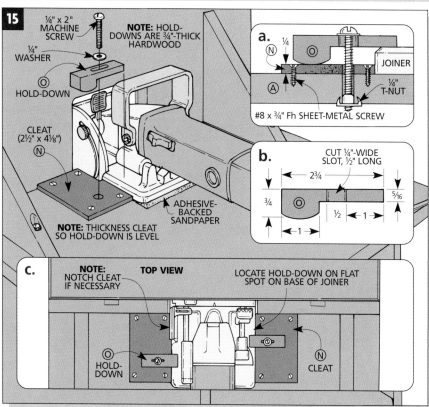

Pre-drilled holes in the base of some plate joiners can be used to screw it in place directly onto the table.

enough so the arm contacts a flat place on the end of the joiner.

Note: This may be above or below the power cord (see photo below).

Once the height is established, just glue up two pieces of ³⁄₄"-thick stock to make the pivot block. After installing a carriage bolt that will be used to hold the arm in place, the mounting plate is simply screwed to the bottom *(Fig. 17a)*.

ARM SUPPORT. At this point, you can turn your attention to building an arm support. It holds up the "free" end of the arm. And it serves as a platform for the block that the cable passes through.

Here again, the arm support (T) consists of two glued-up pieces of ³⁄₄"-thick hardwood *(Fig. 18)*. And a ¹⁄₄" hardboard arm support plate (U) is screwed to the bottom. But this time, an upper stop block (V) with "stepped holes" drilled in it is glued to the top *(Fig. 18a)*.

ASSEMBLY. Now you can begin assembling the parts. Attaching the arm is easy. Just slip it onto the end of the carriage bolt in the pivot block and thread on a knob. With the arm in place, you're ready to position the pivot block and arm support.

The goal here is to be able to push the arm all the way forward so it won't "bottom out" on the stop block *(Fig. 19)*.

Note: Set the plate joiner for the maximum depth of cut.

The best way I found to do this is to temporarily clamp the pivot block in place and check the operation of the arm.

Start by positioning the front edge of the arm (the edge nearest the pivot point) so it's parallel with the back of the base *(Fig. 19)*. Also, check that the wheel is centered on the end of the joiner.

Now push the arm all the way forward *(Fig. 19)*. There should be about ¹⁄₂" clearance between the stop block and the arm. Finally, screw both mounting plates to the base with woodscrews.

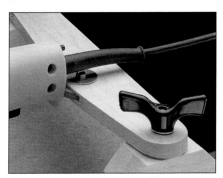

With some plate joiners (like the one shown above), you'll need to position the arm below the power cord.

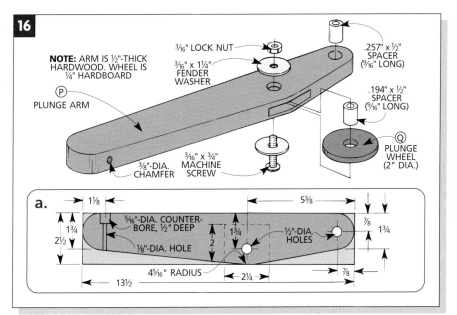

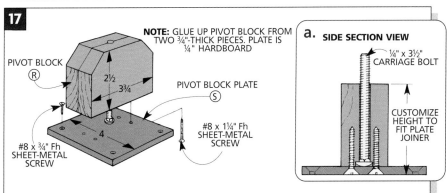

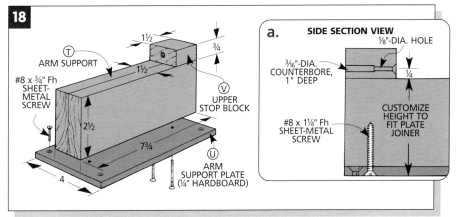

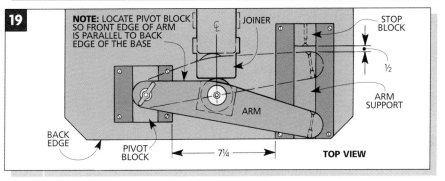

SHOP TIP

Installing a T-Nut

To install a T-nut into a tight space, start by threading a bolt all the way into the T-nut. Then slip the bolt and the barrel of the T-nut into a pre-drilled hole. To seat the T-nut, just thread a wing nut on the end of the bolt. Tightening the wing nut draws the prongs into the workpiece (see photo).

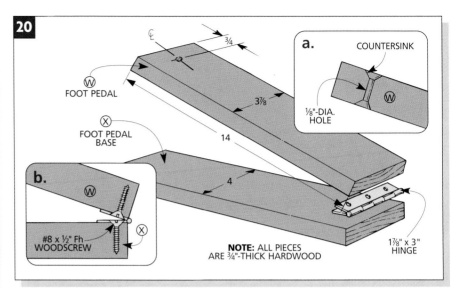

20

FOOT PEDAL

X — FOOT PEDAL BASE

3/4

3⅞

14

4

a. COUNTERSINK

⅛"-DIA. HOLE

b. #8 x ½" Fh WOODSCREW

1⅞" x 3" HINGE

NOTE: ALL PIECES ARE ¾"-THICK HARDWOOD

FOOT PEDAL

With the plunge mechanism in place, the last thing to do to complete the table is add the foot pedal *(Fig. 21)*. It works like the pedal on an automobile. Only this pedal plunges the blade of the plate joiner through the opening in the fence and into the workpiece.

What makes this work is a wire cable that slides inside a flexible plastic sleeve. Depressing the pedal pulls the cable, then the cable transfers this movement to the arm behind the plate joiner.

PEDAL. I started work by making a ¾"-thick hardwood foot pedal (W) and foot pedal base (X) *(Fig. 20)*. These pieces are identical in length. But to keep the pedal from binding when a frame is added later, the pedal is ⅛" narrower than the base. After drilling a hole in the pedal for the cable *(Fig. 20a)*, just hinge the two pieces together *(Fig. 20b)*.

FRAME. To provide support for the pedal and base, a hardwood frame is added. It consists of two foot pedal sides (Y) that are screwed to the base and a top (Z) that holds them together *(Fig. 21)*.

Before screwing the foot pedal top (Z) in place, you'll need to glue on a lower stop block (AA) and drill a series of "stepped" holes for the cable and sleeve that are added next *(Fig. 21a)*.

CABLE AND SLEEVE. There isn't anything unusual about either the cable or the flexible sleeve. (I picked both of them up from the local bike shop.) Just be sure they're long enough so you can put the pedal in a convenient place.

INSTALL CABLE. To install the cable, start by sticking one end through the holes in the top of the foot pedal and fasten it to the end of the pedal with a panhead screw and both a flat and a lock washer *(Fig. 22)*. Then slip the sleeve over the cable until it "bottoms out" in the stop block. To avoid getting a kink in the cable, slide a spring over the sleeve and push it into the stop block *(Fig. 22a)*.

SPRING. Before connecting the opposite end of the cable to the arm, I attached

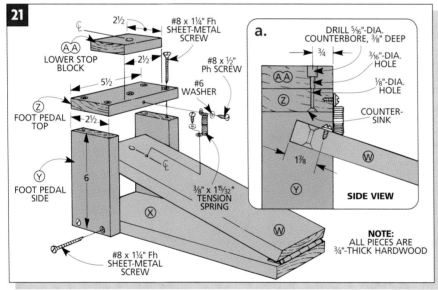

21

2½

#8 x 1¼" Fh SHEET-METAL SCREW

AA — LOWER STOP BLOCK

2½

#8 x ½" Ph SCREW

#6 WASHER

5½

Z — FOOT PEDAL TOP

2½

Y — FOOT PEDAL SIDE

6

X

3/8" x 1¹⁵/₃₂" TENSION SPRING

#8 x 1¼" Fh SHEET-METAL SCREW

a. DRILL ⁵/₁₆"-DIA. COUNTERBORE, ⅜" DEEP

3/4

AA

Z

³/₁₆"-DIA. HOLE

⅛"-DIA. HOLE

COUNTERSINK

1⅞

W

Y

SIDE VIEW

NOTE: ALL PIECES ARE ¾"-THICK HARDWOOD

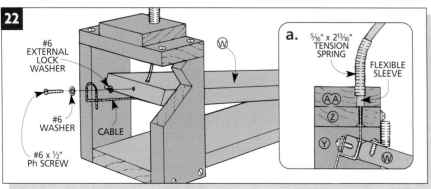

22

#6 EXTERNAL LOCK WASHER

#6 WASHER

CABLE

#6 x ½" Ph SCREW

W

a. ⁵/₁₆" x 2¹³/₁₆" TENSION SPRING

FLEXIBLE SLEEVE

AA

Z

Y

W

a tension spring to the pedal (W) and top (Z). The spring retracts the foot pedal after you've stepped down on it.

CRIMP-ON STOP. At this point, there's just one last thing to do. That's to run the wire cable through the upper stop block and arm, then secure it with a crimp-on stop *(Fig. 23)*.

The goal is to seat the stop in the counterbore when the arm is "at rest." To do this, you'll need to push the arm forward just a bit. Then, when the spring-loaded base of the joiner pushes the arm back, the stop will be at the correct place. ■

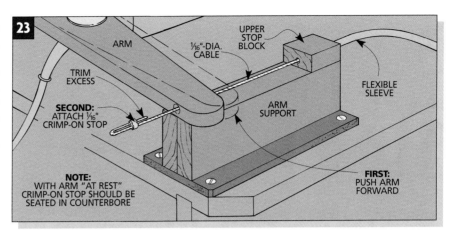

23

ARM

1/16"-DIA. CABLE

UPPER STOP BLOCK

FLEXIBLE SLEEVE

TRIM EXCESS

SECOND: ATTACH 1/16" CRIMP-ON STOP

ARM SUPPORT

NOTE: WITH ARM "AT REST" CRIMP-ON STOP SHOULD BE SEATED IN COUNTERBORE

FIRST: PUSH ARM FORWARD

TECHNIQUE .... *Making Plate Joints*

The Plate Joiner Table makes it easy to cut the slots for a biscuit, whether you're cutting just one or several. And it only takes a few minutes to set it up.

SETUP

To set up the joiner table, start by clamping the base of the table to your workbench. Then raise (or lower) the sliding table so the blade will cut the slot at the desired height.

The up and down location of this slot is determined by the thickness of the workpiece, and by the "side" of the workpiece that's face down on the table. So to ensure that the two mating pieces will be flush after they're assembled, you'll want to cut the slots in both pieces with the "show" side facing down.

LAYOUT. An easy way to keep the faces straight is to make all your marks on the opposite face. This means you'll need to mark the layout lines for the joints on the opposite side. To do this, simply butt the pieces together and make a mark across the joint line.

When cutting a slot, align each mark with the index line on the plate joiner guard or the table depending on how the workpiece is positioned (see photos).

TYPES OF CUTS

There are three basic cuts you'll make most often on the Plate Joiner Table: edge joints (used mostly when gluing up solid wood panels), end grain (typically used in place of a mortise and tenon joint), and face cuts (to strengthen a butt joint).

EDGE JOINTS. Probably the most common type of joint used with a plate joiner, edge joints are easy to cut. Just align the layout mark for the slot with the index line on the fence guard. Then hold the workpiece firmly against the fence with both hands as you step on the foot pedal (far left photo below).

END GRAIN. Another joint that benefits greatly from using the joiner table is an end grain joint. Here, the adjustable stop is clamped to the sliding table after positioning the workpiece. Then the rotation of the blade won't cause the piece to "walk" to the side (middle photo).

FACE CUTS. Cutting a slot in the face of a workpiece takes a slightly different setup. First, this is one operation where you'll need to make your layout mark on the show side of the workpiece, since you'll have to remove the guard and hold the piece against the fence. Then, with the layout mark on the workpiece aligned with the index line on the table, hold the workpiece securely against the tall fence as you make a cut (right photo below).

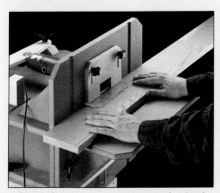

Edge Joints. It's easy to cut a slot in the edge of a board. Just align the layout mark for the slot with the index line on the guard. Then hold the workpiece firmly against the fence with both hands as you step on the foot pedal.

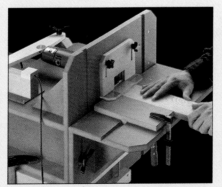

End Grain. You can also cut a slot in the end of a workpiece. Only here, the adjustable stop is clamped to the sliding table so the rotation of the blade doesn't cause the workpiece to "walk" to the side and cut a slot that could end up too long.

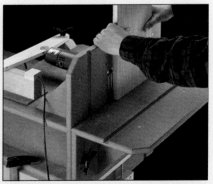

Face Cuts. To cut a slot in the face of a workpiece, first remove the guard. Then, with the layout mark on the workpiece aligned with the index line on the table, hold it securely against the tall fence as you make the cut.

Mortising Machine

This shop-built Mortising Machine, with a router carriage that moves up and down and a table that slides in four directions, lets you set up the machine and cut a perfect mortise in less than a minute.

For years now, I've been cutting mortises by using my drill press to drill a series of overlapping holes, then using a chisel to square the corners and remove the ridges. This method has worked fine, especially when I only had a few mortises to cut.

But then I started building a large project that required cutting over a hundred mortises. That's when I decided to put off hand-cutting the mortises for awhile and build a project that's been on the back burner for quite some time — a shop-made Mortising Machine.

ROUTER AND SPIRAL BIT. This mortiser works together with a router and a spiral end mill bit to cut the mortises. It's quick, accurate, and a great way to make mortises, even if you only have a few to cut.

SLIDING TABLE. The way the Mortising Machine works is simple. First, the workpiece is clamped on a table that slides in four directions: in and out to position the router bit on the thickness of the workpiece. And side to side to establish the exact length and location of the mortise. Then a pair of adjustable stops allow you to lock in the mortise length.

CARRIAGE. To provide the up and down movement that's needed to cut the depth of the mortise, the router is mounted to a sliding carriage. Turning a crank lowers the carriage and plunges the spinning bit into the workpiece. And a depth gauge allows you to see when the mortise is cut to the desired depth.

Note: The mortiser can rout mortises up to 3" long in a single setup. The depth of the mortise depends mostly on the length of the spiral end mill bit you use.

MATERIALS. The base and carriage are made almost entirely of Baltic birch plywood. I used medium-density fiberboard (MDF) for the sliding table. There's a lot of hardware required for this project, but most of it can be found at home centers and hardware stores. I've also listed suppliers in Sources on page 126.

EXPLODED VIEW

OVERALL DIMENSIONS:
28W x 20D x 37½H
(WITH CARRIAGE FULLY RAISED)

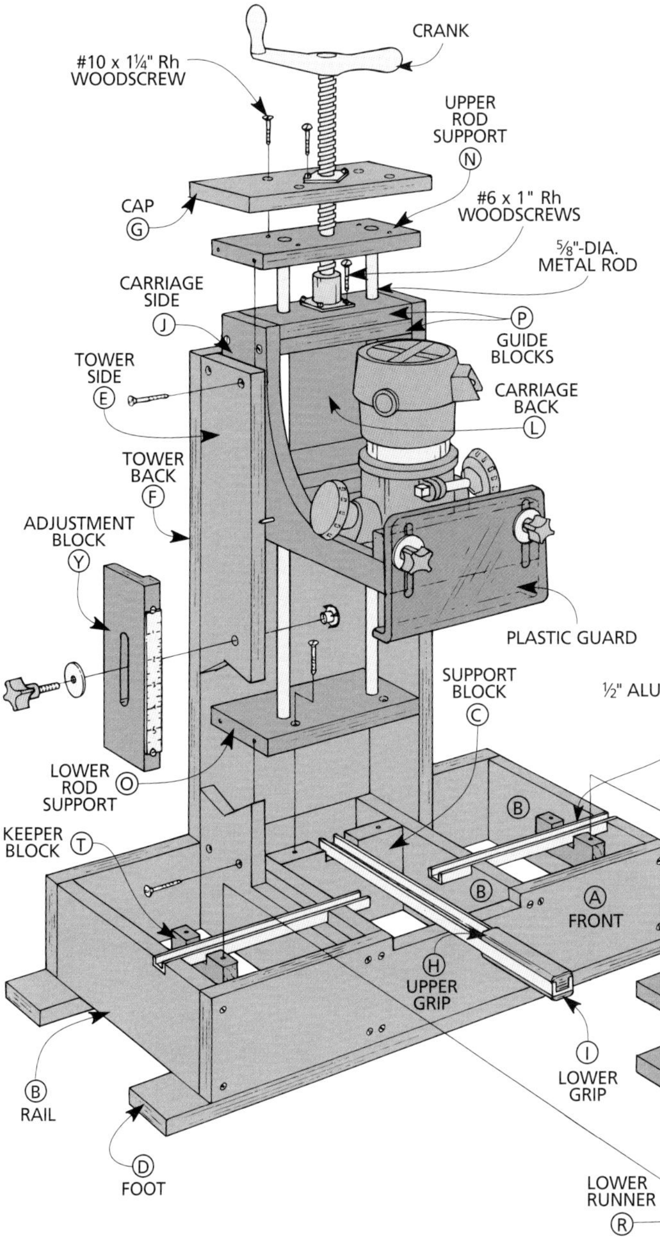

CRANK
#10 x 1¼" Rh WOODSCREW
UPPER ROD SUPPORT N
CAP G
#6 x 1" Rh WOODSCREWS
⅝"-DIA. METAL ROD
CARRIAGE SIDE J
P GUIDE BLOCKS
TOWER SIDE E
CARRIAGE BACK L
TOWER BACK F
ADJUSTMENT BLOCK Y
PLASTIC GUARD
SUPPORT BLOCK C
½" ALUMINUM CHANNEL
LOWER ROD SUPPORT O
KEEPER BLOCK T
B
B
A FRONT
H UPPER GRIP
I LOWER GRIP
B RAIL
D FOOT

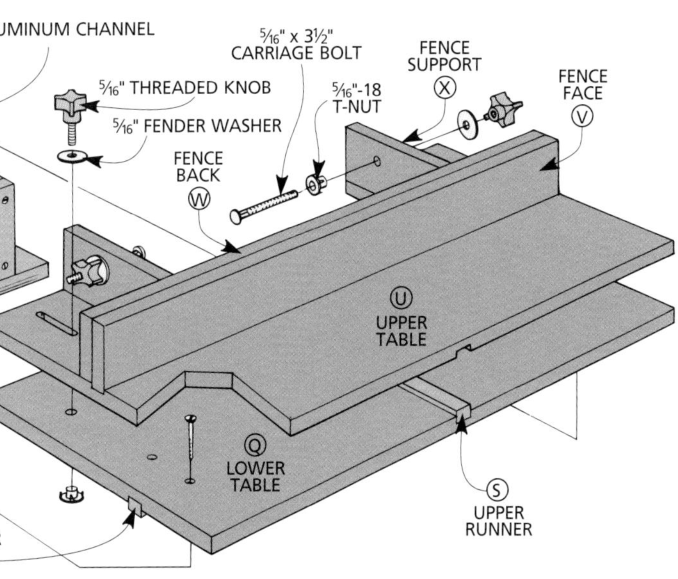

⁵⁄₁₆" x 3½" CARRIAGE BOLT
⁵⁄₁₆" THREADED KNOB
⁵⁄₁₆" FENDER WASHER
⁵⁄₁₆"-18 T-NUT
FENCE SUPPORT X
FENCE FACE V
FENCE BACK W
U UPPER TABLE
Q LOWER TABLE
LOWER RUNNER R
S UPPER RUNNER

CUTTING DIAGRAM

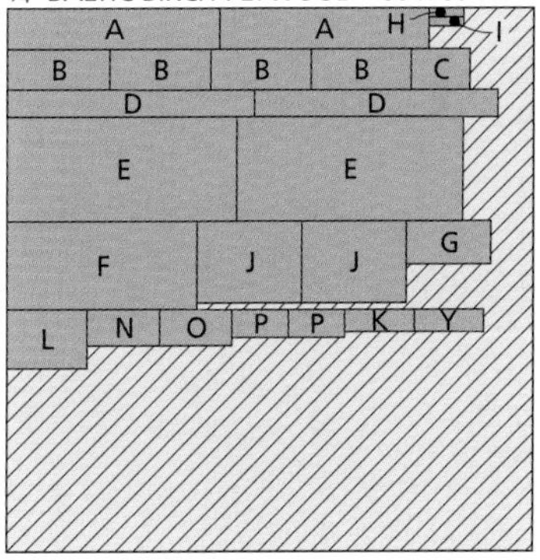

¾" BALTIC BIRCH PLYWOOD - 60 x 60
A
A
H
I
B
B
B
B
C
D
D
E
E
F
J
J
G
L
N
O
P
P
K
Y

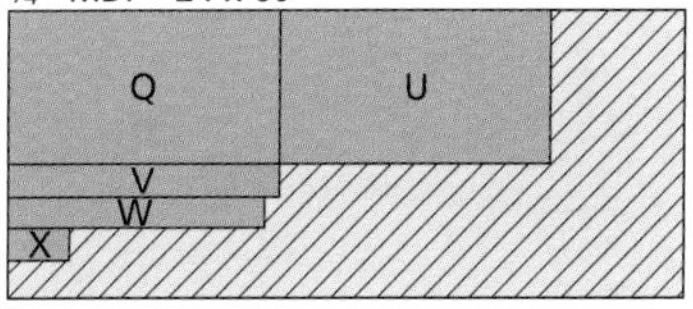

¾" MDF - 24 x 60
Q
U
V
W
X

NOTE: ALSO NEED A 2" x 12" PIECE OF ¾"-THICK STOCK FOR PART T

MATERIALS LIST

WOOD

- **A** Base Front/Back (2) ¾ ply - 4½ x 24
- **B** Rails (4) ¾ ply - 4½ x 11½
- **C** Support Block (1) ¾ ply - 4½ x 6¾
- **D** Feet (2) ¾ ply - 3 x 28
- **E** Tower Sides (2) ¾ ply - 11½ x 26
- **F** Tower Back (1) ¾ ply - 9¾ x 21½
- **G** Cap (1) ¾ ply - 4¾ x 9¾
- **H** Upper Grip (1) ⅝ ply - 1 x 4
- **I** Lower Grip (1) ¼ ply - 1 x 4
- **J** Carriage Sides (2) ¾ ply - 9 x 12
- **K** Carriage Front (1) ¾ ply - 2½ x 8
- **L** Carriage Back (1) ¾ ply - 6½ x 9
- **M** Mounting Plate (1) ⅜ pnlc.* - 6¾ x 10¾
- **N** Upr. Rod Support (1) ¾ ply - 4 x 8¼
- **O** Lwr. Rod Support (1) ¾ ply - 4 x 8¼
- **P** Guide Blocks (2) 1½ ply - 3⅛ x 6½
- **Q** Lower Table (1) ¾ MDF - 13 x 24
- **R** Lower Runners (2) ⅜ pnlc.* - ¾ x 11
- **S** Upper Runner (1) ⅜ pnlc.* - ¾ x 8⅛
- **T** Keeper Blocks (2) ¾ x 1½ - 4½
- **U** Upper Table (1) ¾ MDF - 13 x 24
- **V** Fence Face (1) ¾ MDF - 2⅞ x 24
- **W** Fence Back (1) ¾ MDF - 2¾ x 24
- **X** Fence Supports (2) ¾ MDF - 2¾ x 5½
- **Y** Adjustment Block (1) ¾ ply - 2½ x 8

*Parts are phenolic plastic

HARDWARE SUPPLIES

- (4) No. 8 x 2" Fh woodscrews
- (81) No. 8 x 1½" Fh woodscrews
- (27) No. 8 x 1¼" Fh woodscrews
- (8) No. 8 x ¾" Fh woodscrews
- (2) No. 10 x 1¼" Rh woodscrews
- (2) No. 8 x 1¼" Rh woodscrews
- (1) No. 8 x 1" Rh woodscrew
- (2) No. 8 x ½" Rh woodscrews
- (4) No. 6 x 1" Rh woodscrews
- (7) ⁵⁄₁₆"-18 T-nuts (w/ prongs)
- (7) ⁵⁄₁₆" fender washers
- (1) ³⁄₁₆" washer
- (1) No.12 flat washer
- (1) ¼" x 1¼" hex bolt
- (1) ¼" lock nut
- (2) ⁵⁄₁₆" x 3½" carriage bolts
- (2) ⁵⁄₁₆" knobs (w/ through hole)
- (3) ⁵⁄₁₆" knobs (w/ 1" stud)
- (2) ⁵⁄₁₆" knobs (w/ 1½" stud)
- (2) ⅝" x 21¼" metal rods
- (4) ⅝" I.D. x ¾" O.D. - 1" bronze bushings
- (2) ½" x 1" - 9¾" aluminum channel (⅛" thick)
- (1) ½" x 1" - 16" aluminum channel (⅛" thick)
- (1) ¹¹⁄₁₆"-dia. crank (9" long)
- (1) ¼" I.D. x ¾" O.D. sealed ball bearing
- (1) Plastic bit guard
- (1) 6" steel rule
- (1) 8d finish nail

BASE

I began by making the base of the Mortising Machine. The base provides a mounting surface for a metal track that guides the sliding tables *(Fig. 1)*. It also serves as a foundation for a tall, vertical tower that houses the router carriage.

FRAME. The base starts out as a simple plywood frame. The front and back (A) of this frame are identical in size *(Fig. 2)*. But to allow clearance for a handle, you'll need to cut a long notch in the front piece.

The front and back are connected by four rails (B) that are notched to accept the metal track. To prevent the table from binding in the metal tracks, it's important for these notches to line up.

An easy way to make sure that all of the notches align is to use a simple stop block on your miter gauge for consistent cuts. To do this, first mount a $3/4$"-wide dado blade in the table saw. Then butt each rail against a stop block that you've clamped to an auxiliary fence on the miter gauge *(Fig. 3)*. After making a single pass for each rail, reposition the stop block and make a second pass to complete each of the notches.

SUPPORT BLOCK. Before assembling the base, I added a plywood support block (C) to hold the end of the handle. After notching the support block to accept the handle, it's screwed to the two inside rails to form an H-shaped assembly. Then just screw the rails to the front and back.

FEET. This is also a good time to add two feet (D) to the bottom of the base *(Fig. 1)*. These long strips of plywood extend past the base so you can clamp the mortising machine to your bench.

TOWER

Once the base is assembled, the next step is to add the tower. Basically, it's a tall, open box that provides rigid support for the carriage assembly.

SIDES. The main parts of the tower are two L-shaped sides (E). To cut the long "leg" of each side, I ran a large plywood

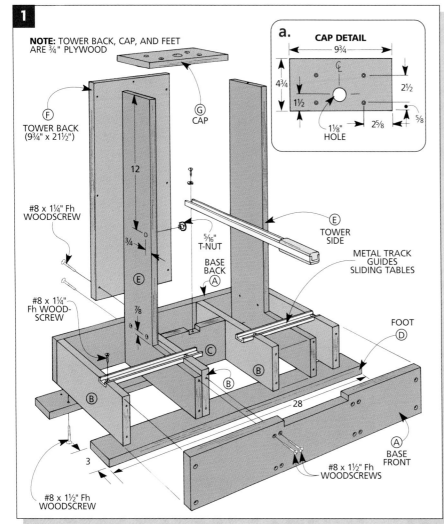

1

NOTE: TOWER BACK, CAP, AND FEET ARE $3/4$" PLYWOOD

a. CAP DETAIL

$9^3/4$

$4^3/4$ $2^1/2$ $1^1/2$

$1^1/8$" HOLE $2^5/8$ $5/8$

(F) TOWER BACK ($9^3/4$" x $21^1/2$")

(G) CAP

#8 x $1^1/4$" Fh WOODSCREW

12

$3/4$

$5/16$" T-NUT

(E) TOWER SIDE

BASE BACK (A)

METAL TRACK GUIDES SLIDING TABLES

(E)

#8 x $1^1/4$" Fh WOODSCREW

$7/8$

FOOT (D)

(C)

(B)

(B)

(B)

28

(A) BASE FRONT

3

#8 x $1^1/2$" Fh WOODSCREWS

#8 x $1^1/2$" Fh WOODSCREW

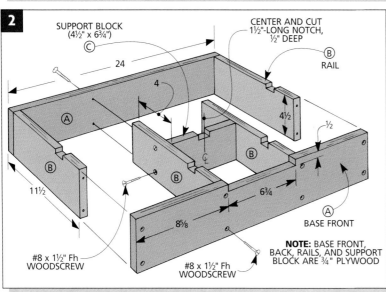

2

SUPPORT BLOCK ($4^1/2$" x $6^3/4$") (C)

24

4

CENTER AND CUT $1^1/2$"-LONG NOTCH, $1/2$" DEEP

(B) RAIL

$4^1/2$

$1/2$

(A)

(B)

(B)

(B)

$11^1/2$

$6^3/4$

$8^5/8$

(A) BASE FRONT

NOTE: BASE FRONT, BACK, RAILS, AND SUPPORT BLOCK ARE $3/4$" PLYWOOD

#8 x $1^1/2$" Fh WOODSCREW

#8 x $1^1/2$" Fh WOODSCREW

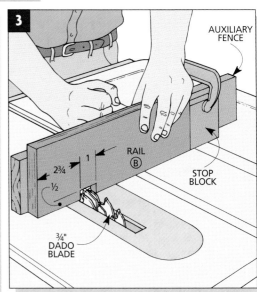

3

AUXILIARY FENCE

RAIL (B)

STOP BLOCK

$2^3/4$ 1

$1/2$

$3/4$ DADO BLADE

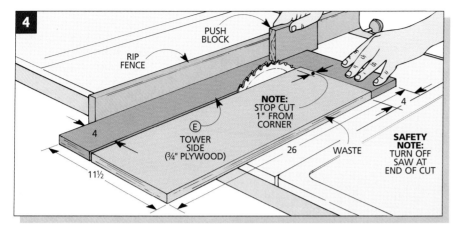

The aluminum channel used for the track and the handle is quite soft, so when it was time to cut it I used a good carbide-tipped saw blade. To support the channel, I attached an auxiliary fence to my miter gauge.

blank against the rip fence on the table saw *(Fig. 4)*. But because the saw blade won't make a square corner, I stopped the cut about 1" from the layout line.

Now it's just a matter of cutting the short "leg" of the sides *(Fig. 4)*. I stopped the cut before getting to the corner. Then I trimmed off the waste with a hand saw.

Before attaching the sides, it's best to drill two countersunk shank holes near the inside corner of each piece *(Fig. 1)*. (This simplifies assembly of the carriage later.) I also installed a T-nut in the left side for a depth gauge that's added later.

Now glue and clamp the sides of the tower to the inside rails. Then add screws through the front and back into the sides.

BACK. Next, to prevent the tower from racking, I added a $3/4$" plywood tower back (F). It's cut to fit flush with the top edge and outside face of each side.

CAP. After screwing the back in place, all it takes to enclose the top of the tower is a plywood cap (G) *(Figs. 1 and 1a)*. Before you add it, first drill a hole in the

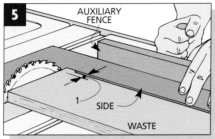

cap to accept the crank that's added later. Here again, predrill the holes for fastening the cap to the carriage assembly.

TRACK. Now you can make the metal track that guides the table side to side. The track consists of two pieces of aluminum channel that fit into the notches in the rails *(Fig. 6)*. The two pieces create an opening for the handle to swing back and forth. After cutting the two pieces of track to final length (see the Shop Tip above), they're screwed to the rails.

HANDLE. The aluminum channel is also a good material to use for the handle that moves the table from side to side.

A couple of scraps of plywood make a comfortable grip and prevent the channel from digging into my hand *(Fig. 6)*. The upper grip (H) starts out as an extra-long strip that's resawed to $5/8$" thick *(Fig. 7)*. Round over the top edges of this strip *(Fig. 7a)*, and rabbet it to fit inside the channel *(Fig. 7b)*. For the lower grip (I), I resawed a scrap to $1/4$" thick. After fitting the upper grip in the channel, the lower grip is screwed in place *(Fig. 6a)*. Then file and sand the edges smooth.

ATTACH HANDLE. Once the grip is completed, the opposite end of the handle can be screwed in place *(Fig. 6)*.

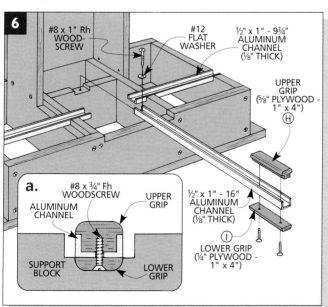

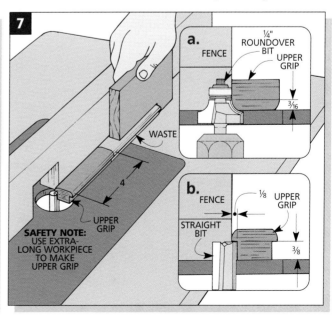

The carriage assembly consists of two main parts: a carriage that holds the router, and a guide system that allows the carriage to travel up and down a pair of metal rods *(Fig. 8)*.

To provide easy access to the router (and clearance for the router handles), the carriage is left open in front. And on each side of the carriage, I cut out a large, sweeping curve *(Fig. 8)*.

Note: Before cutting any parts, be sure to have your router on hand so you can adjust the size of any pieces as needed.

CONSTRUCTION. The two sides (J), front (K), and back (L) of the carriage are all made of $3/4$" plywood *(Fig. 9)*. To hold a mounting plate for the router, you'll need to cut a groove in each piece. As for the curved sides, don't worry about their exact shape. Just be sure there's enough clearance for the router handles.

The next step is to notch the bottom corners of the front (K) to fit over the sides *(Fig. 9a)*. I also drilled two $5/16$"-dia. shank holes on the front and installed two T-nuts to provide a way to attach a guard for the router bit later.

MOUNTING PLATE. Now you're ready to add the mounting plate *(Fig. 10)*. To provide solid support for the router, I made the plate from a rigid plastic material called phenolic. Phenolic is available in several different thicknesses (mine is $3/8$" thick). For sources, see page 126.

To create an opening for the router bit, there's a large hole cut in the mounting plate *(Fig. 10)*. The hole I cut is much

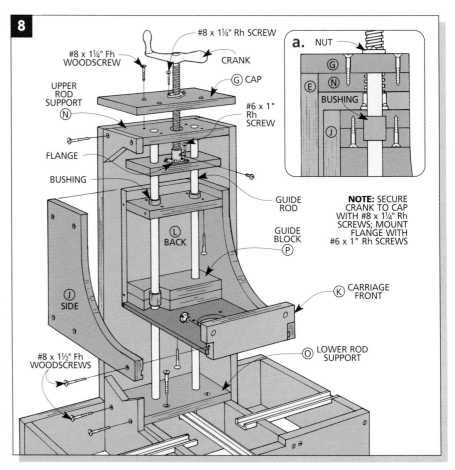

larger than necessary. But I did it this way because I wanted to create a large "window" that makes it easier to see the layout markings on the workpiece when setting up the Mortising Machine.

In addition to the large hole, you'll need to drill two holes near the back edge of the mounting plate to slip over the

metal rods *(Fig. 10)*. Plus, a countersunk shank hole can be drilled in between these two holes (from the bottom). This hole is for a woodscrew that's used to secure the mounting plate to a guide block that's added later. Finally, don't forget to locate and drill mounting holes in the mounting plate for your router.

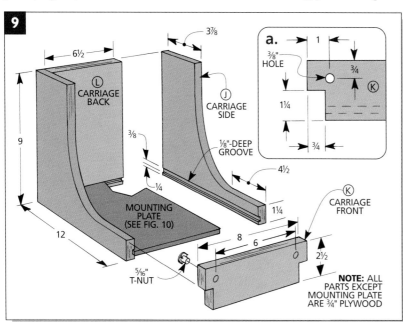

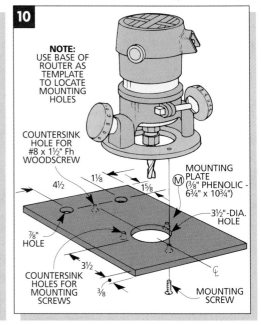

Set the carriage pieces aside for awhile and concentrate on the guide system.

GUIDE RODS. The heart of this system is a pair of metal guide rods *(Fig. 11)*. These rods pass through a number of plywood blocks and the mounting plate. (I bought a long metal rod and cut each guide rod to final length with a hacksaw.)

SUPPORT BLOCKS. The ends of the rods are held in place by an upper (N) and lower rod support (O). Two thick guide blocks (P) attached to the carriage slide up and down the rods as you turn the crank on top of the machine *(Fig. 8)*.

Note: Each guide block starts out as two oversize pieces of $3/4$" plywood.

BUSHINGS. To eliminate "play" in the carriage, the rods slip through bushings captured inside pockets in the guide blocks *(Fig. 8a and photo below)*. But the bushings don't ensure the carriage will slide smoothly without binding. That depends on the rods being parallel to each other. (The holes in one block need to line up with the holes in the others.)

To do this, start with six identical support blocks (one block each for the upper and lower rod support, and four for the guide blocks). Then clamp two stop blocks to the drill press fence to position each piece *(Fig. 12)*.

DRILL HOLES. To form the pockets for the bronze bushings, begin by drilling $3/4$"-dia. counterbores $1/2$" deep in the pieces that make up the guide blocks (P) *(Fig. 11)*. Then follow up with $5/8$" through holes for the guide rods. I also drilled the holes in the upper rod support (N) all the way through. But to prevent the guide rods from slipping through the lower rod support (O), I drilled stopped holes ($5/8$" deep) in it.

After completing all the holes in the supports and guide blocks, you can fit the bushings into the pockets and screw the guide blocks together. Then trim the waste off the ends and the back edges of the guide blocks.

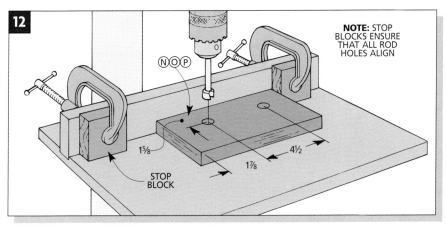

Bronze bushings that slip over the metal guide rods eliminate "play" to create an accurate guide system for the carriage. The 1"-long bushings are captured inside pockets in the guide blocks.

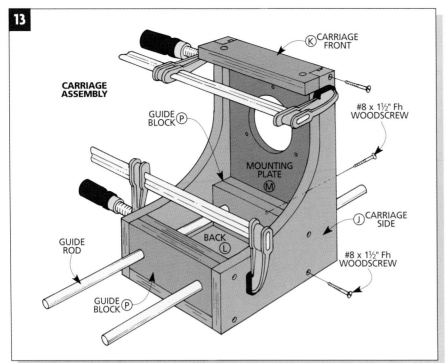

13

CARRIAGE
ASSEMBLY

(K) CARRIAGE FRONT

GUIDE BLOCK (P)

#8 x 1½" Fh WOODSCREW

MOUNTING PLATE (M)

(J) CARRIAGE SIDE

BACK (L)

GUIDE ROD

GUIDE BLOCK (P)

#8 x 1½" Fh WOODSCREW

CARRIAGE ASSEMBLY. At this point, you're ready to assemble the carriage. To do this, start by sliding the rods through the guide blocks and mounting plate. Then, after clamping the sides (J), front (K), and back (L) in place around the guide blocks, simply screw the carriage assembly together *(Fig. 13)*.

Before installing this assembly, you'll need to screw the lower rod support (O) to the base (refer to *Fig. 8* on page 30). Then after drilling a hole in the upper rod support (N) to accept the crank, slip the rod support over the guide rods.

Now set this assembly inside the tower and fit the rods into the holes in the lower rod support. It's secured by driving screws through the sides of the tower into the upper rod support. Attaching the cap (G) with screws will make it easy to install the crank.

MOUNT CRANK. First remove the mounting flange from the end of the crank. (A single screw holds it in place.) After inserting the threaded part of the shaft through the top of the tower, just screw the "nut" on the crank to the cap.

Once the crank is secured, you can mark the location for the flange on the upper guide block. But in order to attach the flange, you'll need some knuckle room. I found it easiest to remove the upper rod support, cap, and crank. (This entire assembly is held in place with the four screws that hold the upper rod support.) Finally, screw the flange in place and reassemble the parts.

ACCESSORIES .... *Router Bit Guard*

Routers are like any other shop tool. They're only as safe as the person using them. Table-mounted routers not only provide you with an easy way to get the most from this portable tool, they also have guards to protect the user from getting too close to the spinning bit. Since the bit is exposed below the carriage in the Mortising Machine, it's a good idea to add a guard for safety as well.

Note: The guard shown is made from scrap pieces of material, but commercial blade guards are available. For more information on commercial guards, see Sources on page 126.

Making the guard is quite simple. In fact, there are only two pieces: a shield (mine is safety orange in color) and a hardwood guard block (see drawing).

SHIELD. The shield is just a piece of acrylic plastic with a couple of adjustment slots that allow you to raise and lower the guard depending on the thickness of your workpiece. (For a tip on drilling and cutting acrylic plastic, see the Shop Tip on page 15.)

Note: You can find acrylic plastic at most home centers and hardware stores.

GUARD BLOCK. Although the shield extends down in front of the carriage, I also wanted part of the guard to extend underneath. So I attached the guard block to the bottom edge with screws. (Commercial guards are usually made

from one piece of plastic that curls underneath the router carriage assembly.)

MOUNTING. To hold the guard in place, I used a couple of plastic star knobs and a pair of fender washers. The knobs are threaded into the T-nuts that are added to the front (K) of the carriage (see detail 'a' in drawing).

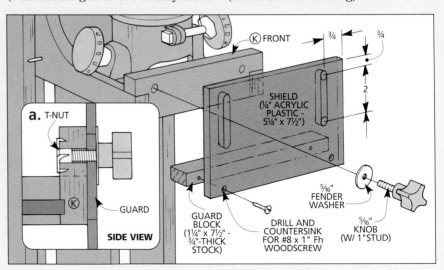

(K) FRONT

¾

¾

2

SHIELD (¼" ACRYLIC PLASTIC - 5¼" x 7½")

a. T-NUT

(K)

GUARD

SIDE VIEW

GUARD BLOCK (1¼" x 7½" - ¾"-THICK STOCK)

DRILL AND COUNTERSINK FOR #8 x 1" Fh WOODSCREW

⁵⁄₁₆" FENDER WASHER

⁵⁄₁₆" KNOB (W/ 1" STUD)

LOWER TABLE

This Mortising Machine is designed with two sliding tables. A lower table moves from side to side *(Fig. 14)*. And an upper table (that rides piggy-back on top) is designed to slide in and out.

To provide the movement that's needed to cut a mortise to length, the lower table slides back and forth in the metal track in the base.

NOTCH. The lower table (Q) is just a piece of ³⁄₄" MDF with a wide notch cut in the back edge *(Fig. 15)*. This notch should be wide enough to provide clearance around the tower as the lower table moves from side to side.

RUNNERS. To guide the table, I made two lower runners (R) that fit inside the aluminum track. These runners fit in a groove cut in the bottom of the table. In addition, a third runner attached to the top of the table serves as a track for the upper table. This upper runner (S) fits in a dado cut in the top of the table.

After cutting all the phenolic runners to size, the next step is to screw the two lower runners in place so they're flush with the ends of the table. This creates an opening between the runners for a ball bearing that fits into the groove under the lower table *(Fig. 15b)*.

BEARING. The purpose of this bearing is simple. When the table is installed, the bearing fits inside the channel that forms the handle *(Fig. 14a)*. As you move the handle back and forth, it exerts pressure against the bearing which slides the table smoothly from side to side.

The bearing is secured to the table with a bolt and lock nut. And I used these same fasteners to secure the upper runner. The nut sits in a recess that's formed by drilling a counterbore in the runner *(Fig. 15a)*. This prevents the upper table from hitting the lock nut as it slides on the runner.

T-NUTS. With the upper runner bolted in place, I drilled two pilot holes and added the T-nuts to the bottom of the table, one near each of the back corners *(Fig. 15)*. Later, the T-nuts are used to hold the two sliding tables together.

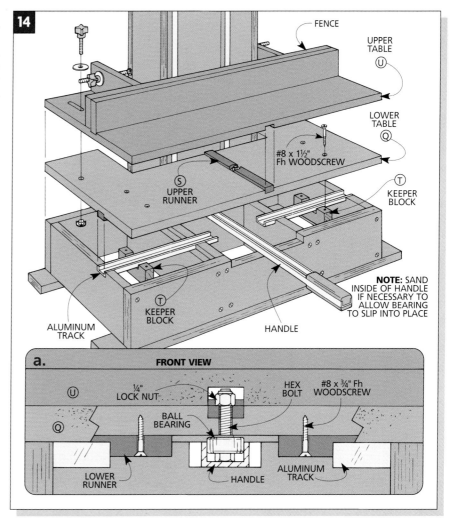

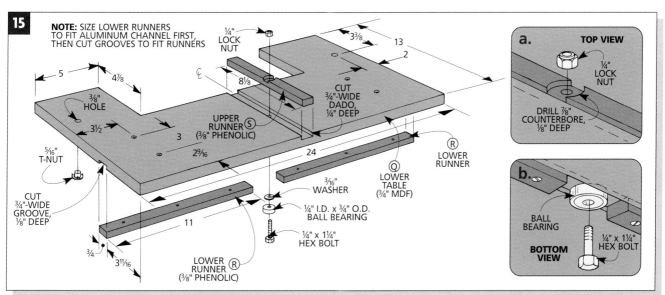

INSTALL LOWER TABLE. Now you're ready to install the lower table. You may have to jockey it around a bit to fit the bearing down in the handle and to get the runners to slip into the track.

KEEPER BLOCKS. With the table in place, I added two hardwood keeper blocks (T) (refer to *Fig. 14* on page 33). These U-shaped blocks prevent the table from lifting up when working with long pieces that hang over the base. To keep this from happening, I notched the blocks to fit around the T-track and lower runners and screwed it to the table.

UPPER TABLE

At this point, you can turn your attention to building the upper table *(Fig. 16)*. This table slides in and out on the runner that's mounted to the top of the lower table. Plus, it provides a platform for a sturdy multi-part fence that's used to clamp the workpiece in place.

It's this forward and backward movement that lets you establish the location of the mortise on the edge of a workpiece. To get the mortise to end up exactly where you want it, you simply slide the table in or out to position the workpiece under the bit. Then, by tightening a pair of knobs and locking the two tables together, they'll move as a single unit when cutting the mortise.

CONSTRUCTION. The upper table (U) is identical in size to the lower table. And once again, it has a wide U-shaped notch that provides clearance around the tower. But this time, I cut a pair of adjustment slots in the table *(Fig. 16)*. Also, cutting a dado in the bottom of the table allows it to fit over the upper runner. What you want here is to size the dado to create a smooth, sliding fit.

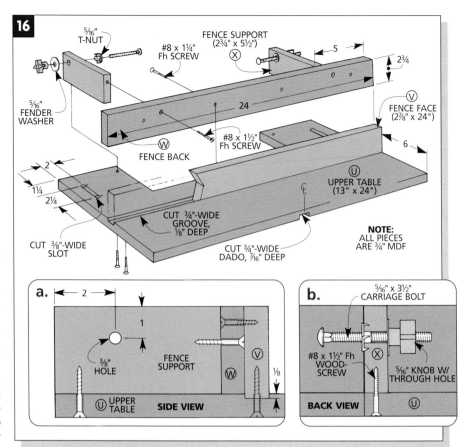

There's just one thing left to do before adding the fence assembly. That's to cut a groove in the top of the table to accept one of the fence pieces *(Fig. 16)*.

FENCE

In addition to supporting a workpiece, the fence provides a way to mount a stop system that controls the side to side movement of the sliding tables.

The fence is made up of several parts. To position the workpiece on the table, the fence face (V) is a long strip of $3/4$"

MDF that's screwed into the groove in the top of the table *(Fig. 16)*. To strengthen the face, I added a back (W) and two supports (X). Before screwing these pieces together, it's best to install in each support a T-nut that's part of the stop system. Then screw the supports to the table and fasten the fence back (W) and face (V) together with screws.

INSTALL UPPER TABLE. Now you can install the upper table. Doing this is just a matter of setting it in place and fastening the upper and lower tables together with two threaded knobs. The knobs pass through the slots in the upper table and thread into the T-nuts in the lower table *(Figs. 17 and 17a)*.

STOP SYSTEM. All that's left is to add the stop system *(Fig. 16b)*. The stop system determines the amount of side to side movement of the tables. The key to the stop is a $3^1/2$"-long carriage bolt that threads into the T-nut in each support. When you slide the table to the right, the head of the bolt in the left support contacts the tower and "stops" the table. The opposite stop works the same way.

To adjust the stops, it's just a matter of threading the bolts in or out. Then tightening a knob on the end of each bolt locks in the adjustment.

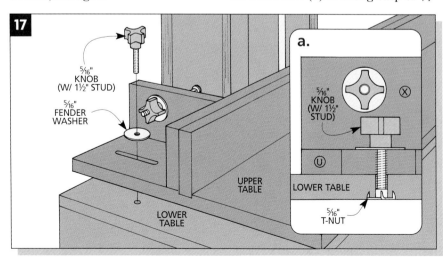

DEPTH GAUGE

To see at a glance when the mortise is cut to the desired depth, I added a depth gauge to the side of the tower.

There's nothing complicated about the depth gauge. It's just a 6" metal rule attached to a plywood adjustment block (Y) *(Fig. 18)*. A long slot in the adjustment block lets you raise and lower the depth gauge. Also, I cut a wide rabbet to form a lip that fits over the edge of the tower *(Fig. 18a)*. This lip keeps the rule and the depth gauge aligned as you move the gauge up and down.

ATTACH RULE. The metal rule is attached with two roundhead woodscrews. Tightening the screw heads against the rule holds it securely in place.

INSTALL GAUGE. Now you can install the depth gauge. A threaded knob that passes through the adjustment block and into the T-nut (installed earlier) is all that's needed here.

INDICATOR. To make it easy to "read" the depth gauge, I added a small indicator to the side of the carriage. It's just a nail with the head snipped off. File the end of the nail and drill a hole, before using some epoxy to hold it in place.

SETUP. To use the depth gauge, lower the carriage until the tip of the bit just touches the workpiece. Then adjust the

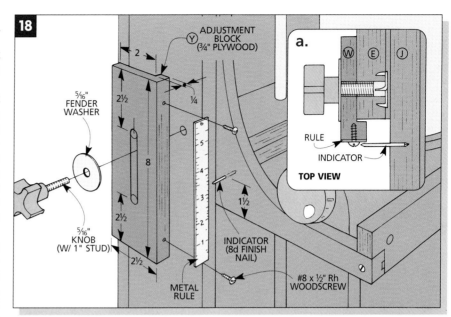

gauge so the indicator points to the final depth of the mortise. As you lower the carriage to make a series of successive cuts, the indicator will eventually point to the bottom end of the rule. That's when you know the mortise has been cut to the correct depth. ■

A handy feature of the mortiser is the depth gauge. It allows you to see when the mortise is cut to the right depth without having to remove the workpiece.

SHOP INFO .... *Spiral End Mill Bits*

When making mortises with the Mortising Machine, you want to make a clean cut that doesn't clog up. That's why I use a spiral end mill bit.

There are two types of spiral end mill bits: upcut and downcut. Upcut bits pull the chips up toward the router and out of the kerf for fast cutting. (This is what I used.) The downward cutting action of a downcut bit works best in materials prone to chipout on the top (such as plywood). For sources of bits, see page 126.

CLEAN CUT. You could use a straight bit to cut the mortise, but because of its spiral design, the cutting edges of a spiral end mill bit contact the wood at an angle. So instead of chopping the wood fibers like a straight bit, it produces a clean, slicing cut. This reduces chipout along the edges of the mortise.

CHIP CLEARANCE. Plus, the spiral design of these specialty bits also allows

for fast chip clearance. Unlike a straight bit that shoots chips out to the side and clogs up the cut, an upcut spiral end mill bit pulls most of the chips up and out. This means no more digging chips out of the mortise after it's been cut.

NO BURN. And since the chips are removed faster, the bit doesn't have a chance to heat up. So there's less tendency for the wood to burn. This means the bit lasts longer too — especially if you use a solid-carbide bit.

Spiral Bits. *To cut a mortise using the Mortising Machine, I found that a spiral upcut router bit produced a clean cut with little (if any) tearout. These bits are available in a number of sizes. Use a bit with a ¹/₂" shank to reduce vibration.*

Cutting mortises with the machine is easy — all it takes is a little planning and an accurate setup. First, mark out the mortise on your workpiece. Setting up the machine is just a matter of positioning the piece on the sliding table, clamping it in place, then adjusting the stops that limit the length of the mortise.

POSITION WORKPIECE. After the mortise has been laid out, setting up the mortiser takes just a few steps. The first involves adjusting the upper table to position the workpiece under the bit.

UPPER TABLE. Begin by positioning the workpiece on the sliding table with one edge butted against the fence face. Then lower the carriage so that the bit just touches the top of the workpiece. Now slide the upper table in or out to center the bit over the mortise (*Step 1*). Once it's centered, tighten the knobs that lock the upper table in place.

Now position the plastic router bit guard up or down with the workpiece in place (*Step 1*).

LOWER TABLE. With the upper table set, next you'll need to position the lower table. The lower table slides back and forth to provide the movement that's needed to cut a mortise to length.

CLAMP WORKPIECE. To position the lower table, first slide the workpiece along the fence until the bit is centered on the length of the mortise. Then clamp the workpiece to the fence (*Step 2*).

SET STOPS. Now you can set the stops that limit the length of the mortise. To do this, start by sliding the handle to the left until the bit aligns with the right end of the mortise. Adjust the bolt so it touches the tower and tighten the knob on the end of the bolt to lock it in place (*Step 3*). Repeat the process to set the stops on the other side.

SET DEPTH GAUGE. The next adjustment determines the depth of the mortise. All that's needed to do this is to set the depth gauge (with the bit still touching the workpiece) so the indicator points to the final depth of the mortise (*Step 4*). With the depth gauge set, once again you'll need to tighten the knob that locks it in place.

MAKE THE FIRST CUT. Now you're ready to cut a mortise in your workpiece. To start, you'll need to first turn on the router and crank the carriage assembly down, lowering it until it plunges into the workpiece.

I find it's safest to make several shallow cuts with the router (about 1/8" deep works best), slowly turning the crank clockwise to lower the spiral end mill bit (*Step 5*).

COMPLETE THE MORTISE. I make the first cut with the bit positioned at the right end. Slide the handle to the right until it stops. Then lower the carriage another 1/8" and push the handle all the way back in the opposite direction (*Step 6*). The spiral end mill bit is an upcut bit, which means the spirals draw the chips up and out, clearing them from the workpiece (see the Shop Info box on page 35).

Continue this process until the gauge reaches the bottom end of the rule and the mortise is cut to the desired depth.

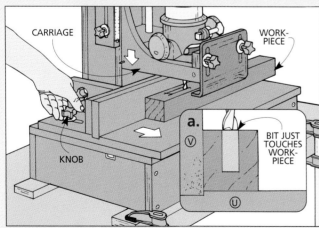

1 To set up the Mortising Machine, lay out the mortise and butt the workpiece against the fence. Now lower the carriage, slide the table in or out (so the bit will cut the mortise at the desired location), and lock the knobs.

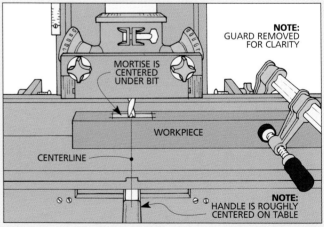

2 All it takes to establish the final position of the workpiece is to slide it along the fence until the bit is positioned over a centerline on the length of the mortise. Then simply clamp the workpiece to the fence.

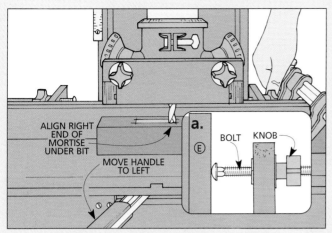

3 To set the stops, slide the handle to the left until the bit aligns with the right end of the mortise. Then adjust the carriage bolt so it contacts the tower side. After locking the stop, repeat the process for the other side.

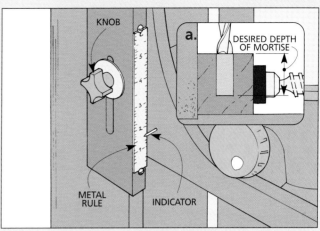

4 With the tip of the router bit still touching the workpiece, you can adjust the depth gauge so the indicator points to the desired depth of the mortise. Then tighten the depth gauge knob to lock the gauge in place.

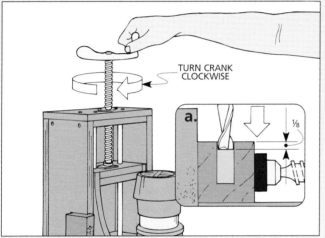

5 Now you're ready to flip the switch on the router and start cutting the mortise. To do this, turn the crank to lower the carriage and plunge the spinning bit into the workpiece. A shallow (1/8" deep) cut works best.

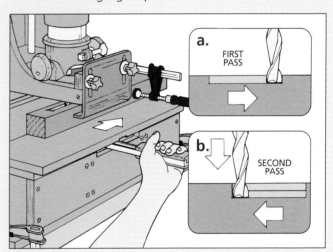

6 After sliding the handle to the right until it stops, lower the carriage assembly another 1/8" or so and push the handle all the way in the opposite direction. Continue this process, making several passes, until the mortise is cut to the desired depth.

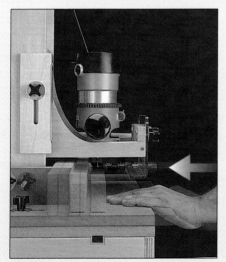

Mortise Location. It's easy to establish the location of the mortise on a workpiece. Just slide the table in or out to position the piece under the bit.

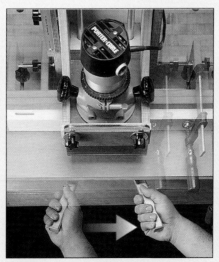

Mortise Length. To cut the mortise to length, use the handle to slide the table from side to side. Two stops control the amount of movement.

Depth of Mortise. Turning a crank raises and lowers the router carriage assembly and provides all the control you'll need over the depth of the mortise.

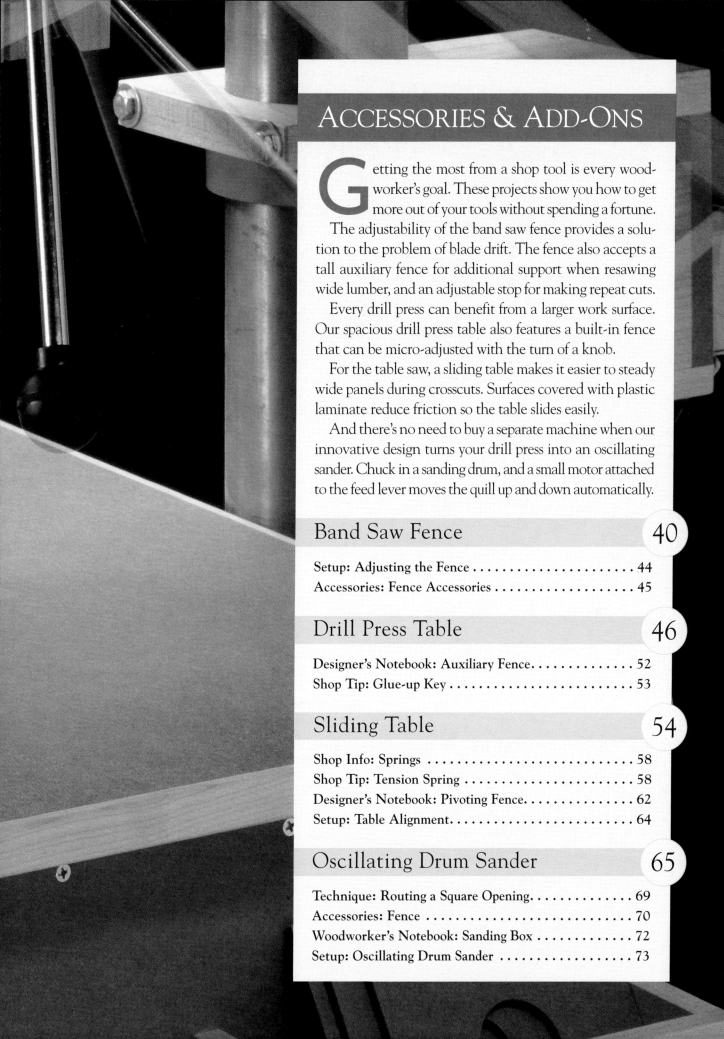

ACCESSORIES & ADD-ONS

Getting the most from a shop tool is every wood-worker's goal. These projects show you how to get more out of your tools without spending a fortune. The adjustability of the band saw fence provides a solution to the problem of blade drift. The fence also accepts a tall auxiliary fence for additional support when resawing wide lumber, and an adjustable stop for making repeat cuts.

Every drill press can benefit from a larger work surface. Our spacious drill press table also features a built-in fence that can be micro-adjusted with the turn of a knob.

For the table saw, a sliding table makes it easier to steady wide panels during crosscuts. Surfaces covered with plastic laminate reduce friction so the table slides easily.

And there's no need to buy a separate machine when our innovative design turns your drill press into an oscillating sander. Chuck in a sanding drum, and a small motor attached to the feed lever moves the quill up and down automatically.

Band Saw Fence

With this unique fence system, it's easy to get straight cuts on your band saw every time. The fence features a built-in clamping system, adjustable rails, and a pair of handy fence accessories.

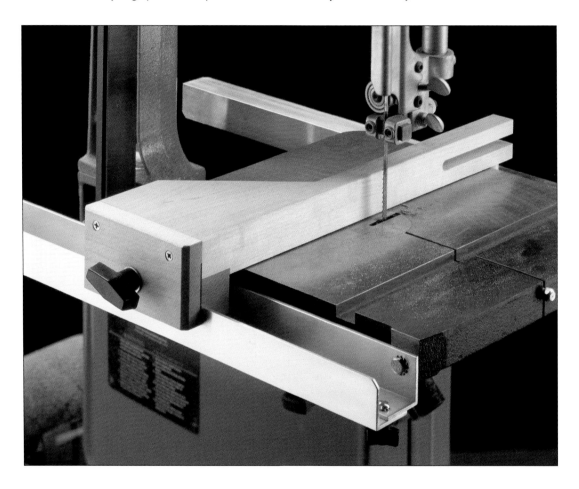

How many times have you clamped a scrap piece of wood to the table of your band saw as a fence, then spent the next hour fiddling around with it just to get a straight cut?

The solution is simple — add a fence system. But this is an expensive option for most saws. So I decided to build my own. The system I came up with consists of two main parts: a wood fence and a set of metal rails that guide it.

FENCE. The fence determines the width (thickness) of the cut and supports the workpiece. To make sure it stays in place after it's been positioned, there's a simple, but effective, fence clamp. Once it's tightened down, the fence is rock solid — there's no side to side play.

While the wide end of the fence provides plenty of clamping pressure on the rail, the other end is narrow to give you as much clearance as possible between the blade and the riser of the saw.

RAILS. The fence fits into a set of aluminum angle rails: a two-piece front rail and a single back rail. The two-piece front rail allows you to quickly and easily adjust the angle of the fence in relation to the blade to get a straight cut. (Details about adjusting the fence are on page 44.)

In addition to being adjustable, the fence system is also designed so that you can easily lift the fence off the rails whenever it isn't being used.

ACCESSORIES. There's a slot cut in the end of the fence to accept two optional accessories. One is a simple block that acts as an adjustable stop for repeat cuts. The other is a tall auxiliary fence that provides added support when resawing wider stock. Instructions for these easy-to-make add-ons are on page 45.

MATERIALS. Despite all the features, there isn't much material required to build the fence system. You may have enough wood in your scrap bin to build the fence. And all of the hardware is readily available at most hardware stores.

EXPLODED VIEW

OVERALL DIMENSIONS:
$23^7/_8$W x $19^1/_8$D x $5^7/_8$H

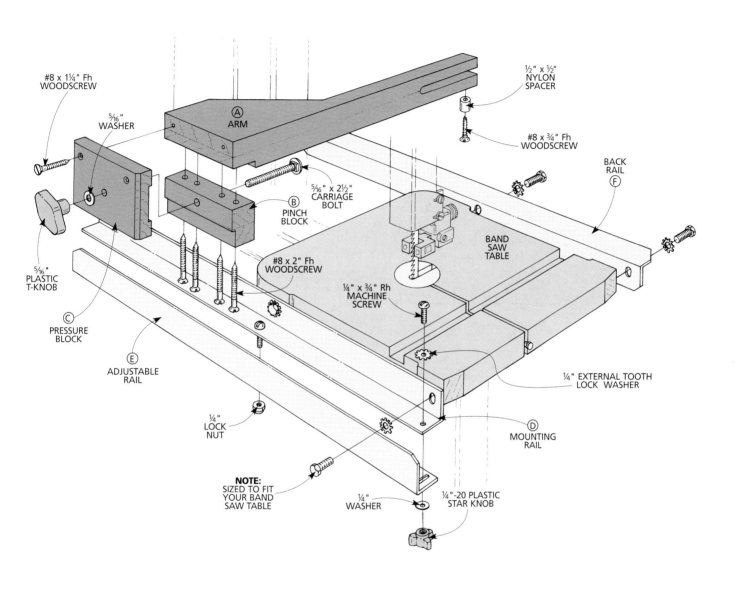

#8 x 1¼" Fh WOODSCREW

⁵⁄₁₆" WASHER

Ⓐ ARM

½" x ½" NYLON SPACER

#8 x ¾" Fh WOODSCREW

BACK RAIL Ⓕ

⁵⁄₁₆" x 2½" CARRIAGE BOLT

Ⓑ PINCH BLOCK

⁵⁄₁₆" PLASTIC T-KNOB

BAND SAW TABLE

#8 x 2" Fh WOODSCREW

¼" x ¾" Rh MACHINE SCREW

Ⓒ PRESSURE BLOCK

Ⓔ ADJUSTABLE RAIL

¼" EXTERNAL TOOTH LOCK WASHER

Ⓓ MOUNTING RAIL

¼" LOCK NUT

NOTE: SIZED TO FIT YOUR BAND SAW TABLE

¼" WASHER

¼"-20 PLASTIC STAR KNOB

MATERIALS LIST

MATERIALS

A	Arm (1)	$1^1/_2$ x 5 - $17^3/_4$
B	Pinch Block (1)	$1^1/_2$ x $1^3/_8$ - 5
C	Pressure Block (1)	$^3/_4$ x $2^3/_4$ - 5
D	Mounting Rail (1)	$1^1/_2$ x $1^1/_2$ alum. angle - $23^7/_8$
E	Adjustable Rail (1)	$1^1/_2$ x $1^1/_2$ alum. angle - $23^7/_8$
F	Back Rail (1)	$1^1/_2$ x $1^1/_2$ alum. angle - $23^7/_8$

HARDWARE SUPPLIES

(4) No. 8 x 2" Fh woodscrews
(2) No. 8 x 1¼" Fh woodscrews
(1) No. 8 x ¾" Fh woodscrew
(2) ¼"-20 x ¾" Rh machine screws
(1) ¼"-20 lock nut
(1) ¼" external tooth lock washer
(1) ¼"-20 plastic star knob
(1) ¼" washer
(1) ⁵⁄₁₆" x 2½"-long carriage bolt

(1) ⁵⁄₁₆" washer
(1) ⁵⁄₁₆" plastic T-knob
(1) ½" x ½" round nylon spacer
(4) Hex-head machine bolts w/ lock washers to fit your band saw table*

*For mounting rails to saw table

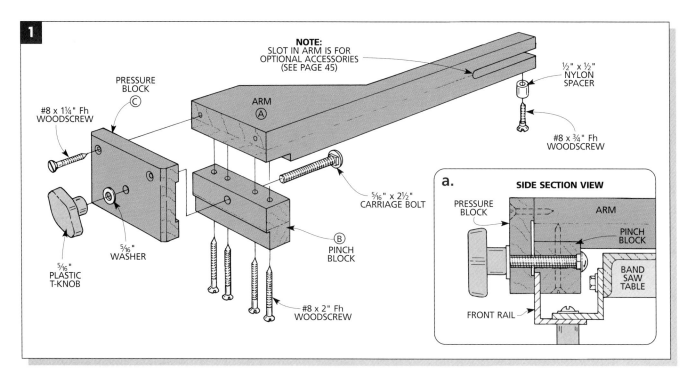

1

NOTE:
SLOT IN ARM IS FOR
OPTIONAL ACCESSORIES
(SEE PAGE 45)

PRESSURE
BLOCK
Ⓒ

ARM
Ⓐ

½" x ½"
NYLON
SPACER

#8 x 1¼" Fh
WOODSCREW

#8 x ¾" Fh
WOODSCREW

5⁄16" x 2½"
CARRIAGE BOLT

5⁄16"
WASHER

Ⓑ
PINCH
BLOCK

5⁄16"
PLASTIC
T-KNOB

#8 x 2" Fh
WOODSCREW

a.

SIDE SECTION VIEW

PRESSURE
BLOCK

ARM

PINCH
BLOCK

BAND
SAW
TABLE

FRONT RAIL

FENCE

The heart of the band saw system is the fence *(Fig. 1)*. It consists of three hardwood parts: an arm, a pinch block, and a pressure block. The pinch block and pressure block create a slot that supports the arm on the front rail *(Fig. 1a)*.

ARM

I started work by making the arm. It's shaped like the letter "d" — wide at the front to provide a large clamping surface, and narrow at the end to clear the throat of the band saw (see photo below).

The arm (A) is made by gluing up two 5"-wide blanks of ³⁄4"-thick stock face to face *(Fig. 2)*. (I used hard maple.) To

determine the length of these blanks, measure the length (depth) of your band saw table and add 5". (In my case, the blanks were 17³⁄4" long.) After the glue dries, cut the arm to shape and sand the edges smooth *(Fig. 2)*.

SLOT. If you're planning on making the fence accessories shown on page 45, now is the time to cut a slot in the arm *(Fig. 2)*. I did this by laying out the location of the slot on the *inside* face of the arm. That way, the arm can rest on the flat edge while you are drilling a ³⁄8"-dia. hole at the end of the slot. Finally, remove the remaining waste with the band saw.

RABBET. The arm slides on a rail and is held on this rail by a pinch block and a pressure block *(Fig. 1a)*. To prevent the pinch block from twisting when it's

screwed to the arm later, I cut a ¹⁄4"-deep rabbet in the front of the arm to "lock" it in place *(Figs. 1 and 2)*.

PINCH BLOCK

The next step is to make the pinch block that fits in the rabbet you just cut in the arm *(Fig. 3)*. This block forms the rear "jaw" of the clamp that holds the arm in place on the front rail *(Fig. 1a)*.

To make the pinch block (B), start by gluing up two pieces of ³⁄4"-thick stock to make a blank about 8" long. Then rip this blank to match the width of the rabbet (1³⁄8") *(Fig. 3a)*.

LIP. Next, to create a "lip" so the pinch block can ride on the front rail, a rabbet is cut on the edge of the blank *(Fig. 3a)*.

2

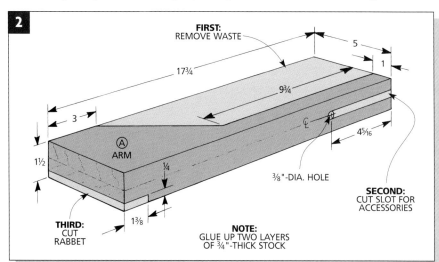

FIRST:
REMOVE WASTE

5

1

17³⁄4

9³⁄4

3

Ⓐ
ARM

¼

1½

³⁄8"-DIA. HOLE

4⁵⁄16

SECOND:
CUT SLOT FOR
ACCESSORIES

THIRD:
CUT
RABBET

1³⁄8

NOTE:
GLUE UP TWO LAYERS
OF ³⁄4"-THICK STOCK

The "d"-shaped arm of the fence allows it to wrap around the riser of the band saw. This way, you can slide it all the way to the left to accommodate wide pieces.

After the lip has been created, all that remains is to trim the pinch block to match the width of the arm (5") and screw it in place *(Fig. 3)*. I used four screws here so the pinch block will resist twisting when the pressure block is tightened down. And note that the screws are positioned so that a hole can be drilled through the center of the block later.

PRESSURE BLOCK

All that's left is to add the pressure block (C) to the arm *(Fig. 1)*. Since it's a short piece, I once again started with an extra-long blank. Then cut this blank to match the combined height of the pinch block and arm (2¾") *(Fig. 4)*.

SHALLOW GROOVE. To help concentrate clamping pressure on the front rail, a shallow groove is cut in one face of the pressure block *(Fig. 4)*.

After the groove is cut, trim the block to match the width of the arm (5"), and chamfer the outside corners *(Fig. 4)*.

CLAMP. The pressure block is attached to the arm with two woodscrews. Clamping pressure is exerted by a carriage bolt and a T-knob (or a wing nut). You should be able to find this hardware locally, but if you can't, some mail order sources are listed on page 126.

The carriage bolt passes through both the pressure block and the pinch block *(Fig. 1a)*. When the T-knob is tightened on the end of the bolt, it pinches the guide rail and locks the fence in place.

TEMPLATE. The tricky part to all this is getting the screw and bolt holes to align perfectly in both pieces.

To solve this problem, I drilled three holes in the pressure block first *(Fig. 4)*. Then I used carpet tape to fasten the pres-

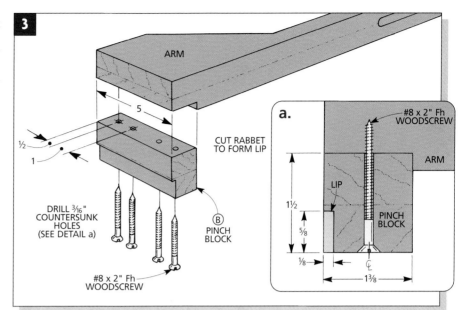

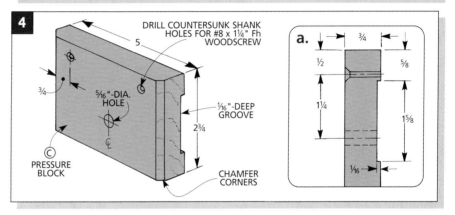

sure block to the arm and used the holes as a template to drill through the pinch block and into the arm *(Fig. 5)*.

ASSEMBLY. After the holes are drilled, the fence can be assembled. To do this, drive the carriage bolt into the pinch block. Then, screw the pressure block to the arm. Now place a washer over the

carriage bolt and thread on the T-knob (or a wing nut) *(Fig. 1a)*.

NYLON SPACER. To complete the fence, screw a round nylon spacer to the narrow end of the arm *(Fig. 6)*. This spacer will ride on the back rail and support the fence when the arm doesn't rest directly on the saw table.

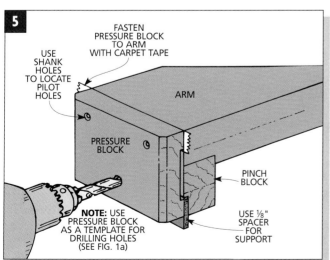

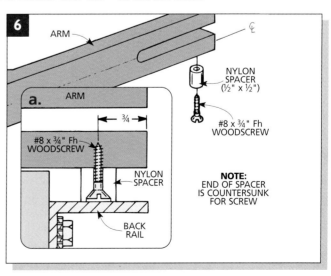

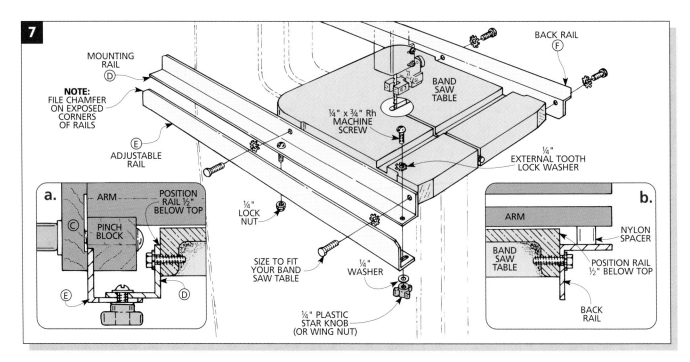

7

MOUNTING RAIL (D)

NOTE: FILE CHAMFER ON EXPOSED CORNERS OF RAILS

(E) ADJUSTABLE RAIL

BAND SAW TABLE

¼" x ¾" Rh MACHINE SCREW

BACK RAIL (F)

¼" EXTERNAL TOOTH LOCK WASHER

a.

ARM

POSITION RAIL ½" BELOW TOP

(C) PINCH BLOCK

(E)   (D)

¼" LOCK NUT

SIZE TO FIT YOUR BAND SAW TABLE

¼" WASHER

¼" PLASTIC STAR KNOB (OR WING NUT)

b.

ARM

NYLON SPACER

BAND SAW TABLE

POSITION RAIL ½" BELOW TOP

BACK RAIL

RAILS

With the fence complete, work can begin on the rails that attach to the band saw table. There is a two-piece front rail and a single back rail *(Fig. 7)*.

ALUMINUM ANGLE. All three rail pieces are made from 1½" x 1½" aluminum angle (available at most hardware stores). I used a hacksaw to cut three equal-length rails from a single six-foot length of angle (each piece is just under 24" long).

FRONT RAIL. Two pieces of angle make up the front rail *(Fig. 7)*. A mounting rail (D) attaches to the table of your band saw. An adjustable rail (E) attaches to the mounting rail and pivots so you can adjust your fence to get a straight cut.

The pivot point is centered on the length of the rails. A slot on one end allows you to adjust the rail in or out and then "lock" it in position.

SPACER BLOCK. The tricky part is drilling the holes in both rail pieces so they align. The solution is to clamp a spacer block between the rails *(Figs. 8 and 8a)*. Then lay out and drill the holes.

MAKE SLOT. Next, to create the slot in the adjustable rail (E), I drilled a series of holes and filed the slot smooth *(Fig. 8b)*.

SETUP . . . . *Adjusting the Fence*

The most unique feature of this fence system is its ability to compensate for drift. Drift is the tendency of the blade to "pull" one way or the other while cutting. Just about every band saw blade will have a certain amount of drift. It can be made worse by a dull blade, or a blade with uneven set.

Although it may sound like a constant headache, the solution is simple. All you need to do is adjust the angle of your fence to match the drift.

ALIGN FENCE. The first step is to align the band saw fence so it's parallel to your miter gauge slot.

Start by positioning the fence next to the edge of the miter gauge slot and lock it in place. Then loosen the star knob on the adjustable rail (E) (see detail 'a'). Next, pivot the adjustable rail until the arm of the fence aligns with the edge of the slot, and tighten the star knob.

TEST CUT. To check the fence system, make a test cut. Start by standing a scrap piece of wood on edge (see drawing). Then position the fence to cut the scrap in half and resaw the board. If the cut is straight, no more adjustment is needed.

DRIFT. If the cut isn't straight, move the fence so you can kick out the end of the board until the blade begins to follow a straight line. After cutting several inches of a straight line, turn off the saw, but don't move the workpiece. Then pivot the adjustable rail until the fence matches the angle of the workpiece (see detail 'a').

Now you should be able to cut a straight line with the workpiece against the fence.

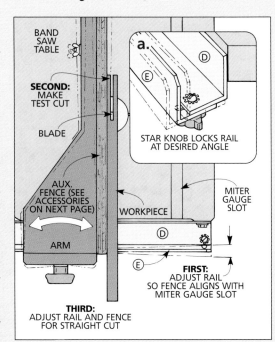

BAND SAW TABLE

a.

(D)

(E)

SECOND: MAKE TEST CUT

BLADE

STAR KNOB LOCKS RAIL AT DESIRED ANGLE

AUX. FENCE (SEE ACCESSORIES ON NEXT PAGE)

ARM

WORKPIECE

MITER GAUGE SLOT

(D)

(E)

FIRST: ADJUST RAIL SO FENCE ALIGNS WITH MITER GAUGE SLOT

THIRD: ADJUST RAIL AND FENCE FOR STRAIGHT CUT

MOUNT RAIL. To mount the front rail, two oversized holes are drilled in the mounting rail (D) for bolts. These bolts thread into the pre-drilled holes in your tabletop *(Fig. 7)*.

Note: If your band saw doesn't have these holes, you'll need to drill them.

The important thing is that you locate the rail so it's ½" below the top of the table *(Fig. 7a)*. This way, you'll still be able to get the bar of your miter gauge in and out of the slot *(Fig. 7)*.

BACK RAIL. Once the front rail is bolted into place, the only thing left is to add the back rail (F) *(Fig. 7)*. It bolts to the rear of the table to support the narrow end of the fence *(Fig. 7b)*.

All you need to do is drill two over-sized mounting holes and bolt it to the band saw table.

CHAMFER CORNERS. And as a finishing touch to the rails, file off the sharp exposed corners *(Fig. 7)*.

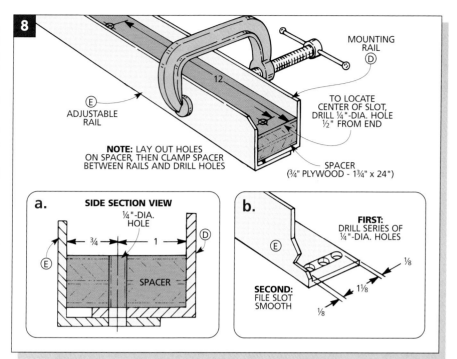

ACCESSORIES . . . . *Fence Accessories*

There are two accessories for the Band Saw Fence that I find myself reaching for all the time. One is a tall auxiliary fence that makes resawing safe and simple *(Fig. 1)*. The other is an adjustable block that's handy for making stopped cuts (like cutting tenons) *(Fig. 2)*.

AUXILIARY FENCE

The auxiliary fence offers additional support to your workpiece when resawing. It's just a piece of plywood cut to match the length of the arm (17¾") *(Fig. 1)*.

This fence attaches to the arm with a bolt and a wing nut *(Fig. 1)*. To prevent your workpiece from catching on the bolt, counterbore the hole *(Fig. 1a)*.

STOP BLOCK

The stop block is a piece of scrap hardwood with a hole drilled at one end for a carriage bolt. Locating the hole near one end allows you to flip the block and position it either close to the blade, or back by the end of the arm *(Fig. 2)*.

To complete the stop block, chamfer the two opposing corners of the block *(Fig. 2)*. This prevents sawdust from building up between the stop block, the table, and the workpiece.

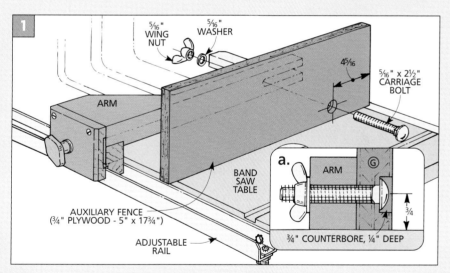

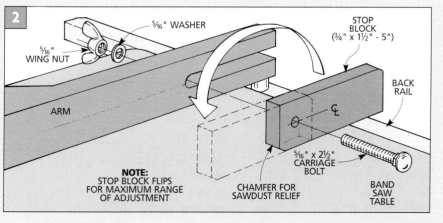

Drill Press Table

Stock drill press tables have a small work surface. And trying to position a fence on one is next to impossible. This table gives you a larger work area and features a built-in micro-adjustable fence.

Anyone who has ever spent too much time positioning a fence on a drill press will appreciate this add-on table. It combines a large work surface with an easily adjustable fence that's actually part of the table.

NO CLAMPS. Attaching the fence to the table solves a couple of problems. For instance, there's no need to fumble around with clamps to hold an auxiliary fence in place. And this fence won't get lost like the ones made of scrap wood.

TWO-PART TOP. Nevertheless, making the fence part of the table does present a challenge. How do you make the fence adjustable? The secret is a table top that's built in two parts. One part (the middle section) is bolted to the metal drill press table. The other part (surrounding the

middle) slides forward and backward quickly with just a push or a pull.

By attaching the fence to the sliding part of the table, you can position it exactly where you want. When you're through drilling, the table slides back to move the fence out of the way.

Another advantage to this two-part table is that it provides a larger work surface than the metal table of the drill press.

MICRO-ADJUSTER. And if you need to move the fence just a hair to fine-tune its position, simply turn a knob at the side of the table. It's connected to an adjusting mechanism located underneath the table.

BRAKE. Once the fence is positioned, another knob locks it in place. Like the adjusting mechanism, the brake can be operated with one hand.

MATERIALS. I used ³/₄" MDF for most of the table. The top of the table is covered with hardboard. And the center piece of hardboard is removable so that it can be replaced if it gets chewed up.

OPTIONAL FENCE. A ³/₄"-thick fence provides a sturdy bearing surface while allowing the most clearance possible between the drill bit and the fence. For jobs that don't require that much clearance, I built a second, removable fence that lets me add on a couple of useful accessories. A T-slot in the top of the fence accepts a stop block for precise and repeatable positioning of workpieces. A material hold-down also fits into the slot to act as a "third hand" while drilling. Details about this are in the Designer's Notebook on page 52.

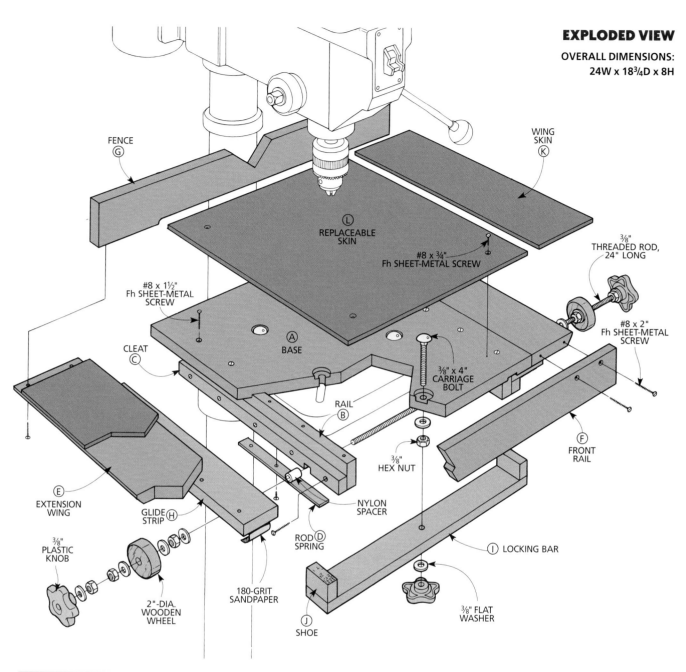

EXPLODED VIEW

OVERALL DIMENSIONS:
24W x 18¾D x 8H

FENCE
Ⓖ

WING
SKIN
Ⓚ

Ⓛ
REPLACEABLE
SKIN

#8 x ¾"
Fh SHEET-METAL SCREW

⅜"
THREADED ROD,
24" LONG

#8 x 1½"
Fh SHEET-METAL
SCREW

CLEAT
Ⓒ

Ⓐ
BASE

⅜" x 4"
CARRIAGE
BOLT

#8 x 2"
Fh SHEET-METAL
SCREW

RAIL
Ⓑ

⅜"
HEX NUT

Ⓕ
FRONT
RAIL

EXTENSION
WING
Ⓔ

GLIDE
STRIP
Ⓗ

NYLON
SPACER

⅜"
PLASTIC
KNOB

ROD Ⓓ
SPRING

2"-DIA.
WOODEN
WHEEL

180-GRIT
SANDPAPER

Ⓘ LOCKING BAR

Ⓙ
SHOE

⅜" FLAT
WASHER

MATERIALS LIST

WOOD
A Base (1)　　　　　¾ MDF - 16 x 18
B Rails (2)　　　　　¾ MDF - 1⅞ x 15
C Cleats (2)　　　　¾ MDF - 1 x 15
D Rod Springs (2)　¾ x ⅛ - 8
E Extension Wings (2)　¾ MDF - 4 x 18
F Front Rail (1)　　¾ MDF - 2¾ x 24
G Fence (1)　　　　¾ MDF - 3¼ x 24
H Glide Strips (2)　¾ MDF - 2½ x 15
I Locking Bar (1)　¾ MDF - 2 x 17⅛
J Shoes (2)　　　　¾ MDF - 1¼ x 2
K Wing Skins (2)　¼ hdbd. - 4½ x 17¼
L Replaceable Skin (1)　¼ hdbd. - 15 x 17¼

HARDWARE SUPPLIES
(4) No. 8 x 2" Fh sheet-metal screws
(14) No. 8 x 1½" Fh sheet-metal screws
(20) No. 8 x 1¼" Fh sheet-metal screws
(8) No. 8 x ¾" Fh sheet-metal screws
(4) ⅜" x 2" carriage bolts*
(1) ⅜" x 4" carriage bolt
(11) ⅜" hex nuts
(14) ⅜" flat washers
(1) ⅜" threaded rod, 24" long
(3) ⅜" plastic knobs
(2) 2"-dia. x ⅝" wooden wheels (⅜" bore)
(2) 1"-long nylon spacers (.385" I.D. x .5" O.D.)
(2) 1" x 15" 180-grit sandpaper
* Size may vary depending on your drill press

CUTTING DIAGRAM

¾" MDF - 24 x 48

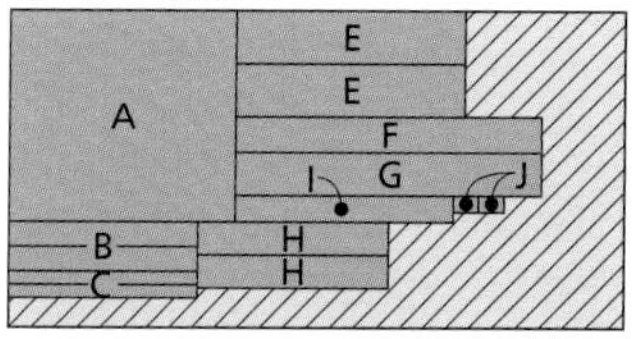

	E	
A	E	
	F	
	I	G	J
B			
C	H	
	H	

¼" TEMPERED HARDBOARD - 24 x 48

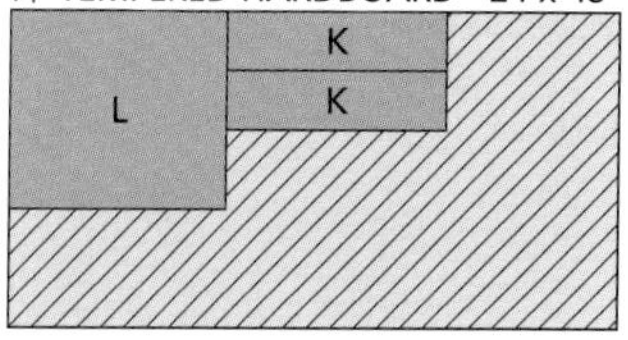

| | K | |
| L | K | |

ALSO NEED: 8"-LONG PIECE OF
¾"-THICK SCRAP FOR PART D

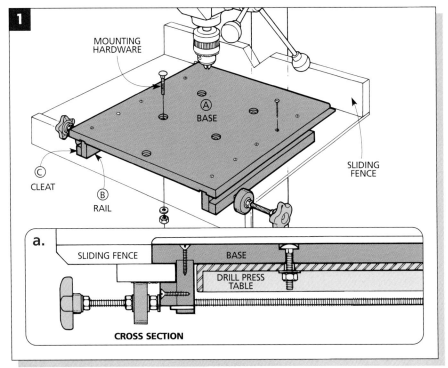

1

MOUNTING HARDWARE

(A) BASE

SLIDING FENCE

(C) CLEAT

(B) RAIL

a.

SLIDING FENCE

BASE

DRILL PRESS TABLE

CROSS SECTION

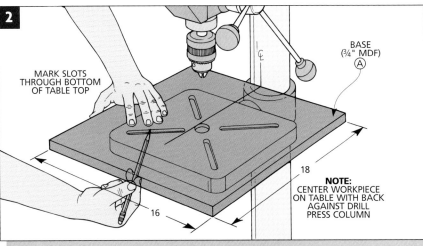

2

MARK SLOTS THROUGH BOTTOM OF TABLE TOP

BASE (3/4" MDF) (A)

18

16

NOTE: CENTER WORKPIECE ON TABLE WITH BACK AGAINST DRILL PRESS COLUMN

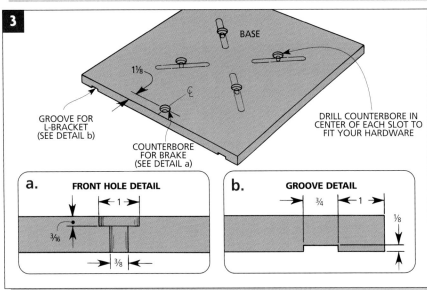

3

BASE

1 1/8

GROOVE FOR L-BRACKET (SEE DETAIL b)

COUNTERBORE FOR BRAKE (SEE DETAIL a)

DRILL COUNTERBORE IN CENTER OF EACH SLOT TO FIT YOUR HARDWARE

a. FRONT HOLE DETAIL

1

3/16

3/8

b. GROOVE DETAIL

3/4

1

1/8

I made most of this Drill Press Table from 3/4" medium-density fiberboard (MDF) and 1/4" hardboard — two engineered wood products that are strong, stable, and inexpensive. But you could also use 3/4"-thick plywood.

Note: MDF is prone to splitting when screws are driven into its edges. It's important that you drill properly-sized pilot holes and use straight-shanked screws. Refer to the Shop Tip on page 11 for more about this.

The Drill Press Table consists of two main parts — a base and a sliding fence. The base is attached to the metal table of the drill press. The fence fits around the base. I began with the base.

BASE. The base (A) provides a large work surface and supports the sliding fence. It's just a piece of MDF that's cut to size *(Fig. 2)*, and then bolted to the table of the drill press *(Fig. 1)*.

To locate the holes for the mounting hardware, first center the base (A) on the table of the drill press, with the back against the column *(Fig. 2)*.

Then mark the location of the mounting holes by tracing the slots in the table to the bottom of the base (A). Once the slots are traced, flip the workpiece over and drill a counterbored hole in the center of each slot for mounting hardware that fits your table *(Fig. 3)*. I used 3/8" carriage bolts *(Fig. 1a)*.

This is also a good time to drill a 3/8"-dia. counterbored hole near the front edge of the base. This is for a brake that's added later *(Fig. 3a)*.

GROOVES. Once the counterbored holes are drilled, the next step is to cut two 1/8"-deep grooves on the bottom of the base *(Figs. 3 and 3b)*. These grooves each accept an L-bracket that support a pair of extension wings and a sliding fence that are added later.

L-BRACKETS. The L-brackets are simple assemblies. Each one is just two pieces of MDF glued and screwed together to form an "L" *(Fig. 4)*. I cut the rails (B) and cleats (C) for the L-brackets 3" shorter than the grooves they fit in. There are two reasons for this.

First, the front of each bracket is set back 1/2" from the front of the base to prevent sawdust from building up when the fence is adjusted. Second, the brackets are positioned 2 1/2" from the back to allow room to turn the crank when adjusting the height of the table.

Once the rails and cleats are cut to size, you are ready to glue and screw the parts together *(Fig. 4b).*

Note: In the next step, a $1/2$"-wide notch is cut in each L-bracket. So locate the screws outside of the area to be notched *(Figs. 4a and 4b).*

Now you can cut the notch in each bracket. These are for nylon spacers used with the adjustment rod *(Figs. 4a and 5).*

Once the notches have been cut, you can glue and screw the L-brackets into the dadoes in the base *(Fig. 4b).*

ADJUSTMENT ROD. With the L-brackets in place, all that's left to complete the base is to add a micro-adjustment rod. This rod rests in the notches you cut in the L-brackets *(Fig. 6).*

The adjustment rod is a length of threaded rod with two knobs and two wooden wheels *(Fig. 5).* A set of hex nuts and washers are tightened against the knobs and wheels so that they will turn along with the rod *(Fig. 5a).*

But before threading on the knobs and wheels, push on two nylon spacers to prevent the rod from wearing on the notches in the L-brackets. (*Woodsmith Project Supplies* offers a hardware kit that includes all these pieces. See Sources on page 126 for details.)

The threaded rod is held in place by an unusual method — a couple of rod springs (D) made from narrow strips of hardwood pressing against the nylon spacers *(Fig. 6).* I ripped these $1/8$"-wide pieces from the edge of a $3/4$"-thick blank.

As either knob is turned, the threaded rod and the wheels rotate. When this happens, the wheels press against the bottom of the extension wings (added in the next step) and move the fence back and forth (see the photo below).

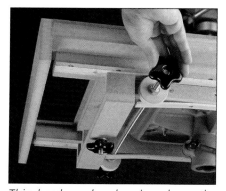

Thin hardwood rod springs keep the adjustment assembly pressed against the table when making micro-adjustments, yet allow the table to slide forward and back easily for rough positioning.

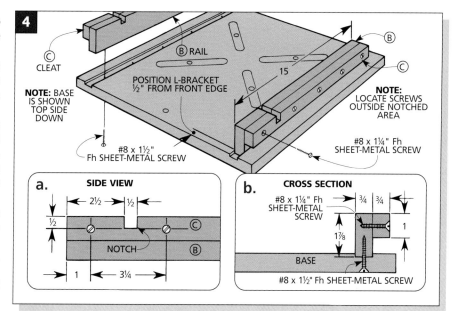

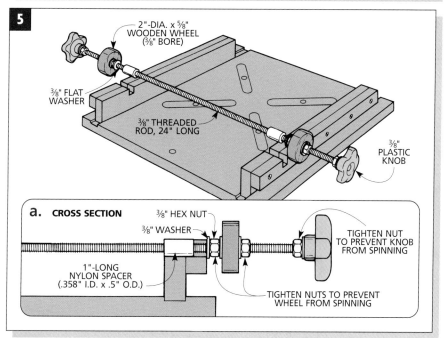

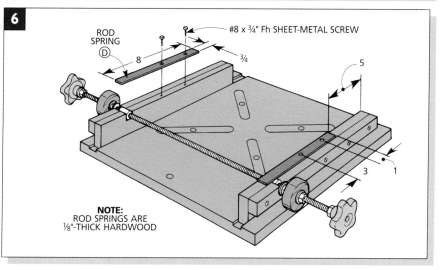

SLIDING FENCE

With the base complete, the next step is to build a sliding fence to fit around the base. It consists of an extension wing on either side of the base, a front rail, and a fence at the back *(Fig. 7)*.

WINGS. The extension wings (E) enlarge the work surface and support the fence. Each wing is cut to match the length of the base (18") *(Fig. 8)*. And to provide clearance when turning either knob on the adjustment rod, the outside edge is chamfered *(Fig. 8)*.

RAIL AND FENCE. To determine the length of the front rail and fence, temporarily clamp the extension wings to the sides of the base *(Fig. 8)*. Then measure across the combined width. (In my case, it was 24".)

After the front rail (F) is cut to length it can be glued and screwed to the front edge of the wings.

Note: To allow room for hardboard skins added later, position the front rail $^1/_4$" above the wings *(Fig. 8a)*.

Before attaching the fence (G), two more things need to be done to it. To allow clearance for the drill press chuck, a V-notch is cut on the top edge (see photo below). And to keep sawdust from building up, a $^3/_8$"-deep notch is routed along the bottom edge *(Fig. 8a)*.

GLIDE STRIPS. Next, to support the sliding fence on the base and allow it to move back and forth, add a pair of glide strips (H) *(Fig. 9)*. They're cut to match

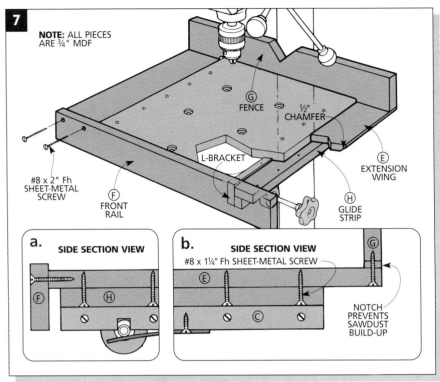

7

NOTE: ALL PIECES ARE ¾" MDF

FENCE (G)
½" CHAMFER
L-BRACKET
#8 x 2" Fh SHEET-METAL SCREW
(F) FRONT RAIL
(E) EXTENSION WING
(H) GLIDE STRIP

a. SIDE SECTION VIEW
(F) (H)

b. SIDE SECTION VIEW
#8 x 1¼" Fh SHEET-METAL SCREW
(E) (C) (G)
NOTCH PREVENTS SAWDUST BUILD-UP

When you need to drill close to the fence with a short bit, a V-shaped notch in the top of the fence provides clearance for the drill press chuck.

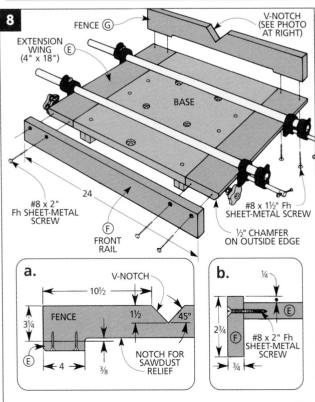

8

FENCE (G)
V-NOTCH (SEE PHOTO AT RIGHT)
EXTENSION WING (E) (4" x 18")
BASE
#8 x 2" Fh SHEET-METAL SCREW
24
(F) FRONT RAIL
#8 x 1½" Fh SHEET-METAL SCREW
½" CHAMFER ON OUTSIDE EDGE

a.
V-NOTCH
10½
FENCE
3¼
1½
45°
(E)
4
⅜
NOTCH FOR SAWDUST RELIEF

b.
¼
(E)
2¾
(F)
#8 x 2" Fh SHEET-METAL SCREW
¾

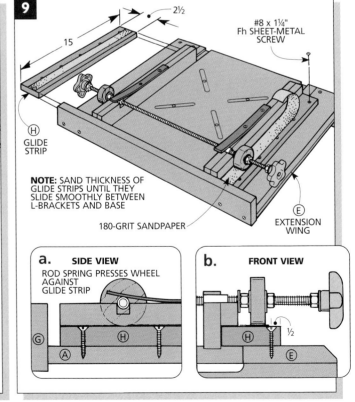

9
2½
15
#8 x 1¼" Fh SHEET-METAL SCREW
(H) GLIDE STRIP
NOTE: SAND THICKNESS OF GLIDE STRIPS UNTIL THEY SLIDE SMOOTHLY BETWEEN L-BRACKETS AND BASE
180-GRIT SANDPAPER
(E) EXTENSION WING

a. SIDE VIEW
ROD SPRING PRESSES WHEEL AGAINST GLIDE STRIP
(G) (H)
(A)

b. FRONT VIEW
(H) (E)
½

the length of the L-brackets (15") and are screwed to the bottom of the wings.

To make sure the glide strips slide smoothly on the L-brackets, first place the base and the fence together upside-down on a flat surface *(Fig. 9)*. Then sand them until they slide easily.

Finally, glue a strip of 180-grit sand-paper to the bottom of each glide *(Fig. 9)*. This gives the wheels something to "bite" into when you turn the knob.

BRAKE

All that's left to complete the Drill Press Table is to add a simple brake assembly to lock the sliding fence in place. The U-shaped brake hangs from a bolt that passes through the counterbored hole drilled earlier in the base *(Fig. 10)*.

BRAKE. The brake consists of a locking bar, two shoes, and a plastic knob that threads onto a carriage bolt *(Fig. 10)*. When the knob is tightened, the shoes press against the bottom of the glide strips (H) and prevent the fence from sliding. When the knob is loosened, the fence slides freely.

To determine the length of the locking bar (I), flip the Drill Press Table over on its top. Then measure the distance between the outside edges of the L-brackets and add $1\frac{5}{8}$" *(Figs. 11 and 11a)*.

Now the brake can be completed by drilling a hole in the center of the locking bar for a carriage bolt. Then glue on the two shoes (J) *(Fig. 11)*.

Once the brake is attached to the base, the table and fence can be mounted to the metal table on your drill press *(Fig. 12)*. When you position this assembly, remember to butt it up against the column of the drill press so you can get max-imum use of the work surface.

SKINS. To protect the table and keep sawdust out of the glide strips, I glued a pair of wing skins (K) to the extension wings *(Figs. 12 and 12a)*. A replaceable skin (L) is screwed to the base also. ∎

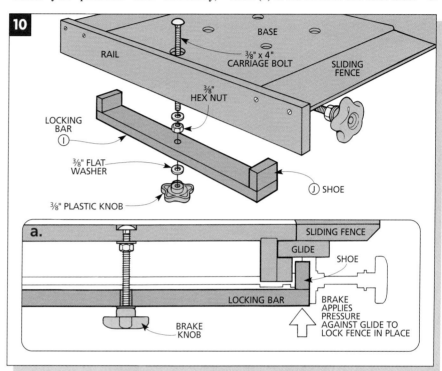

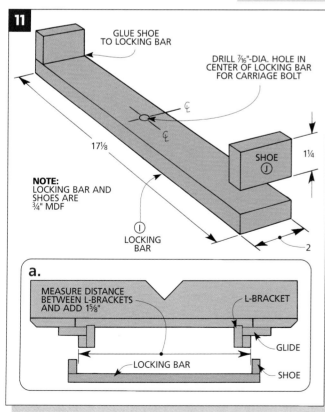

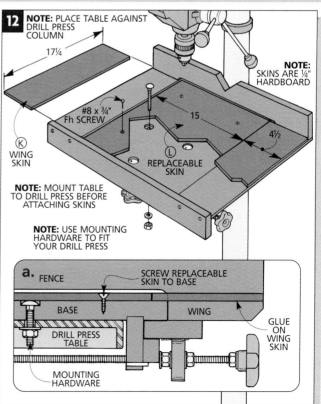

DESIGNER'S NOTEBOOK

For more accuracy and repeatable results, add this Auxiliary Fence to the Drill Press Table. It gives you extra "hands," including a hold-down and a material stop.

CONSTRUCTION NOTES:

■ This Auxiliary Fence is designed to attach to the existing fence of the Drill Press Table. It accepts a stop that is used to position the workpiece. Then a hold-down "locks" the workpiece in place for drilling.

A T-slot in the fence allows you to slide the stop or hold-down where needed, then secure them in place.

■ To add the hold-down and stop system to the Drill Press Table, start by cutting two fence pieces (M) from ³/₄"-thick stock *(Fig. 1)*. (I used hard maple.)

■ Then, to accept the hold-down and stop block shown on the next page, a T-slot is cut along the top edge of the fence. This slot is formed by cutting a ⁵/₁₆"-deep kerf in each piece before gluing them together *(Fig. 1a)*. (To keep the fence pieces aligned as you glue them up, see the Shop Tip on the facing page.)

■ When the glue is dry, the T-slot can be completed by cutting a groove centered along the top edge of the fence *(Fig. 1b)*.

■ Next, cut a notch in the center of the fence for chuck clearance *(Fig. 2)*.

■ Then rout a chamfer along the front bottom edge for sawdust relief *(Fig. 1)*.

■ Now all you need to do is screw (or bolt) the auxiliary fence to your existing drill press fence *(Fig. 2)*.

■ Once the fence is completed, you can move on to building the hold-down bracket and the stop block that slide in the T-slot. These are shown on the next page.

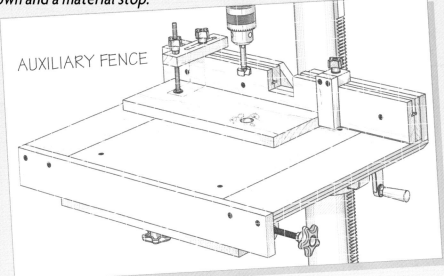

AUXILIARY FENCE

1

FENCE
(M)

NOTE: FENCE PIECES CUT FROM ³/₄"-THICK STOCK

3

24

NOTE: ROUT ⅛" CHAMFER ON FRONT EDGE ONLY

a. FIRST CUT ⅛"-WIDE KERF, THEN GLUE UP PIECES (SEE SHOP TIP ON NEXT PAGE)

1   ⅛

⁵/₁₆

b. ³/₈

FLIP PIECE END-FOR-END TO CENTER GROOVE

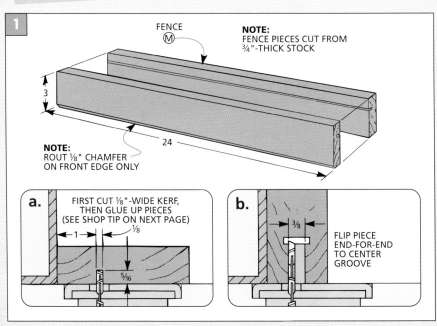

2

#8 x 2" Fh WOODSCREW

2½   1½

AUX. FENCE

NOTE: AUXILIARY FENCE SCREWED (NOT GLUED) TO EXISTING FENCE

MATERIALS LIST

NEW PARTS

M	Fence (2)	³/₄ x 3 - 24
N	Hold-down (1)	³/₄ x 1½ - 6
O	Stop (1)	³/₄ x 1½ - 3⁵/₈
P	Rail (1)	³/₄ x 1½ - 1½

HARDWARE SUPPLIES

(6) No. 8 x 2" Fh woodscrews
(2) No. 8 x 1½" Fh woodscrews
(3) ⁵/₁₆" threaded plastic knobs
(2) ⁵/₁₆" x 1³/₄"-long toilet bolts
(1) ⁵/₁₆" x 5"-long carriage bolt
(2) ⁵/₁₆" washers
(1) ⁵/₁₆" hex nut
(1) ⁵/₁₆" T-nut

HOLD-DOWN

■ The hold-down bracket "locks" a workpiece in place on the Drill Press Table. In fact, you may want to make two or three hold-downs to help when securing longer workpieces and to allow you to clamp on both sides of the drill press chuck.

The hold-down slides in the T-slot in the fence so it can be placed anywhere along its length.

■ The hold-down (N) is just a 3/4"-thick piece of stock (I used hard maple) (Fig. 3).

■ In order to slide the hold-down in and out for different size workpieces, a slot is cut near one end. A toilet bolt passes through this slot and the head rides in the T-slot in the fence.

■ To make the slot, I first drilled a series of overlapping holes centered on the width of the hold-down (Fig. 4). Then I used a chisel to clean out the remaining waste and smooth out the sides.

■ Once you've completed the slot, a hole is drilled in the other end for a 5/16" T-nut (Fig. 4). The T-nut will hold a 5"-long carriage bolt (Fig. 3). This bolt applies clamping pressure to the workpiece to hold it firmly against the table top.

■ After driving the T-nut into place, thread the carriage bolt through it, install a jam nut (hex nut), and tighten a plastic knob against the jam nut (Fig. 3).

■ Finally, the hold-down can be mounted to the fence with a toilet bolt, a washer, and a threaded knob (Fig. 3).

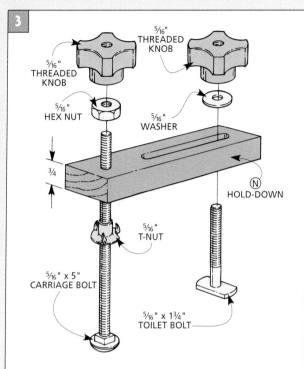

3

5/16" THREADED KNOB

5/16" THREADED KNOB

5/16" WASHER

5/16" HEX NUT

3/4

HOLD-DOWN (N)

5/16" T-NUT

5/16" x 5" CARRIAGE BOLT

5/16" x 1¾" TOILET BOLT

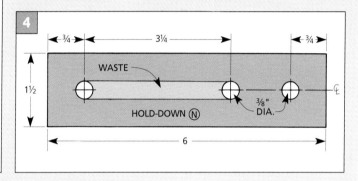

4

3/4   3¼   3/4

1½

WASTE

HOLD-DOWN (N)

3/8" DIA.

6

SHOP TIP

Glue-up Key

When gluing up the fence, it's important that the kerfs in the two pieces stay aligned. Otherwise, the head of the toilet bolt won't fit. An easy way to do this is to cut a key from 1/8" hardboard to fit in the kerfs. Give the key a heavy coat of wax so that any glue squeezeout won't stick to it.

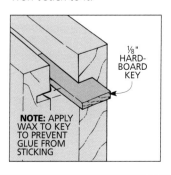

1/8" HARD-BOARD KEY

NOTE: APPLY WAX TO KEY TO PREVENT GLUE FROM STICKING

STOP BLOCK

■ The last item to build for the auxiliary fence is an adjustable stop block. It's used to accurately position a workpiece to be drilled. It's especially useful when you need to drill identically-placed holes in several workpieces. And used along with the hold-down bracket, it helps prevent the workpiece from shifting.

■ The stop block is just an L-shaped bracket consisting of two parts: a stop (O) and a rail (P) (Fig. 5). And like the hold-down, the stop block attaches to the fence by way of a toilet bolt that slides in the T-slot cut in the fence.

■ Since both the stop and the rail are such small parts, it's a good idea to start with an extra-long blank.

■ After drilling holes for woodscrews and a toilet bolt, cut the stop and rail to final length from the blank (Fig. 5).

Note: The stop is cut 1/8" shorter than the combined height of the fence and the rail to provide sawdust relief.

■ Now the parts can be glued and screwed together to form the L-shaped stop block (Fig. 5).

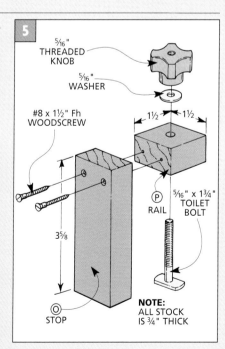

5

5/16" THREADED KNOB

5/16" WASHER

#8 x 1½" Fh WOODSCREW

1½   1½

3⅝

(P) RAIL

5/16" x 1¾" TOILET BOLT

(O) STOP

NOTE: ALL STOCK IS 3/4" THICK

■ Finally, push a toilet bolt through the hole, thread on a washer and plastic knob, and slide the toilet bolt into the T-slot.

Sliding Table

With this shop-built table installed on your table saw, you can work like the pros in cabinet shops. They use sliding tables because they provide more support and safety when making crosscuts.

Crosscutting a wide panel on the table saw can be a real juggling act. One hand is kept busy balancing the workpiece because the saw table in front of the blade is too small to provide much support. And the other is struggling to steady the miter gauge (that is, if the runner hasn't already come out of the slot). Not the safest situation.

MORE SUPPORT. One solution I've seen in a lot of production cabinet shops is a sliding table. To provide more support for the workpiece, a sliding table extends in front of the saw table.

There's only one drawback with most commercial tables. They're expensive.

So I decided I could build my own shop-made version for less.

CONSIDERATIONS. I had two things in mind when working on this Sliding Table. First, it had to crosscut workpieces up to 24" wide. And second, I wanted a table that was easy to build and didn't have a lot of complicated hardware.

SIMPLE DESIGN. The end result is a table with a simple, straightforward design. It slides on two rails that are supported by a shallow tray. And instead of using complicated hardware to make the table slide easily, I used plastic laminate. It creates a slick, durable surface for the table to slide across.

FENCE. To ensure accuracy when crosscutting, this table also features a fence that can be adjusted so it's precisely 90° to the saw blade. And when you're not using the table, just loosen a pair of knobs to remove the fence.

You can also build a pivoting fence that makes it easy to cut angles. The Designer's Notebook on page 62 shows how to add this option.

REPLACES EXTENSION. Like most commercial tables, this sliding table replaces the left extension wing on your saw table. To provide clearance when you pull the table back, you'll need to move (or cut off) the rails that guide the rip fence.

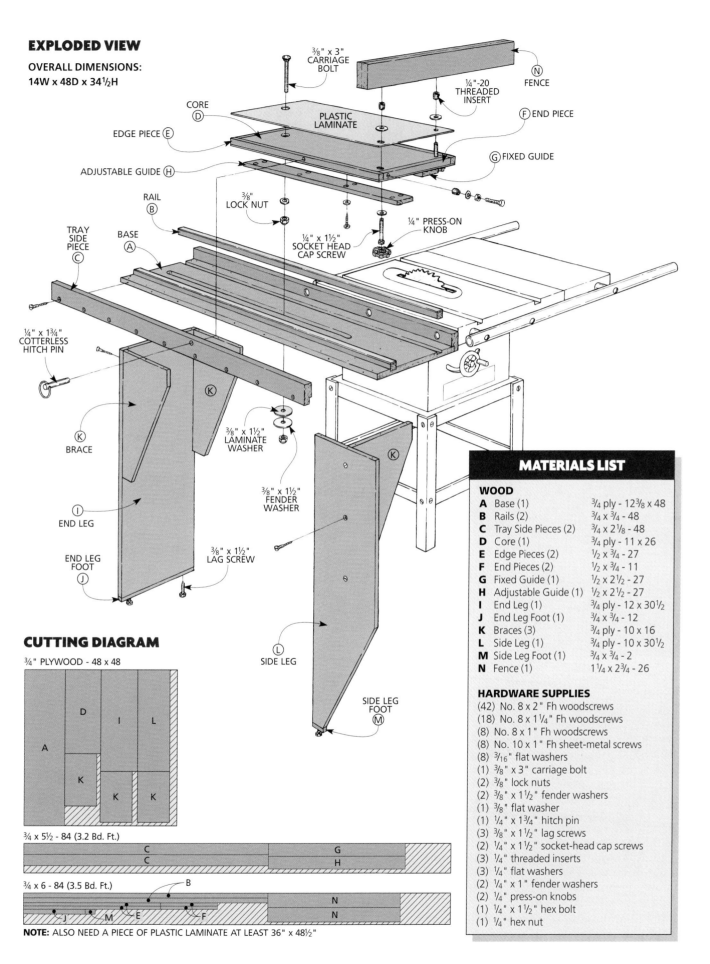

EXPLODED VIEW

OVERALL DIMENSIONS:
14W x 48D x 34½H

³⁄₈" x 3" CARRIAGE BOLT

FENCE (N)

CORE (D)

PLASTIC LAMINATE

¼"-20 THREADED INSERT

EDGE PIECE (E)

(F) END PIECE

ADJUSTABLE GUIDE (H)

(G) FIXED GUIDE

RAIL (B)

³⁄₈" LOCK NUT

¼" x 1½" SOCKET HEAD CAP SCREW

¼" PRESS-ON KNOB

TRAY SIDE PIECE (C)

BASE (A)

¼" x 1¾" COTTERLESS HITCH PIN

(K) BRACE

(K)

³⁄₈" x 1½" LAMINATE WASHER

(K)

³⁄₈" x 1½" FENDER WASHER

(I) END LEG

END LEG FOOT (J)

³⁄₈" x 1½" LAG SCREW

SIDE LEG (L)

SIDE LEG FOOT (M)

CUTTING DIAGRAM

¾" PLYWOOD - 48 x 48

A | D | I | L
K
K | K

¾ x 5½ - 84 (3.2 Bd. Ft.)

C
C | G
H

¾ x 6 - 84 (3.5 Bd. Ft.)

B
J | M | E | F
N
N

NOTE: ALSO NEED A PIECE OF PLASTIC LAMINATE AT LEAST 36" x 48½"

MATERIALS LIST

WOOD

A	Base (1)	¾ ply - 12³⁄₈ x 48
B	Rails (2)	¾ x ¾ - 48
C	Tray Side Pieces (2)	¾ x 2⅛ - 48
D	Core (1)	¾ ply - 11 x 26
E	Edge Pieces (2)	½ x ¾ - 27
F	End Pieces (2)	½ x ¾ - 11
G	Fixed Guide (1)	½ x 2½ - 27
H	Adjustable Guide (1)	½ x 2½ - 27
I	End Leg (1)	¾ ply - 12 x 30½
J	End Leg Foot (1)	¾ x ¾ - 12
K	Braces (3)	¾ ply - 10 x 16
L	Side Leg (1)	¾ ply - 10 x 30½
M	Side Leg Foot (1)	¾ x ¾ - 2
N	Fence (1)	1¼ x 2¾ - 26

HARDWARE SUPPLIES

(42) No. 8 x 2" Fh woodscrews
(18) No. 8 x 1¼" Fh woodscrews
(8) No. 8 x 1" Fh woodscrews
(8) No. 10 x 1" Fh sheet-metal screws
(8) ³⁄₁₆" flat washers
(1) ³⁄₈" x 3" carriage bolt
(2) ³⁄₈" lock nuts
(2) ³⁄₈" x 1½" fender washers
(1) ³⁄₈" flat washer
(1) ¼" x 1¾" hitch pin
(3) ³⁄₈" x 1½" lag screws
(2) ¼" x 1½" socket-head cap screws
(3) ¼" threaded inserts
(3) ¼" flat washers
(2) ¼" x 1" fender washers
(2) ¼" press-on knobs
(1) ¼" x 1½" hex bolt
(1) ¼" hex nut

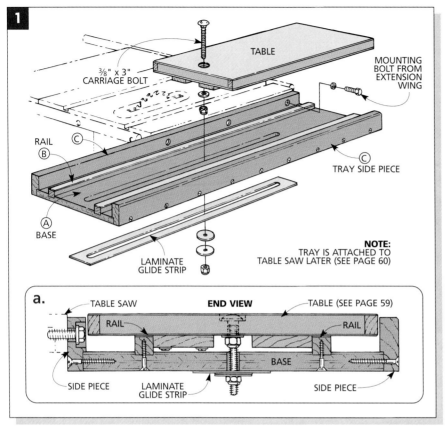

1

⅜" X 3"
CARRIAGE BOLT

TABLE

MOUNTING
BOLT FROM
EXTENSION
WING

RAIL
Ⓒ
Ⓑ

Ⓒ

TRAY SIDE PIECE

Ⓐ
BASE

NOTE:
TRAY IS ATTACHED TO
TABLE SAW LATER (SEE PAGE 60)

LAMINATE
GLIDE STRIP

a.

TABLE SAW

END VIEW

TABLE (SEE PAGE 59)

RAIL

RAIL

BASE

SIDE PIECE

LAMINATE
GLIDE STRIP

SIDE PIECE

This creates a hard, slick surface for the table to slide back and forth on.

Attaching the laminate strips is easy. Just cut oversize pieces and glue them in place with contact cement. The only problem is the rails are narrow, so it's hard to hold the router steady when trimming the edges flush. To keep the router from tipping, I used carpet tape to stick a support block to the base *(Fig. 2b)*.

I also wanted a durable, slick surface on the bottom of the base. That's because the hardware that secures the table to the tray rides against the bottom as you make a cut *(Fig. 1a)*.

GLIDE STRIP. Here again, I used a strip of laminate to create a slippery surface. After laying out the location of this "glide strip" *(Figs. 5 and 5a)*, I ran pieces of masking tape around the lines to avoid slopping contact cement onto the base. The edges of the tape also help position the strip. I held the strip on edge and moved it across the tape until it reached the edge. Then I just laid the strip down in the contact cement and pressed it firmly in place with a roller.

SLOT. The next step is to cut a slot in the base to accept a bolt that will hold the table in place *(Fig. 1a)*. To prevent the bolt from binding as the table slides back and forth, I cut a ½"-wide slot *(Fig. 5a)*. To do this, drill a ½"-dia. hole at each end of the layout lines. Then attach an edge guide to your jig saw and cut between the edges of the holes.

TRAY

The heart of the Sliding Table is a long tray that mounts to the side of the saw table. This tray replaces the left extension wing. Because the tray will extend past the back edge of the table, you'll need to move the rails that guide the rip fence to the right (or cut them off) (see the photo on the opposite page).

BASE. I started work on the tray by making the plywood base (A) *(Figs. 1 and 2)*. The length of the base determines how far you can slide the table back and forth. To provide enough travel to crosscut a 24"-wide panel, I made the base 48" long *(Fig. 2)*.

RAILS. After cutting the base to size, the next thing to do is to add a pair of rails. The rails act as glides for the table to slide across *(Figs. 1 and 1a)*. And they're part of the system that makes the table track in a straight line.

The rails (B) are narrow strips of hardwood that fit in shallow grooves cut in the base *(Fig. 2a)*. I cut the grooves first. That way, I could cut the rails close to finished size and plane them until they fit snug in the grooves.

To prevent the table from binding, the important thing is that these grooves are parallel to each other. An easy way to

ensure this is to cut one groove, reposition the fence, and then run the same edge against the rip fence to cut the second groove *(Figs. 3 and 4)*.

LAMINATE. After screwing the rails in place, the next step is to apply a strip of plastic laminate to the top of each rail.

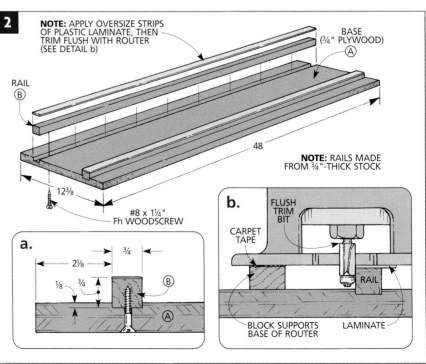

2

NOTE: APPLY OVERSIZE STRIPS
OF PLASTIC LAMINATE, THEN
TRIM FLUSH WITH ROUTER
(SEE DETAIL b)

BASE
(¾" PLYWOOD)
Ⓐ

RAIL
Ⓑ

48

NOTE: RAILS MADE
FROM ¾"-THICK STOCK

12⅜

#8 x 1¼"
Fh WOODSCREW

a.

2⅛

¾

⅛
¾

Ⓑ

Ⓐ

b.

FLUSH
TRIM
BIT

CARPET
TAPE

RAIL

BLOCK SUPPORTS
BASE OF ROUTER

LAMINATE

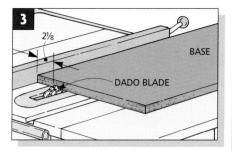

3
2⅛
BASE
DADO BLADE

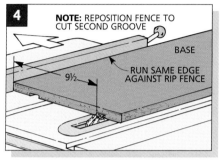

4
NOTE: REPOSITION FENCE TO CUT SECOND GROOVE
BASE
RUN SAME EDGE AGAINST RIP FENCE
9½

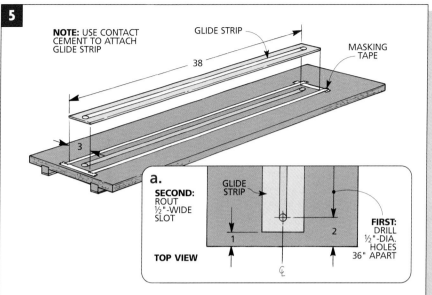

5
NOTE: USE CONTACT CEMENT TO ATTACH GLIDE STRIP
GLIDE STRIP
MASKING TAPE
38
3

a.
GLIDE STRIP
SECOND: ROUT ½"-WIDE SLOT
TOP VIEW
1
2
FIRST: DRILL ½"-DIA. HOLES 36" APART

SIDES. All that's left to complete the tray is to add two tray side pieces (C) *(Fig. 6)*. These pieces stiffen the plywood base. Both pieces are made from ¾"-thick hardwood and are rabbeted to fit the edge of the base *(Fig. 6a)*.

But before attaching the side pieces, you'll need to drill holes in one of them so the tray can be installed on the saw table. I used the holes in the edge of the saw table as a template *(Fig. 7)*.

Note: Secure the side piece ⅛" below the saw table, flush at the end *(Fig. 7a)*.

DRILL HOLES. Now it's just a matter of drilling holes for the mounting bolts. The size of these holes depends on the bolts that held your extension wing in place.

The thing to keep in mind is to drill the counterbores large enough so you can get a socket wrench inside to tighten the bolts *(Fig. 7a)*. Then drill oversize shank holes to allow the tray to be adjusted up and down. (I drilled ½"-dia. shank holes for ⁷⁄₁₆"-dia. bolts.)

ATTACH SIDES. After gluing and screwing the side pieces to the base, the tray is complete. But don't attach it to the saw table just yet. This makes it easier to work on the table that's added next and the legs that are added later.

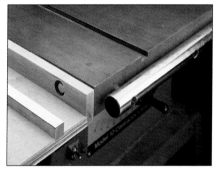

To provide clearance for the sliding table, reposition (or cut) the rails that guide the rip fence so they're flush with or just inside the edge of the saw table.

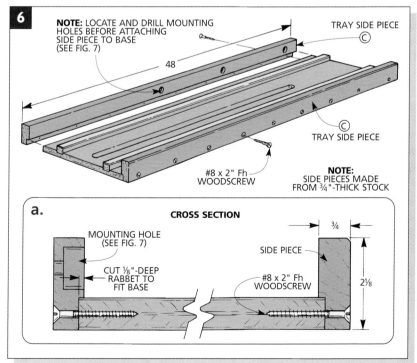

6
NOTE: LOCATE AND DRILL MOUNTING HOLES BEFORE ATTACHING SIDE PIECE TO BASE (SEE FIG. 7)
TRAY SIDE PIECE
C
48
C
TRAY SIDE PIECE
#8 x 2" Fh WOODSCREW
NOTE: SIDE PIECES MADE FROM ¾"-THICK STOCK

a. CROSS SECTION
MOUNTING HOLE (SEE FIG. 7)
CUT ⅛"-DEEP RABBET TO FIT BASE
SIDE PIECE
¾
#8 x 2" Fh WOODSCREW
2⅛

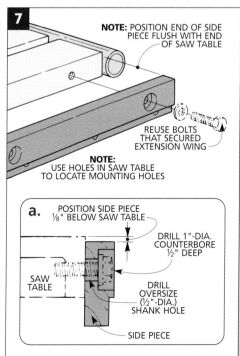

7
NOTE: POSITION END OF SIDE PIECE FLUSH WITH END OF SAW TABLE
REUSE BOLTS THAT SECURED EXTENSION WING
NOTE: USE HOLES IN SAW TABLE TO LOCATE MOUNTING HOLES

a. POSITION SIDE PIECE ⅛" BELOW SAW TABLE
DRILL 1"-DIA. COUNTERBORE ½" DEEP
SAW TABLE
DRILL OVERSIZE (½"-DIA.) SHANK HOLE
SIDE PIECE

Springs aren't typical hardware in most of my projects. But they are key to the operation of a couple of projects in this book (the Plate Joiner Table on page 16 and the Edge Sander on page 110). And while the Sliding Table doesn't need a spring to operate, I found it handy to use one to help position pieces temporarily during assembly (see the Shop Tip below).

There are two different types of springs: compression springs (like those in a ball point pen) and extension springs (like you'd see on a screen door). Which one you choose depends on the job you want the spring to do.

Note: Both types of springs come in a wide variety of lengths, diameters, and gauges. They are readily available at most hardware stores and home centers.

COMPRESSION

A compression spring is designed to push. To make this work, it consists of a series of open wire coils (on the right in the photo). When the coils are compressed, the ends of the spring exert pressure outward.

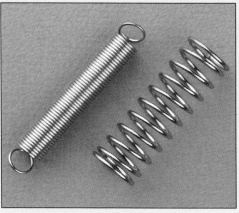

QUICK RELEASE. Because of this, I often use compression springs as a "quick release" on a jig that has a built-in clamp *(Fig. 1)*. When you loosen the wing nuts, the springs automatically pop up the bar that holds the workpiece down. This frees up your hands so you can quickly reposition another workpiece.

CONSTANT PRESSURE. Another place I've found where compression springs work well is when you need to exert constant pressure. For instance, to keep a machine screw that's used as a micro-adjustable "stop" from vibrating

out of adjustment, just slip a spring over the shank of the screw *(Fig. 2)*. In a similar way, compression springs help keep tension on the sanding belt of the Edge Sander (refer to page 119).

EXTENSION

Unlike a compression spring, the wire coils on an extension spring are wound tightly together (left spring in photo). When the coils are stretched apart, the tension that's produced pulls the spring back together.

RETURN. This makes it an ideal choice when you want to return something to its starting point (as with the foot pedal of the Plate Joiner Table; refer to page 24). A common use is to fasten an extension spring between the carriage of a radial arm saw and an anchor point to pull the blade safely back behind the fence after you make a cut *(Fig. 3)*.

HOLD-DOWN. But an extension spring can also be used to apply pressure downward. For example, when ripping thin stock that has a tendency to "chatter," I use a simple spring-loaded hold-down *(Fig. 4)*. This is just a piece of wood that pivots on an auxiliary fence as you slide a workpiece underneath. As the spring tries to pull back to its relaxed position, the hold-down applies pressure downward on the workpiece.

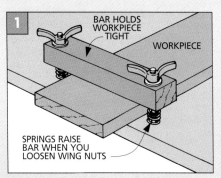

Quick Release. *To quickly position a workpiece, compression springs pop up the bar on this shop-built clamp.*

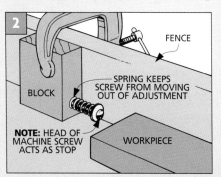

Constant Pressure. *A spring holds the machine screw on this micro-adjustable stop exactly where you want it.*

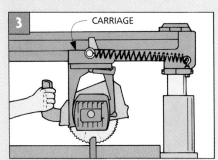

Return. *After you make the cut, the expansion spring returns the radial arm saw carriage to its starting point.*

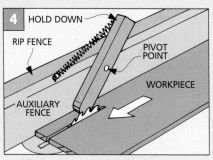

Hold-down. *This spring-loaded hold-down prevents thin stock from chattering as you make a cut.*

SHOP TIP

Tension Spring

When drilling the pilot holes for the adjustable guide on the Sliding Table, a compression spring keeps tension on the adjustable guide so it stays pressed against the rail.

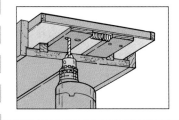

With the tray complete, work can begin on the table. To produce accurate cuts, the table needs to be flat and sturdy.

So I built it up from a plywood core (D) and wrapped hardwood edge (E) and end pieces (F) around it *(Fig. 9)*. The edging is sized so the completed table will fit in the tray with $1/16$" of clearance on each side (12"). And it's 27" long, to match the length of my saw table.

Next, I covered both sides of the table with oversized pieces of plastic laminate. Then I trimmed the laminate with a flush trim bit in a hand-held router. And finally, to avoid accidentally "catching" the laminate, I routed a small ($1/8$") chamfer around the top edges *(Fig. 9a)*.

Note: If you plan to add the optional pivoting fence, a slot needs to be cut in the table at this point. Refer to the Designer's Notebook on page 62 for details.

MOUNTING SYSTEM. The table is held in place with a carriage bolt that passes through a counterbored shank hole drilled in the table and then through the slot in the tray *(Figs. 8a and 9)*.

In use, this bolt is held in place with two lock nuts *(Fig. 8a)*. After slipping on a special washer cut from laminate, the bottom lock nut is tightened just enough to hold the table in place, yet still allow the table to slide easily.

GUIDES. But the bolt doesn't keep the table from moving from side to side. So I added a pair of guides to the bottom *(Fig. 10)*. These guides run against the inside edges of the rails so the table tracks in a straight line *(Figs. 10a and 10b)*.

To make this work, one of the guides is fixed (G), and the other is adjustable (H). (I drilled a series of overlapping holes to form adjustment slots.) Attaching the fixed guide is easy. It's screwed in place $2^{11}/_{16}$" in from the edge of the table. The challenge comes when you need to position the adjustable guide.

What you're looking for here is to get the guide so it's snug against the rail, but not so tight it's hard to push the table. The thing that worked well for me is to temporarily fit a compression spring between the guides at each end of the table (see the Shop Tip on the opposite page).

LOCK PIN. Finally, to keep the table from sliding when it's not in use, I added a lock pin. After drilling a hole through the side piece (C) and into the table, I used a cotterless hitch pin that I picked up at the local hardware store *(Fig. 8b)*.

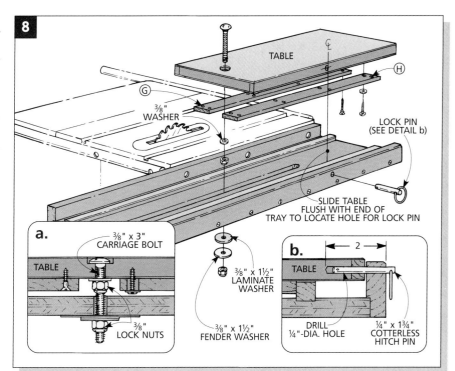

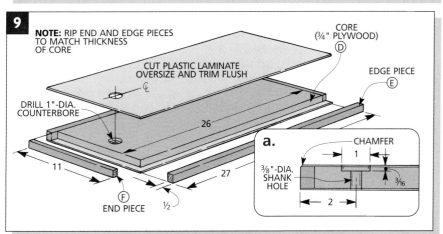

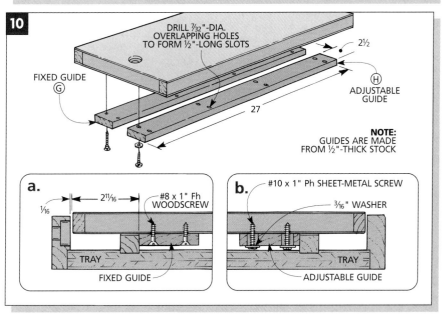

END LEG

After completing the table, I added two wide legs to support it: an end leg and a side leg *(Fig. 11)*. Braces provide additional support for the legs.

The end leg (I) is simple enough. It's just a 12"-wide piece of $3/4$"-thick plywood *(Fig. 12)*. To determine the length of this leg, measure the distance from the top of the saw table to the floor and subtract 4". This accounts for the height (thickness) of the table, and the levelers added next. (In my case, the end leg is $30\frac{1}{2}$".)

LEVELERS. After cutting the leg to size, the next thing to do is to add a pair of levelers to the bottom. This allows you to fine-tune the position of the table after the assembly is attached to the saw. (This procedure is detailed on page 64.) The levelers are nothing more than a couple of lag screws that tighten into a $3/4$"-thick hardwood foot (J) glued to the bottom of the leg *(Figs. 12 and 12a)*.

ATTACH LEG. To make it easy to attach the end leg, I bolted the tray to the saw table and temporarily propped up the opposite end. Then, after positioning the leg so it's centered on the width of the tray and flush with the end, it's simply screwed in place *(Figs. 11 and 11a)*.

BRACES. Next, to help stiffen the leg, I added a pair of braces (K) *(Fig. 12)*. These braces are just triangular-shaped pieces of $3/4$" plywood that are glued and

screwed to the leg and to the base of the tray *(Figs. 11a and 12)*.

SIDE LEG

To support the other end of the tray, the next step is to add a side leg. The side leg (L) is also cut to size from $3/4$" plywood *(Fig. 13)*. To avoid accidentally kicking it, I cut a taper on the lower part of the leg.

Here again, I glued a $3/4$"-thick hardwood foot (M) on the bottom and drilled

a hole for a leveler *(Fig. 13a)*. As before, the side leg is screwed to the base of the tray *(Fig. 11a)*. But this time, I screwed on a single plywood brace (K) that's centered on the width of the leg.

FENCE

This Sliding Table has a fence that can be quickly set so it's 90° to the saw blade. When it's not needed, loosening a couple of knobs allows you to lift the fence off the

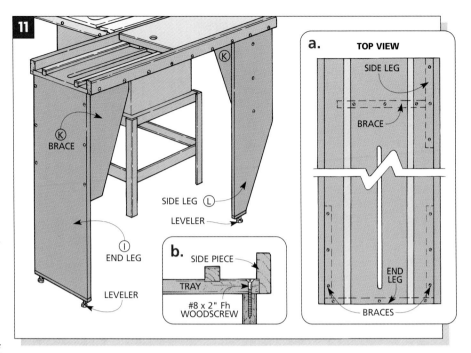

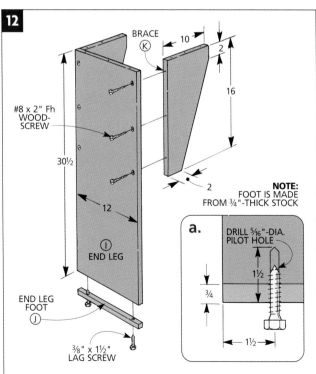

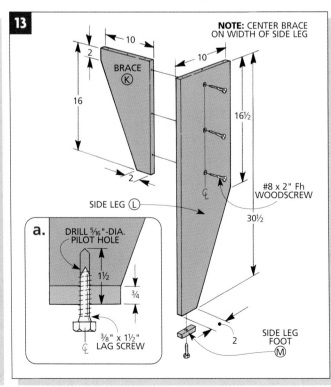

Loosening a pair of knobs makes it easy to remove the fence. When you put the fence back on, a stop system quickly repositions it so it's 90° to the blade.

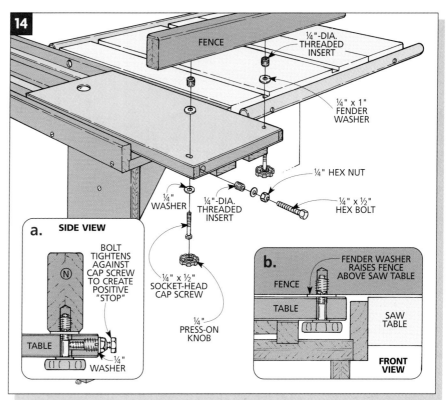

table (see photo above). (For a fence that pivots to allow you to cut angles, see the Designer's Notebook on the next page.)

FENCE. The fence (N) consists of two ⅝"-thick hardwood pieces *(Fig. 15)*. After gluing up the fence, I routed a chamfer around the top and bottom *(Fig. 15a)*.

The fence is held in place with two cap screws that pass through holes in the table and tighten into threaded inserts in the bottom of the fence *(Fig. 14)*. I added press-on knobs to the screws to make the fence easy to remove. Make sure you have clearance between the knobs and the tray *(Fig. 14b)*.

Building in an adjustment so you can square up the fence is easy. Just drill a slotted hole in the table *(Fig. 16)*. But I also wanted to be able to slip the fence off and put it back on without having to reset it square with the blade each time. So to do this, I added a simple "stop."

STOP. The stop is a bolt that threads through an insert in the end of the table until it hits the shank of the cap screw *(Fig. 14a)*. To make this work, you'll need to drill a hole that intersects the adjustment slot *(Figs. 16 and 16a)*.

Next, locate the holes for the threaded inserts in the bottom of the fence. To do this, just square up the fence so the end butts against the saw blade and then transfer the hole locations *(Fig. 17)*.

ATTACH FENCE. After drilling the holes and installing the inserts, you can attach the fence. To prevent it from dragging on the saw table, I slipped a couple of fender washers between the fence and the table *(Fig. 14b)*. Then I threaded a hex nut onto the stop to keep it from loosening up.

As with any precision tool, you'll need to adjust the Sliding Table to get the best results. This procedure isn't complicated. It's outlined on page 64. ∎

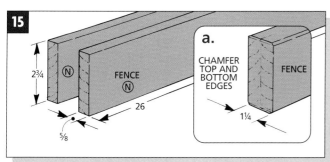

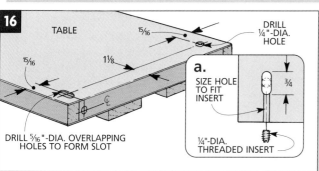

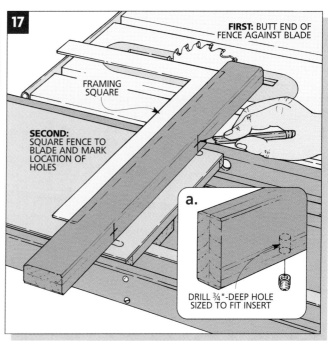

DESIGNER'S NOTEBOOK

Improve the versatility of the Sliding Table fence with these two simple modifications. A slot in the table allows the fence to pivot for cutting angles and a stop block makes repeat cuts a snap.

CONSTRUCTION NOTES:

■ To convert the fence so that it pivots for cutting miters, a couple of curved slots need to be cut in the table. One slot goes through the table and is for the shank of a bolt used to lock the fence in place. The second slot is a counterbore on the bottom of the table that accepts a washer and the head of the bolt.

To cut the slots, I used a router and a trammel. But before you can rout the slots, you'll need to drill starter holes on the bottom side of the table. To do this, start by laying out and drilling a couple of $3/4$"-dia. counterbores $5/16$" deep *(Figs. 1 and 1a)*. Then drill $3/8$"-dia. through holes, centered in the counterbores. These mark the ends of the slot that goes through the table *(Figs. 1 and 1a)*.

■ Next, I made a trammel for my router from $1/4$" hardboard *(Fig. 2)*. Drill an opening for the router bit at one end and use the router base plate to lay out and drill mounting holes for your router.

■ To locate the trammel pivot point, install a $3/8$" straight bit in the router and place the bit into one of the starter holes. Then, using the fence pivot point as a guide, drill a $1/4$" hole through the trammel. A $1/4$" bolt works for a trammel pivot *(Fig. 2)*.

■ Now switch to a $3/4$" straight bit and take several passes to rout a curved slot $5/16$" deep *(Figs. 2 and 2a)*.

■ Next, switch back to a $3/8$" straight bit in the router and finish routing the slot all the way through the table *(Fig. 2b)*.

■ With the slot done, you can complete the table and add the legs to the tray. Then you can begin work on the fence.

■ The body of the fence is built as before. But this time, instead of a stopped hole with a threaded insert towards the outside end of the fence, drill a $5/16$"-dia. through hole *(Fig. 7)*. This is for a bolt that will pass through the fence and into the curved slot in the table.

■ The next thing to do is to cut a $1/2$"-wide groove in one face of the fence, centered on its width *(Fig. 3a)*. This is the first part of a T-slot that will accept a toilet bolt that secures the stop block.

■ After cutting the groove, cut an oversize fence face (O) from $1/4$" hardboard and glue it over the groove *(Fig. 3)*.

■ Once the glue has dried, trim the edges of the face flush with the fence by using

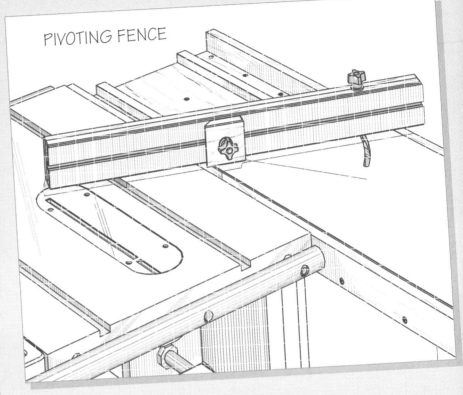

PIVOTING FENCE

MATERIALS LIST

NEW PARTS

O	Fence Face (1)	$1/4$ hdbd. - $2^3/4$ x 26
P	Stop Block (1)	$3/4$ x $2^5/8$ - $2^5/8$

HARDWARE SUPPLIES

(1) $1/4$"-20 x $1^1/2$" socket-head cap screw
(1) $1/4$" press-on knob
(2) $1/4$"-20 threaded inserts
(2) $1/4$" flat washers
(1) $1/4$" fender washer
(1) $5/16$" x 4" hex-head bolt
(1) $5/16$" x $1^3/4$" toilet bolt
(3) $5/16$" flat washers
(1) $5/16$" fender washer
(2) $5/16$" star knobs

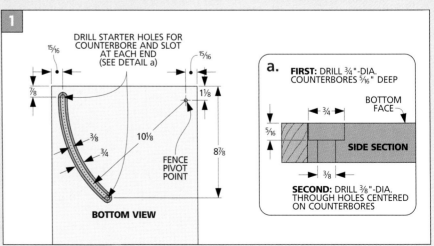

1

DRILL STARTER HOLES FOR COUNTERBORE AND SLOT AT EACH END (SEE DETAIL a)

$15/16$ $15/16$

$7/8$ $1^1/8$

$3/8$ $10^1/8$

$3/4$ $8^7/8$

FENCE PIVOT POINT

BOTTOM VIEW

a. **FIRST:** DRILL $3/4$"-DIA. COUNTERBORES $5/16$" DEEP

BOTTOM FACE

$5/16$ $3/4$

SIDE SECTION

$3/8$

SECOND: DRILL $3/8$"-DIA. THROUGH HOLES CENTERED ON COUNTERBORES

a flush trim bit in the router.

■ Next, set up the rip fence of your table saw so the blade is about centered on the width of the groove in the fence. Then raise the blade to just cut through the hardboard face of the fence *(Fig. 4)*. Make a pass and flip the fence end for end to widen the groove. Then nudge the rip fence and repeat the procedure until the shank of a $5/16$" toilet bolt slides easily in the groove *(Figs. 3a and 7)*.

■ Finally, rout $1/16$" chamfers around the top and bottom edges *(Fig. 3a)*.

■ The last piece to make is the stop block (P). This is just a $2^5/8$"-square piece of $3/4$"-thick stock *(Fig. 5)*. One end is chamfered at 45° to serve as a stop for mitered pieces. Note that the chamfer has a slight shoulder so there isn't a sharp point that might break off.

■ As with the fence, the top and bottom edges of the stop block are eased with $1/16$" chamfers *(Fig. 5)*.

■ A hole drilled in the center of the stop block fits over the shank of the toilet bolt *(Fig. 5)*. Then a plastic star knob with a washer is tightened down to hold the stop block in place.

■ Now all that remains is to mount the fence to the table. To do this, you'll have to locate and drill the mounting holes in the fence *(Fig. 17 on page 61)*. Install a threaded insert in the fence at the pivot point. And drill a $5/16$"-dia. through hole at the other end *(Fig. 7)*.

■ Next, grind the edges off a $5/16$" washer so that it fits in the counterbore in the table *(Fig. 6)*. Then epoxy this washer to the head of a $5/16$" bolt.

■ This bolt, along with a star knob, secures the fence to the table *(Fig. 6)*.

■ Once the fence is installed, and the table has been aligned (see page 64), adjust the fence to cut a perfect 45° miter. Then scribe a line on the table so that you can reset the fence in the future.

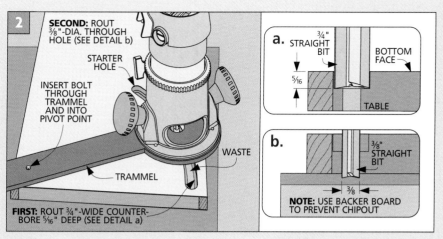

2 SECOND: ROUT $3/8$"-DIA. THROUGH HOLE (SEE DETAIL b)

STARTER HOLE

INSERT BOLT THROUGH TRAMMEL AND INTO PIVOT POINT

WASTE

TRAMMEL

FIRST: ROUT $3/4$"-WIDE COUNTERBORE $5/16$" DEEP (SEE DETAIL a)

a. STRAIGHT BIT $3/4$"   BOTTOM FACE $5/16$ TABLE

b. $3/8$" STRAIGHT BIT $3/8$ NOTE: USE BACKER BOARD TO PREVENT CHIPOUT

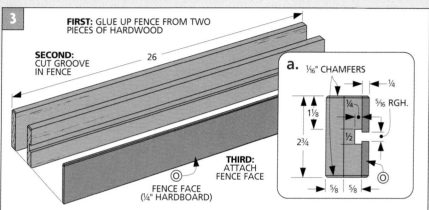

3 FIRST: GLUE UP FENCE FROM TWO PIECES OF HARDWOOD

SECOND: CUT GROOVE IN FENCE   26

THIRD: ATTACH FENCE FACE

FENCE FACE ($1/4$" HARDBOARD)

a. $1/16$" CHAMFERS $1/4$ $1/4$ $5/16$ RGH. $1^1/8$ $1/2$ $2^3/4$ $5/8$ $5/8$

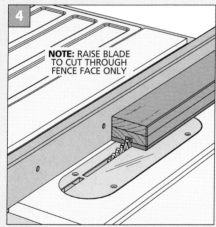

4 NOTE: RAISE BLADE TO CUT THROUGH FENCE FACE ONLY

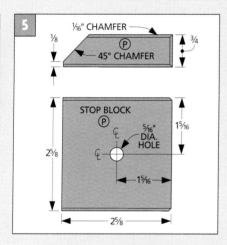

5 $1/16$" CHAMFER $1/8$ $3/4$ 45° CHAMFER   (P)

STOP BLOCK   (P) $5/16$" DIA. HOLE $1^5/16$ $2^5/8$ $1^5/16$ $2^5/8$

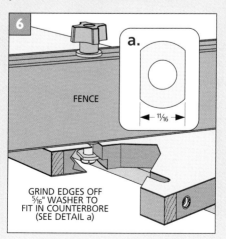

6 **a.**   FENCE $11/16$ GRIND EDGES OFF $5/16$" WASHER TO FIT IN COUNTERBORE (SEE DETAIL a)

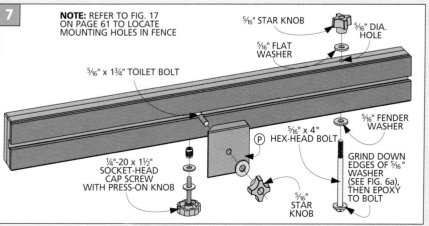

7 NOTE: REFER TO FIG. 17 ON PAGE 61 TO LOCATE MOUNTING HOLES IN FENCE

$5/16$" STAR KNOB $5/16$" DIA. HOLE $5/16$" FLAT WASHER $5/16$" x $1^3/4$" TOILET BOLT $5/16$" FENDER WASHER   (P) $5/16$" x 4" HEX-HEAD BOLT   GRIND DOWN EDGES OF $5/16$" WASHER (SEE FIG. 6a), THEN EPOXY TO BOLT $1/4$"-20 x $1^1/2$" SOCKET-HEAD CAP SCREW WITH PRESS-ON KNOB $5/16$" STAR KNOB

SETUP . . . . Table Alignment

Once the Sliding Table has been attached to your saw, you'll need to adjust it to produce accurate cuts. There are three adjustments that need to be made.

VERTICAL ADJUSTMENT

First, the Sliding Table needs to be flush with the surface of the saw table. This is simply a matter of backing off (or tightening) the levelers to raise (or lower) the tray (*Steps 1 and 2*).

SQUARE FENCE

The next step is to square up the fence relative to the saw blade (*Step 3*). Once this is done, you can make a test cut to check the accuracy of the setup (*Step 4*).

PARALLEL TRAVEL

If the test cut isn't square, chances are the problem is that the table isn't sliding parallel to the blade. To correct this, you'll need to shim one end of the tray out just a bit (*Step 5*).

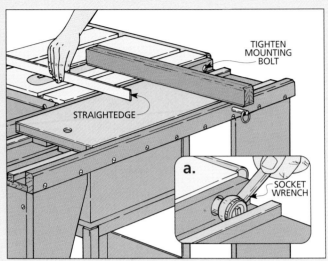

TIGHTEN MOUNTING BOLT

STRAIGHTEDGE

a.

SOCKET WRENCH

1 *Start with the mounting bolts snug, but not tight. Then with a straightedge across the saw table and just the inside edge of the sliding table, raise (or lower) the tray until both surfaces are flush. Then tighten the mounting bolts.*

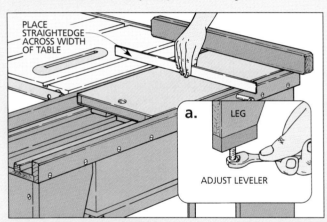

PLACE STRAIGHTEDGE ACROSS WIDTH OF TABLE

a. LEG

ADJUST LEVELER

2 *Now place the straightedge across the full width of the table to check that the outside edge is level with the saw table. To raise (or lower) the table, back out (or screw in) the levelers.*

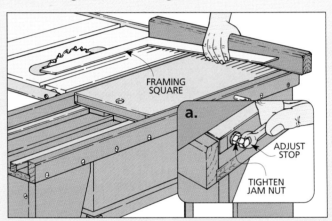

FRAMING SQUARE

a.

ADJUST STOP

TIGHTEN JAM NUT

3 *After squaring the fence up to the blade, tighten the knobs that lock down the fence. Now thread in the stop until it hits the cap screw and tighten the "jam" nut.*

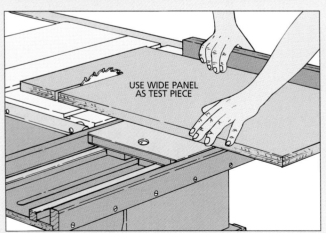

USE WIDE PANEL AS TEST PIECE

4 *The accuracy of the setup can be checked by making a test cut. To provide the best indication of whether or not you'll need to shim the tray, use as wide a panel as possible.*

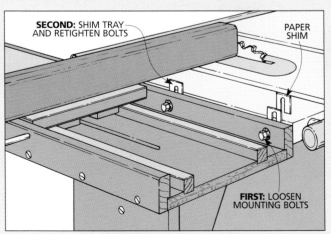

SECOND: SHIM TRAY AND RETIGHTEN BOLTS

PAPER SHIM

FIRST: LOOSEN MOUNTING BOLTS

5 *If you need to shim the tray, loosen two of the mounting bolts and slip paper shims over them. Then retighten the bolts and repeat Steps 3 and 4 to check your adjustments.*

Oscillating Drum Sander

An inexpensive electric motor moves the drill press quill up and down automatically. The large table steadies workpieces. And it's easily disconnected when you need to use the drill press for boring.

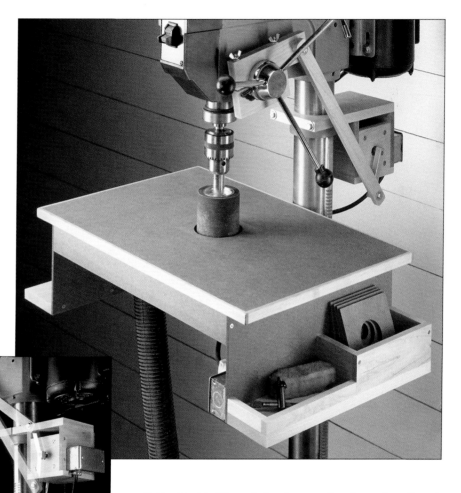

I've always been impressed with oscillating spindle sanders. They make it easy to quickly remove material when sanding the edge of a board.

The basic principle of these spindle sanders is simple. They have a sanding drum that spins around and moves up and down at the same time.

This dual motion was on my mind as I was using a sanding drum on my drill press recently. After all, it already spins around. So all I needed was a way to move it up and down automatically.

GEAR MOTOR. The solution is a small electric gear motor that attaches to the column of the drill press. This motor is connected to the feed lever on the drill press by a long arm. Turn the motor on, and the arm drives the quill feed lever back and forth like the pumping action of an old locomotive (see inset photo).

SANDING PLATFORM. But there's more to this Oscillating Drum Sander than the drive system. A sanding platform also provides a large work surface with an opening for the sanding drum as it moves up and down (main photo).

INSERTS AND STORAGE. It's easy to change the size of this opening for various sizes of sanding drums. Just slip in a different insert. The insert and drum that you remove store conveniently out of the way in two storage racks that hang on the platform like a pair of saddlebags.

FENCE. Finally, the sanding platform can double as a table for drilling. Simply disconnect the drive system and slide a fence onto the platform. This is covered in the Accessories box on page 70.

SANDING BOX. I've also included a design for a simpler drill press sanding box. It doesn't have the oscillating action, but does fit all sizes of sanding drums and has dust extraction. Details about this are on page 72.

EXPLODED VIEW

OVERALL DIMENSIONS:
28W x 16D x 7½H
(SANDING PLATFORM ONLY)

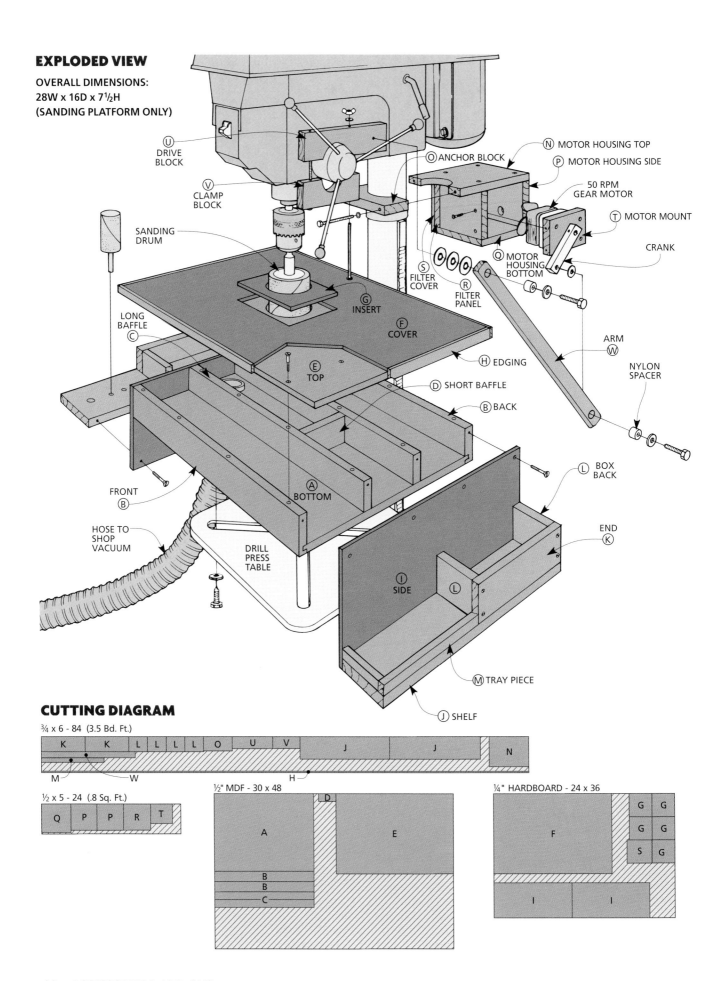

Ⓤ DRIVE BLOCK

Ⓥ CLAMP BLOCK

SANDING DRUM

LONG BAFFLE Ⓒ

FRONT Ⓑ

HOSE TO SHOP VACUUM

DRILL PRESS TABLE

Ⓖ INSERT

Ⓕ COVER

Ⓔ TOP

Ⓐ BOTTOM

Ⓞ ANCHOR BLOCK

Ⓝ MOTOR HOUSING TOP

Ⓟ MOTOR HOUSING SIDE

50 RPM GEAR MOTOR

Ⓣ MOTOR MOUNT

CRANK

Ⓢ FILTER COVER

Ⓡ FILTER PANEL

Ⓠ MOTOR HOUSING BOTTOM

Ⓗ EDGING

Ⓓ SHORT BAFFLE

Ⓑ BACK

ARM Ⓦ

NYLON SPACER

Ⓛ BOX BACK

END Ⓚ

Ⓘ SIDE

Ⓛ

Ⓜ TRAY PIECE

Ⓙ SHELF

CUTTING DIAGRAM

¾ x 6 - 84 (3.5 Bd. Ft.)

K	K	L	L	L	L	O	U	V	J	J	N

M   W   H

½ x 5 - 24 (.8 Sq. Ft.)

Q	P	P	R	T

½" MDF - 30 x 48

D

A

E

B
B
C

¼" HARDBOARD - 24 x 36

F

G	G
G	G
S	G

I   I

MATERIALS LIST

SANDING PLATFORM

A	Bottom (1)	$1/2$ MDF - 15 x 20
B	Front/Back (2)	$1/2$ MDF - 2 x 20
C	Long Baffles (2)	$1/2$ MDF - $1\frac{1}{2}$ x 20
D	Short Baffle (1)	$1/2$ MDF - $1\frac{1}{2}$ x $3\frac{1}{2}$
E	Top (1)	$1/2$ MDF - $15\frac{1}{2}$ x $23\frac{1}{2}$
F	Cover (1)	$1/4$ hdbd. - $15\frac{1}{2}$ x $23\frac{1}{2}$
G	Inserts (5)	$1/4$ hdbd. - $4\frac{1}{2}$ x $4\frac{1}{2}$
H	Edging	$3/4$ x $1/4$ - 84 linear in.
I	Sides (2)	$1/4$ hdbd. - $6\frac{3}{4}$ x $15\frac{1}{2}$
J	Shelves (2)	$3/4$ x $3\frac{3}{4}$ - $15\frac{1}{2}$
K	Ends (2)	$1/2$ x $2\frac{1}{2}$ - $7\frac{1}{2}$
L	Box Front/Bk. (4)	$1/2$ x $2\frac{1}{2}$ - $3\frac{1}{4}$
M	Tray Piece	$1/2$ x $3/4$ - 12 linear in.

MOTOR HOUSING

N	Top (1)	$3/4$ x 5 - $6\frac{3}{4}$

O	Anchor Block (1)	$3/4$ x $2\frac{3}{8}$ - 5
P	Sides (2)	$1/2$ x $4\frac{3}{8}$ - $4\frac{1}{2}$
Q	Bottom (1)	$1/2$ x 5 - $4\frac{3}{4}$
R	Filter Panel (1)	$1/2$ x $4\frac{3}{8}$ - $4\frac{3}{4}$
S	Filter Cover (1)	$1/4$ hdbd. - $4\frac{3}{4}$ x $4\frac{7}{8}$
T	Motor Mount (1)	$1/2$ x $3\frac{1}{2}$ - $3\frac{3}{4}$

DRIVE ASSEMBLY

U	Drive Block (1)	$3/4$ x 2 - 7
V	Clamp Block (1)	$3/4$ x 2 - $4\frac{3}{4}$
W	Arm (1)	$7/16$ x 1 - $16\frac{1}{8}$

HARDWARE SUPPLIES

(12) No. 6 x $1\frac{1}{4}$" Fh woodscrews
(24) No. 6 x 1" Fh woodscrews
(4) No. 6 x $1/2$" Fh woodscrews
(34) No. 6 x 1" Fh sheet-metal screws

(4) $1/4$" x $3/4$" lag screws
(1) $1/4$" x $1\frac{1}{2}$" lag screw
(2) $1/4$" x 5" lag screws
(1) $1/4$"-20 x 1" hex bolt
(2) $1/4$" x $4\frac{1}{2}$" carriage bolts
(2) $1/4$" wing nuts
(11) $1/4$" flat washers
(4) $1/4$" I.D. x 1" O.D. fender washers
(4) 10-32 x 1" Fh machine screws
(1) 10-32 x $1/4$" set screw
(1) $1/2$" x $1/2$" bar stock - $3\frac{3}{4}$"
(2) .257"I.D. x $1/2$"O.D. x $1/2$" nylon spacers
(1) $3\frac{3}{4}$"-dia. dust mask filter
(1) 50 RPM gear motor

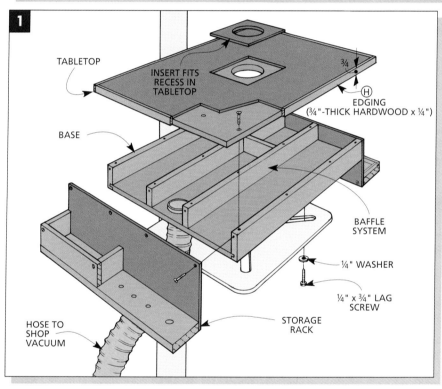

1

TABLETOP

INSERT FITS RECESS IN TABLETOP

BASE

$3/4$

(H)
EDGING
($3/4$"-THICK HARDWOOD x $1/4$")

BAFFLE SYSTEM

$1/4$" WASHER

$1/4$" x $3/4$" LAG SCREW

HOSE TO SHOP VACUUM

STORAGE RACK

SANDING PLATFORM

I began work on the drum sander by making a sanding platform that attaches to the metal table of the drill press. It's a shallow, enclosed box that consists of three sections: a base, a tabletop, and two storage racks *(Fig. 1)*.

Note: The overall width (depth) of the platform is 16". This means it will fit on a drill press with at least 8" of clearance between the column and the center of the chuck. For smaller drill presses, you'll need to reduce the width.

BASE

In addition to supporting the tabletop, the base houses a system of baffles that directs dust into a shop vacuum.

The base starts out as a bottom (A), and a front and back (B) made from $1/2$"-thick MDF *(Fig. 2)*. These pieces are held together with simple tongue and groove joints *(Fig. 2a)*. This joint can be cut on the table saw or with a straight bit in the router table. But before gluing them together, you'll need to cut a hole near one end of the bottom to fit the hose on your shop vacuum *(Figs. 1 and 2)*.

BAFFLE SYSTEM. The next step is to add the H-shaped baffle system. By restricting the area inside the base, it improves the flow of air and dust that's drawn down through an insert in the table top and out into the shop vacuum.

The baffle system is made up of three strips of $1/2$" MDF. Two long baffles (C) run the full length of the base. These pieces are glued and screwed in place on either side of the hole for the shop vacuum hose *(Fig. 2)*. And a short baffle (D) fits between the long baffles.

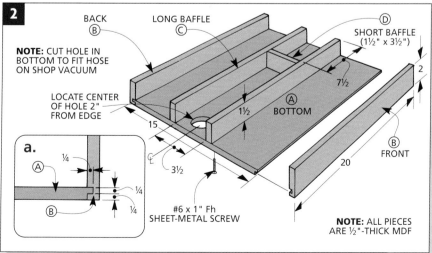

2

BACK
(B)

LONG BAFFLE
(C)

(D)

SHORT BAFFLE
($1\frac{1}{2}$" x $3\frac{1}{2}$")

NOTE: CUT HOLE IN BOTTOM TO FIT HOSE ON SHOP VACUUM

LOCATE CENTER OF HOLE 2" FROM EDGE

$7\frac{1}{2}$

$1\frac{1}{2}$

(A)
BOTTOM

15

a.

$1/4$

(A)

$1/4$

(B)

$1/4$

$3\frac{1}{2}$

#6 x 1" Fh SHEET-METAL SCREW

20

(B)
FRONT

2

NOTE: ALL PIECES ARE $1/2$"-THICK MDF

TABLETOP

With the baffle system in place, you can turn your attention to the tabletop. It serves as a large surface for workpieces to rest on as they are sanded. It also pro-vides an opening for the sanding drum as it moves up and down *(Fig. 1)*.

OPENING. This opening needs to be large enough to accept the biggest sanding drum you have. (Mine is 3".) Yet you still need to be able to reduce the size of the opening for when you use smaller-diameter drums.

The solution is to use a "pop-out" insert with a different size hole for each sanding drum. These inserts fit in a recess in the tabletop.

To form this recess and provide support for the inserts, the tabletop is made up of two parts. The top (E) is a piece of $1/2$" MDF with a large hole cut in the center *(Fig. 3)*. The top is glued and screwed to the base. Then later, a cover with a square opening will be attached to the top *(Fig. 4)*. This way, when you slip an insert into the square opening, it will be supported by the top underneath.

To produce a snug fit, it's best to start with an oversize cover (F) and use the inserts as a gauge when routing the opening. (The way I did this is covered in the Technique box on the facing page.)

INSERTS. Altogether, I made five inserts (G). Four have holes that are $1/4$" larger than each of my sanding drums. And one has a small ($3/4$") finger hole to make it easy to lift out of the tabletop. (This insert is used if you need to cover the hole for regular drilling jobs.)

To cut these holes safely, I tightened each insert in a handscrew, then clamped the handscrew to the drill press table — but there's a slight twist.

To provide clearance for the "wing" on the circle cutter, I set the insert on the threaded rods of the handscrew *(Fig. 5)*.

Note: Place a scrap piece under the insert to protect the cutting edge of the circle cutter *(Fig. 5a)*.

ATTACH COVER. With inserts in hand, I used the one with the largest hole to position the cover on the top during glue-up. To do this, draw centerlines on the insert and top *(Fig. 4)*. Then clamp the insert to the top so the marks align. After applying contact cement to both pieces, lower the cover over the insert.

Now it's just a matter of trimming the edges of the cover with a flush trim bit. After that, I applied strips of hardwood edging (H) around the tabletop to protect the edges (refer to *Fig. 1* on page 67).

STORAGE RACKS

To complete the sanding platform, I added two storage racks, one on each side. These provide the perfect places to keep my sanding drums, the inserts, and other accessories close at hand.

Each rack begins as an L-shaped assembly that consists of a side (I) cut

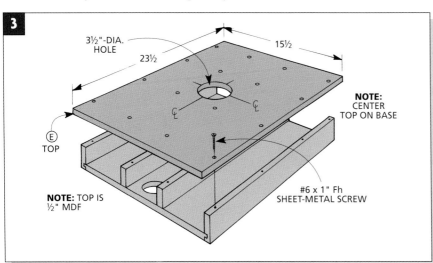

3

3½"-DIA. HOLE

23½

15½

NOTE: CENTER TOP ON BASE

(E) TOP

NOTE: TOP IS ½" MDF

#6 x 1" Fh SHEET-METAL SCREW

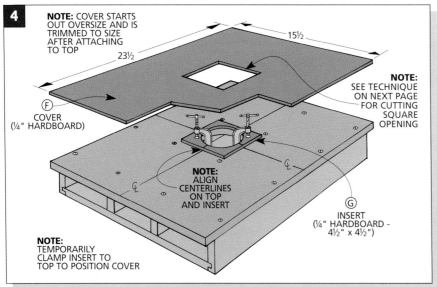

4

NOTE: COVER STARTS OUT OVERSIZE AND IS TRIMMED TO SIZE AFTER ATTACHING TO TOP

23½

15½

(F) COVER (¼" HARDBOARD)

NOTE: SEE TECHNIQUE ON NEXT PAGE FOR CUTTING SQUARE OPENING

NOTE: ALIGN CENTERLINES ON TOP AND INSERT

(G) INSERT (¼" HARDBOARD - 4½" x 4½")

NOTE: TEMPORARILY CLAMP INSERT TO TOP TO POSITION COVER

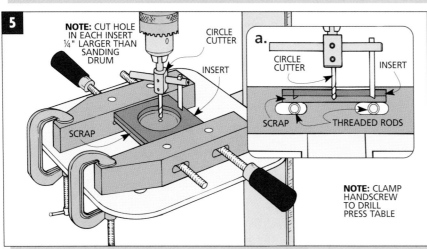

5

NOTE: CUT HOLE IN EACH INSERT ¼" LARGER THAN SANDING DRUM

CIRCLE CUTTER

INSERT

SCRAP

a.

CIRCLE CUTTER

INSERT

SCRAP

THREADED RODS

NOTE: CLAMP HANDSCREW TO DRILL PRESS TABLE

Making the square inserts for the table on the Oscillating Drum Sander is easy. The challenge is cutting a perfectly square opening in the cover so the inserts fit tight — no matter which way you put them in. It took a little head-scratching, but I finally came up with a simple way to rout the opening on the router table.

LAYOUT. Start by laying out the opening so it is centered on an over-sized cover *(Fig. 1)*. (To locate the center of the cover, draw diagonal lines between the corners of the workpiece.) Then cut the opening to rough size with a jig saw *(Fig. 1a)*.

The rest of the material is removed using a straight bit and running the cover against a fence. The idea is to position the

fence so the bit cuts just short of the layout lines. This way, you'll be able to sneak up on the fit.

Note: Because of the large size of the cover, I couldn't use my regular fence.

Instead, I had to clamp a straight piece of scrap to the end of the router table *(Fig. 1)*.

ROUT OPPOSITE SIDES. With the fence in place, lower the cover over the bit. Then push it into the fence and rout along one edge *(Fig. 2)*. After repeating this for the opposite edge, check the fit using one of the inserts (see photo).

If the insert doesn't fit, just nudge the fence away from the bit, and rout one edge only. Continue to make small adjustments until the insert just fits into the opening.

To rout the other two edges, reposition the fence and repeat the process. Once the insert fits between the sides, all that remains is to square up the corners of the opening with a chisel.

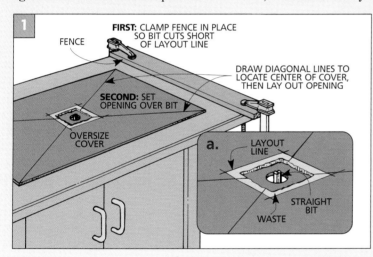

1
FENCE
FIRST: CLAMP FENCE IN PLACE SO BIT CUTS SHORT OF LAYOUT LINE
DRAW DIAGONAL LINES TO LOCATE CENTER OF COVER, THEN LAY OUT OPENING
SECOND: SET OPENING OVER BIT
OVERSIZE COVER
a. LAYOUT LINE
STRAIGHT BIT
WASTE

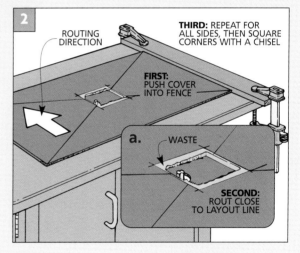

2
ROUTING DIRECTION
THIRD: REPEAT FOR ALL SIDES, THEN SQUARE CORNERS WITH A CHISEL
FIRST: PUSH COVER INTO FENCE
a. WASTE
SECOND: ROUT CLOSE TO LAYOUT LINE

from $\frac{1}{4}$" hardboard and a $\frac{3}{4}$"-thick shelf (J) cut from hardwood *(Fig. 6)*. Before gluing and screwing these pieces together, I drilled a series of holes in the front half of the left-hand shelf to accept the shanks of my sanding drums.

To store sanding sleeves and inserts, I also added a three-sided box to the back half of each rack. It's made up of a $\frac{1}{2}$"-thick hardwood end (K) and a front and back (L). These pieces are just glued and screwed together.

Next, I glued a couple of short tray pieces (M) around the open space of the right-hand storage rack. The idea here is to create a lip that keeps my drill bits and chuck key from falling off the shelf.

Finally, the storage racks are screwed to each side of the sanding platform (refer to *Fig. 1* on page 67).

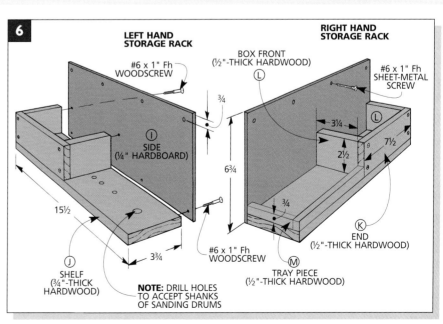

6
LEFT HAND STORAGE RACK
RIGHT HAND STORAGE RACK
BOX FRONT ($\frac{1}{2}$"-THICK HARDWOOD) (L)
#6 x 1" Fh WOODSCREW
#6 x 1" Fh SHEET-METAL SCREW
$\frac{3}{4}$
(I) SIDE ($\frac{1}{4}$" HARDBOARD)
$3\frac{1}{4}$
$7\frac{1}{2}$
$2\frac{1}{2}$
$6\frac{3}{4}$
$\frac{3}{4}$
$15\frac{1}{2}$
$3\frac{3}{4}$
#6 x 1" Fh WOODSCREW
(K) END ($\frac{1}{2}$"-THICK HARDWOOD)
(J) SHELF ($\frac{3}{4}$"-THICK HARDWOOD)
(M) TRAY PIECE ($\frac{1}{2}$"-THICK HARDWOOD)
NOTE: DRILL HOLES TO ACCEPT SHANKS OF SANDING DRUMS

With the addition of this simple fence, you can use your drill press for regular drilling jobs without having to remove the sanding table. It hooks over and clamps onto the lip of the tabletop.

FENCE. The fence starts with two fence pieces (X) glued together, to form an L-shape (see drawing). The pieces are sized $3\frac{1}{8}$" longer than the sanding platform to allow for the clamps that are added next.

CLAMPS. To lock the fence in place, there's a clamp at each end. Each clamp consists of a spacer (Y) and a clamp head (Z) that are aligned with a hardboard key (AA). The key fits into a $\frac{3}{16}$"-deep kerf cut in each piece (detail 'a'). To make these cuts safely, I cut the kerfs on the ends of an extra-long blank, then cut a spacer and a clamp head from the blank. Then I repeated the process for the second clamp head and spacer.

Note: The spacer is sanded slightly thinner than the tabletop before being glued in place. This way, when you tighten the clamp, the clamp head pinches against the bottom of the table.

Next, I stacked the clamp head in position below the spacer and drilled a hole through each end for the assembly. To clamp the fence to the sanding table, a threaded knob is tightened onto a carriage bolt (see detail 'a').

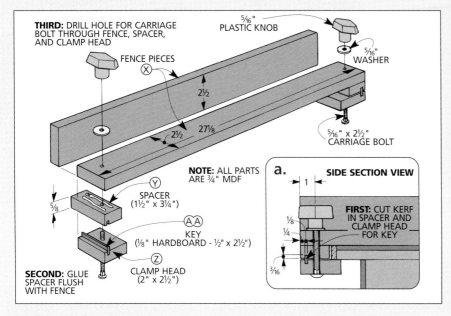

MATERIALS LIST

NEW PARTS

X	Fence Pieces (2)	$\frac{3}{4}$ MDF - $2\frac{1}{2}$ x $27\frac{1}{8}$
Y	Spacers (2)	$\frac{3}{4}$ MDF rgh. - $1\frac{1}{2}$ x $3\frac{1}{4}$
Z	Clamp Heads (2)	$\frac{3}{4}$ MDF - 2 x $2\frac{1}{2}$
AA	Keys (2)	$\frac{1}{8}$ hdbd. - $\frac{1}{2}$ x $2\frac{1}{2}$

HARDWARE SUPPLIES

(2) $\frac{5}{16}$" x $2\frac{1}{2}$" carriage bolts
(2) $\frac{5}{16}$" washers
(2) $\frac{5}{16}$" threaded plastic knobs

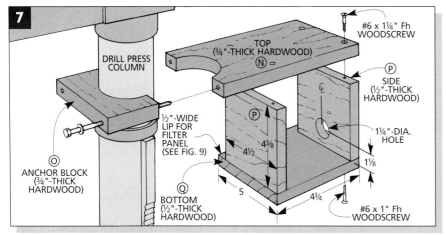

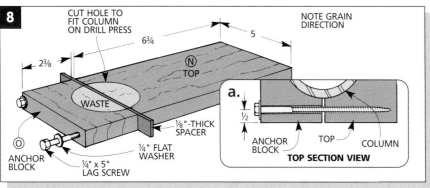

MOTOR HOUSING

The small, 50 RPM motor that drives the Oscillating Drum Sander is enclosed in a wood housing that hangs on the column of the drill press.

COLLAR. The motor housing is supported by a two-piece wood collar with curved openings that fit around the column of the drill press *(Fig. 7)*. A top (N) doubles as the upper part of the motor housing. And an anchor block (O) accepts two lag screws that tighten the collar around the column.

There's one thing to note about these pieces. The grain runs the long way on both pieces. This prevents the anchor block from splitting between the lag bolts. And it means you won't need a wide board (which might cup) for the top.

To get the collar to fit tight, I used a simple trick. Start by slipping a $\frac{1}{8}$" spacer (hardboard) between the two workpieces and "clamp" them together with the lag screws *(Fig. 8)*. After cutting a hole that matches the diameter of the column, the gap created by the spacer allows the collar to pinch tight *(Fig. 8a)*.

MOTOR HOUSING. With the collar complete, I began work on the motor housing. It starts out as a U-shaped assembly that consists of two sides (P) and a bottom (Q) *(Fig. 7).*

Before gluing and screwing this assembly together, drill a hole in the back side piece so you'll be able to feed the wires on the motor out of the housing *(Fig. 10).* Then attach the top (N) with glue and screws.

FILTER & MOTOR MOUNT

At this point, the motor housing is open at each end. But one end will be enclosed by a filter system *(Fig. 9).* And the other will hold a motor mount *(Fig. 10).*

FILTER. To remove dust from the air that's drawn into the motor housing, I used an ordinary filter from a dust mask. It fits in a filter panel (R) with a hole cut in it so air can get through *(Fig. 11).* Routing a rabbet around the hole forms a recess for the filter *(Fig. 11a).* It's held in place by a hardboard filter cover (S) *(Fig. 9).* The hole cut in the filter cover is just less than the diameter of the filter.

MOTOR MOUNT. Now you can add the motor mount (T). It's a ½"-thick piece of hardwood that holds the motor securely in place just above the bottom (Q) of the motor housing *(Fig. 9a).* This makes it easy to slide the motor into the housing.

To vent the air from the housing, the motor mount is shorter (narrower) than the sides. Drilling a hole in the motor mount allows the shaft of the motor to stick through. Also, you'll need to locate and drill holes for machine screws that secure the motor.

Once the motor is attached, simply slide it into the housing. To provide access if you ever need to remove the motor, the motor mount is attached to the sides with screws only (no glue).

CRANK. All that's left is to add a metal crank to the shaft of the motor. Along with a drive assembly that's added later, this crank transfers the rotation of the motor to the feed lever.

The crank is a short piece of ½" metal bar stock *(Fig. 12).* (You can find this at most hardware stores.) A threaded hole on one end accepts a drive arm. And two intersecting holes on the other let you attach the crank to the shaft.

A large, unthreaded hole fits onto the shaft of the motor. And a small, threaded hole accepts a set screw that tightens the crank on the "flat" of the shaft.

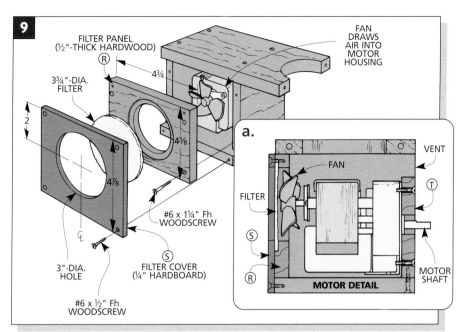

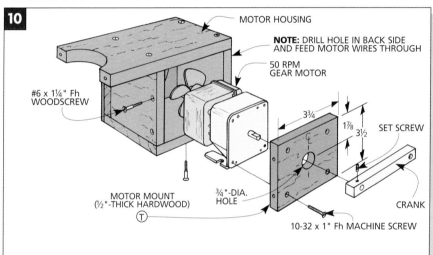

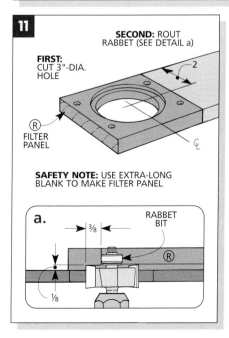

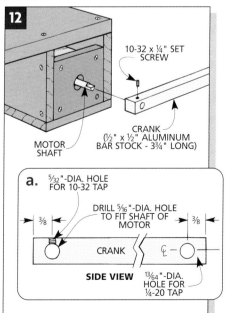

DRIVE SYSTEM

Now that the motor housing is mounted to the drill press column, you're ready to add the drive system.

The idea here is simple. A two-piece pinch block fits around the hub on the feed lever *(Fig. 13)*. This pinch block is attached to an arm that's connected to the crank on the motor. As the crank turns around, the arm drives the pinch block back and forth, which moves the sanding drum up and down.

PINCH BLOCK. The pinch block is similar to the collar for the motor housing. Only this time, curved openings in a drive block (U) and a clamp block (V) fit the hub on the feed lever *(Fig. 14)*. I used the same "spacer" technique to get a tight fit around the hub.

ARM. Now you can add the arm (W) *(Fig. 13)*. It starts out as an extra-long strip of hardwood (18" in my case). It will be cut to length after it is installed.

Later, the bottom end of the arm is attached to the crank with a bolt. To allow the arm to spin freely, the bolt passes through a nylon spacer that fits in a hole drilled in the arm.

Note: To keep the bolt from working loose, the arm is slightly (1/16") thinner than the length of the spacer *(Fig. 13a)*.

To finish setting up the sander, see the opposite page. ◼

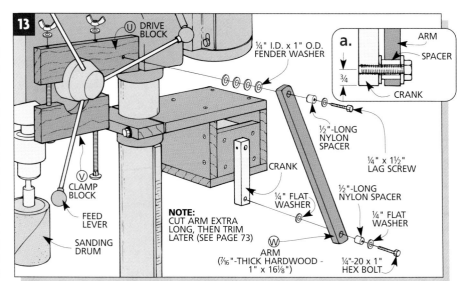

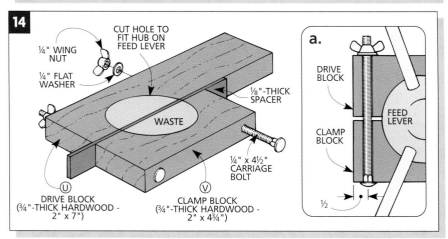

WOODWORKER'S NOTEBOOK

Used with the oscillating drum attachment or without, this reversible table is simpler to build.

SANDING BOX

◼ The Sanding Box has an oversized top and bottom (A) (see drawing). A hole in the top is for large drums. Another hole in the bottom is for small drums. A third hole in a side (B) accepts a vacuum hose.

◼ A hardboard "flop valve" (D) covers the unused hole (detail 'a').

MATERIALS LIST

WOOD

A	Top/Bottom (2)	¾ ply - 14 x 14
B	Box Sides (2)	¾ ply - 2½ x 8
C	Box Front/Back (2)	¾ ply - 2½ x 6½
D	Flop Valve (1)	¼ hdbd. - 6¼ x 6¼

HARDWARE SUPPLIES

(8) No. 8 x 1½" Fh woodscrews

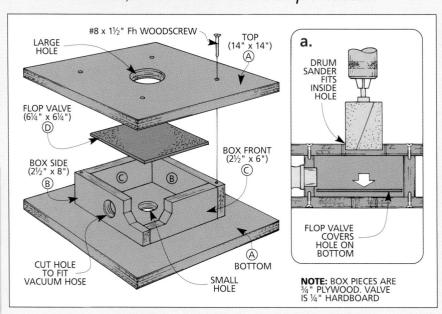

SETUP . . . . *Oscillating Drum Sander*

Setting up the drum sander is just a matter of attaching the arm so it connects the crank on the motor with the pinch block (see drawing).

DEPTH ADJUSTMENT. First, set the drill press depth adjustment so the quill has the maximum amount of travel *(Step 1)*.

STROKE. Then, to keep the quill from hitting the housing of the drill press on its upward stroke, I used a 1¹⁄₂" wide scrap to temporarily position it farther down than the total amount of travel *(Step 2)*.

PINCH BLOCK. Next, tighten the pinch block on the feed lever *(Step 3)*. It's oriented straight up and down, as it will be when the quill is at the bottom of its stroke.

ATTACH ARM. Now you can attach the arm. One end is just bolted to the crank *(Step 4)*. But before you can attach the top end, you'll need to drill holes for the

spacer and lag screw that hold it in place *(Step 5)*. To locate these holes, align the arm with the crank (see drawing). Then check for clearance between the arm and the feed lever and drill the holes.

After removing the scrap, adjust the height and position of the drill press table

so the sanding drum is centered in the opening *(Step 6)*. Then all that's left is to check that the arm moves freely.

To do this, rotate the drive assembly by hand. If it binds, you may need to add or remove one of the washers that are used to shim the arm (detail 'a').

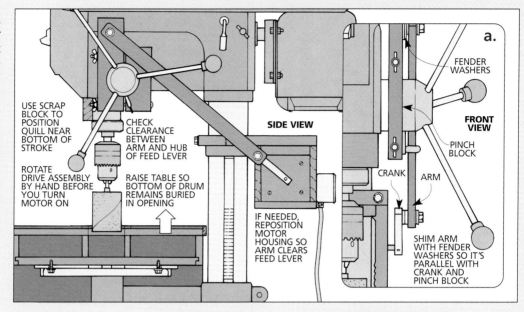

USE SCRAP BLOCK TO POSITION QUILL NEAR BOTTOM OF STROKE

ROTATE DRIVE ASSEMBLY BY HAND BEFORE YOU TURN MOTOR ON

CHECK CLEARANCE BETWEEN ARM AND HUB OF FEED LEVER

RAISE TABLE SO BOTTOM OF DRUM REMAINS BURIED IN OPENING

SIDE VIEW

IF NEEDED, REPOSITION MOTOR HOUSING SO ARM CLEARS FEED LEVER

a.

FENDER WASHERS

FRONT VIEW

PINCH BLOCK

CRANK   ARM

SHIM ARM WITH FENDER WASHERS SO IT'S PARALLEL WITH CRANK AND PINCH BLOCK

1 Start by setting the depth adjustment on the drill press for the maximum amount of travel and lock it in place.

2 Use a 1¹⁄₂"-tall (wide) block to hold the quill down temporarily while the drive assembly is attached.

3 Next, position the pinch block straight up and down and tighten it around the hub of the feed lever.

4 Now bolt the arm to the crank (the arm should pivot) and align the two parts as shown here and in the Side View above.

5 After drilling a hole in the top end of the arm and the pinch block, cut the arm to length and screw it to the pinch block.

6 Finally, remove the scrap block from the quill (see Step 2) and adjust the height of the sanding platform.

SHOP-BUILT MACHINES

You don't have to be a machinist or a mechanic to construct the tools in this section. Regular woodworking tools and creative uses of hardware are the keys to building these industrial-quality machines.

The disc sander and edge sander are self-contained tools, drawing power from their own electric motors. The low-speed grinder relies on the motor of your table saw to save space and expense. Or to keep from tying up your table saw, build the grinder with its own motor as a stand-alone tool.

Finally, the panel saw is a machine that turns your circular saw into a precision tool for cutting sheet goods down to size.

Disc Sander

There's nothing difficult about building this professional-quality power tool for your shop. Inside the sturdy housing and behind the tilting table is just a metal sanding disc attached to an electric motor.

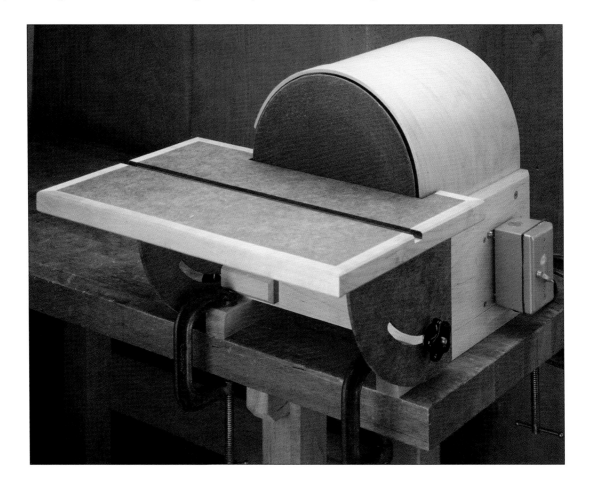

isc sanders are usually found only in production cabinet shops. Their large sanding surface and heavy-duty construction make them ideal for quickly sanding to a line, chamfering, mitering, or removing a lot of stock.

An industrial-quality tool like this would be a great addition to any shop. But the high cost makes it hard to justify buying one. So I decided to build my own and add a number of features to make it easy to use and improve accuracy.

TOP. The most noticeable design feature of this Disc Sander is the top. It's curved to follow the shape of the sanding disc. The top serves as a cover for the motor and helps keep it dust-free. It also protects you by covering the edge of the spinning disc. And it directs sawdust into a built-in vacuum port.

TABLE. The table of the Disc Sander is also unique. First of all, it's larger than the tables found on most sanders, making it easier to support and accurately sand a large piece. And the larger table allows you to use a full-size miter gauge — not the scaled-down ones found on most other power disc sanders.

Another problem with the tables on most disc sanders is you have to find a wrench whenever you want to tilt the table. To get around this, I added a pair of knobs to make it easy to tilt and lock the table firmly in place. And to make changing sanding discs a snap, the table lifts off to give you access to the disc.

BASE. If space is limited in your shop, you can add a pair of "feet" to the sander and clamp it to your workbench (see photo above). Or you can build an optional stand. The stand is wide at the base to provide a stable foundation. And the column is hollow so you can fill it up with sand or bricks. This extra ballast helps to anchor the sander and virtually eliminates vibration. For detailed instructions on how to build this stand, see the Designer's Notebook on page 86.

EXPLODED VIEW

OVERALL DIMENSIONS:
22W x 29D x 16H

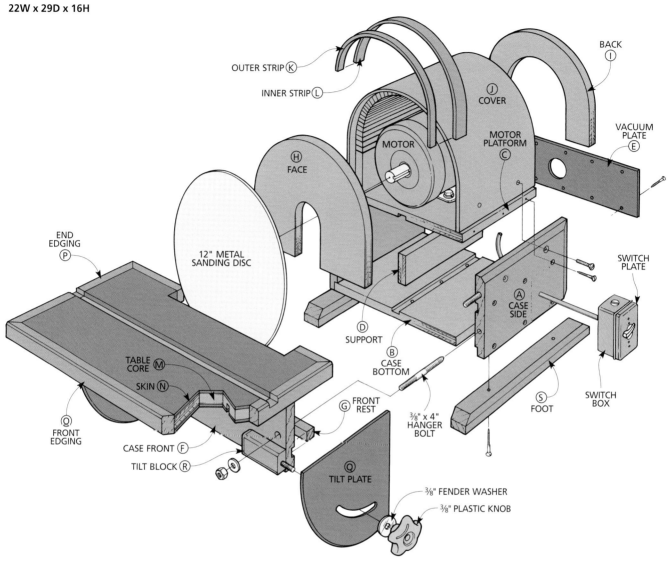

OUTER STRIP (K)
INNER STRIP (L)
BACK (I)
(J) COVER
MOTOR
MOTOR PLATFORM (C)
(H) FACE
VACUUM PLATE (E)
12" METAL SANDING DISC
END EDGING (P)
SWITCH PLATE
(A) CASE SIDE
TABLE CORE (M)
SKIN (N)
(D) SUPPORT
(B) CASE BOTTOM
SWITCH BOX
(Q) FRONT EDGING
(G) FRONT REST
FOOT
(S)
CASE FRONT (F)
TILT BLOCK (R)
³⁄₈" x 4" HANGER BOLT
(Q) TILT PLATE
³⁄₈" FENDER WASHER
³⁄₈" PLASTIC KNOB

MATERIALS LIST

WOOD

A	Case Sides (2)	³⁄₄ x 6³⁄₄ - 12
B	Case Bottom (1)	³⁄₄ ply - 11³⁄₄ x 13
C	Motor Platform (1)	³⁄₄ ply - 11 x 13
D	Support (1)	³⁄₄ ply - 3¹⁄₂ x 11
E	Vacuum Plate (1)	¹⁄₄ hdbd. - 4¹⁄₂ x 13
F	Case Front (1)	³⁄₄ x 6³⁄₄ - 14³⁄₄
G	Front Rest (1)	³⁄₄ x ³⁄₄ - 12¹⁄₂
H	Face (1)	³⁄₄ ply - 12¹⁄₄ x 9⁵⁄₈
I	Back (1)	³⁄₄ ply - 12¹⁄₄ x 9⁵⁄₈
J	Cover (1)	³⁄₄ ply - 11¹⁄₄ x 27 rgh.
K	Outer Strip (1)	¹⁄₈ x 1¹⁄₂ - 27 rough
L	Inner Strip (1)	¹⁄₈ x ⁵⁄₈ - 27 rough
M	Table Core (1)	³⁄₄ ply - 12¹⁄₂ x 20¹⁄₄

N	Skins (2)	¹⁄₄ hdbd. - 12¹⁄₂ x 20¹⁄₄
O	Fr./Bk. Edging (2)	³⁄₄ x 1¹⁄₄ - 21³⁄₄
P	End Edging (2)	³⁄₄ x 1¹⁄₄ - 14
Q	Tilt Plates (2)	¹⁄₄ hdbd. - 8¹⁄₂ x 10
R	Tilt Blocks (2)	³⁄₄ x 1¹⁄₂ - 4
S	Feet (2)	1¹⁄₂ x 1¹⁄₂ - 18

HARDWARE SUPPLIES
(16) No. 5 x ⁵⁄₈" Fh woodscrews
(26) No. 8 x 1¹⁄₂" Fh woodscrews
(4) No. 8 x 2¹⁄₂" Fh woodscrews
(1) 12" metal sanding disc
(1) 1¹⁄₂" x 14" piano hinge
(6) ³⁄₈" x 4" hanger bolts

(4) ³⁄₈" hex nuts
(4) ³⁄₈" flat washers
(2) ³⁄₈" plastic knobs
(2) ³⁄₈" fender washers
(4) ¹⁄₄" x 1¹⁄₂" Fh machine screws
(4) ¹⁄₄" T-nuts
(1) 1725 RPM motor
(1) Switch box
(1) Switch plate
(1) Electrical switch
(1) Electrical cord w/ plug
(4) Bolts, washers, lock washers, and T-nuts to mount motor

CUTTING DIAGRAM

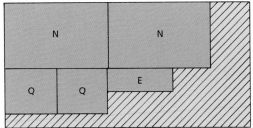

¼" TEMPERED HARDBOARD - 24 x 48

¾" PLYWOOD - 48 x 36

NOTE: YOU CAN GET ALL THE PLYWOOD PARTS FOR BOTH THE DISC SANDER AND THE STAND (SEE PAGE 86) FROM A SINGLE 48" x 96" SHEET OF ¾"-THICK PLYWOOD

¾ x 8 - 84 (4.7 Bd. Ft.)

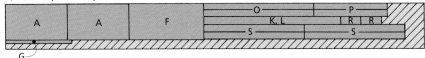

CASE

The Disc Sander is made up of three main parts: a rectangular-shaped case, a half-round top cover, and an adjustable table that tilts so you can sand at an angle. I started by building the case.

Note: The case I built is sized for a standard 12" sanding disc. (To find these discs, see Sources on page 126.)

As you can see, the case is just a rectangular box with tall sides *(Fig. 1)*. The sides extend up to hold the cover in place when it's added later.

SIDES. To make the case, cut a pair of sides (A) to size from ¾"-thick hardwood *(Fig. 2)*. Next, the sides of the case are grooved to accept a motor platform to hold the motor. And they are rabbeted for a plywood bottom *(Fig. 2)*.

In addition to the rabbet for the plywood bottom, you'll also need to rout a rabbet for a vacuum plate that's added later *(Fig. 4)*. This rabbet is on the back edge of each side between the bottom rabbet and the groove *(Fig. 2)*.

While I was at it, I drilled two holes in the front end of each side piece *(Fig. 2)*.

These will be used later to attach the table to the case. But drilling straight, vertical holes on the edge of a workpiece can be difficult. So I used an easy-to-build jig that clamps to the drill press (see the Shop Tip on the next page).

To complete the sides, I knocked down the sharp corners on the case by routing a chamfer on the top and back outside edges of each side *(Fig. 2)*.

BOTTOM AND PLATFORM. Once the sides are complete, the next step is to make the bottom (B) and the motor platform (C). Both of these pieces are cut from ¾"-thick plywood to the same length (13") *(Fig. 3)*. But their widths (depths) are different.

That's because the motor platform (C) needs to be cut ¾" shorter than the bottom (B) *(Fig. 3)*. This creates a pocket for the bottom half of the sanding disc that's added later.

Before assembling the case, you'll need to cut a dado down the center of the platform and bottom. These dadoes are for a support piece *(Fig. 3)*.

After the dadoes are cut, glue and screw the case together *(Fig. 4)*.

Note: The bottom (B) and motor platform (C) are attached flush with the inside edge of the rabbets cut in the sides for the vacuum plate.

SUPPORT. Next, to prevent the motor platform from bowing under the weight of the heavy electric motor, I added a support piece. The support (D) is a piece of ¾" plywood cut to fit in the dadoes in the platform and bottom *(Fig. 4)*.

When you install the support, be sure to position it in the case so it's flush with

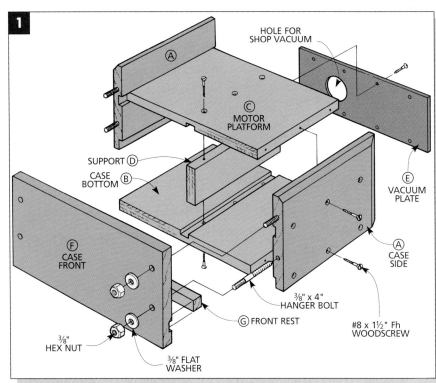

1

HOLE FOR SHOP VACUUM

Ⓐ

Ⓒ MOTOR PLATFORM

SUPPORT Ⓓ

CASE BOTTOM Ⓑ

Ⓔ VACUUM PLATE

Ⓕ CASE FRONT

Ⓐ CASE SIDE

⅜" HEX NUT

⅜" FLAT WASHER

Ⓖ FRONT REST

⅜" x 4" HANGER BOLT

#8 x 1½" Fh WOODSCREW

SHOP TIP

Vertical Drilling Jig

To ensure straight holes when drilling into the end of a workpiece, I use this simple jig for the drill press.

It's made from two scrap pieces of plywood connected at a right angle. Wedge-shaped supports brace the plywood. A cleat serves to hold the workpiece vertical.

For long workpieces, swing the drill press table to the side and allow the workpiece to extend below the jig.

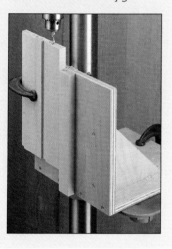

the front edge of the motor platform (not the case bottom) and screw it in place. This leaves some space for the front and front rest that are added later.

VACUUM PLATE. To allow a shop vacuum (or dust collector) to be hooked up to the sander, a $\frac{1}{4}$" hardboard vacuum plate (E) is cut to fit between the rabbets in the sides and flush with the motor platform and bottom *(Fig. 4)*.

Note: It's not necessary to hook up a shop vacuum to the Disc Sander. It works just fine without one. But when it's used, this tool creates a lot of sawdust. So it really helps to have the sander hooked up to some kind of dust collection system to keep floating sawdust particles from filling the air (and your lungs).

Once the vacuum plate is cut to size, drill a hole in it to fit your shop vacuum nozzle (or dust collector) and screw it to the back of the case *(Fig. 4)*.

2

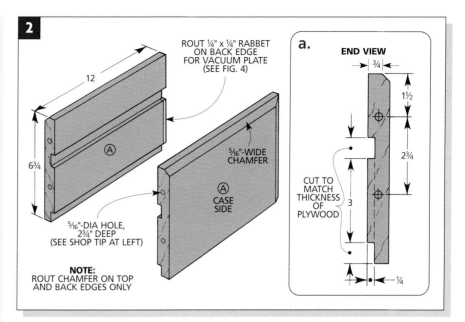

ROUT $\frac{1}{4}$" x $\frac{1}{4}$" RABBET ON BACK EDGE FOR VACUUM PLATE (SEE FIG. 4)

12

6$\frac{3}{4}$

$\frac{5}{16}$"-WIDE CHAMFER

(A)

(A) CASE SIDE

$\frac{5}{16}$"-DIA HOLE, 2$\frac{3}{4}$" DEEP (SEE SHOP TIP AT LEFT)

NOTE: ROUT CHAMFER ON TOP AND BACK EDGES ONLY

a. END VIEW

$\frac{3}{4}$

1$\frac{1}{2}$

2$\frac{3}{4}$

CUT TO MATCH THICKNESS OF PLYWOOD

3

$\frac{1}{4}$

3

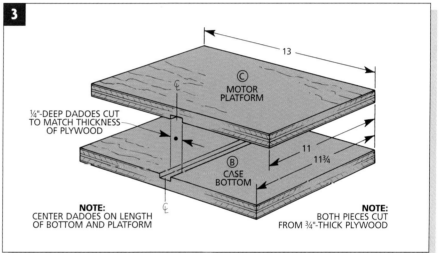

13

(C) MOTOR PLATFORM

$\frac{1}{4}$"-DEEP DADOES CUT TO MATCH THICKNESS OF PLYWOOD

11

11$\frac{3}{4}$

(B) CASE BOTTOM

NOTE: CENTER DADOES ON LENGTH OF BOTTOM AND PLATFORM

NOTE: BOTH PIECES CUT FROM $\frac{3}{4}$"-THICK PLYWOOD

4

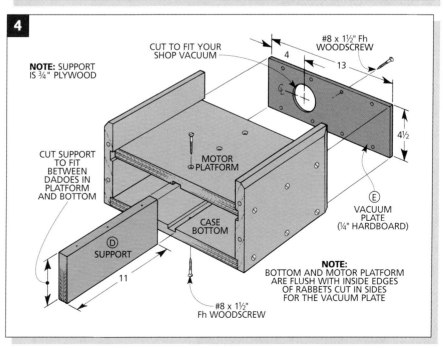

NOTE: SUPPORT IS $\frac{3}{4}$" PLYWOOD

CUT TO FIT YOUR SHOP VACUUM

#8 x 1$\frac{1}{2}$" Fh WOODSCREW

4

13

CUT SUPPORT TO FIT BETWEEN DADOES IN PLATFORM AND BOTTOM

MOTOR PLATFORM

4$\frac{1}{2}$

(E) VACUUM PLATE ($\frac{1}{4}$" HARDBOARD)

(D) SUPPORT

CASE BOTTOM

11

#8 x 1$\frac{1}{2}$" Fh WOODSCREW

NOTE: BOTTOM AND MOTOR PLATFORM ARE FLUSH WITH INSIDE EDGES OF RABBETS CUT IN SIDES FOR THE VACUUM PLATE

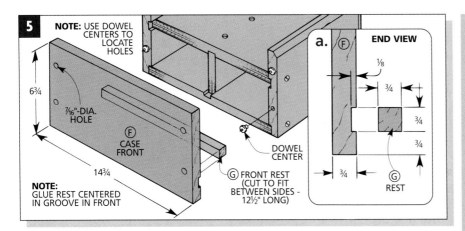

5

NOTE: USE DOWEL CENTERS TO LOCATE HOLES

$6^{3}/_{4}$

$^{7}/_{16}$"-DIA. HOLE

(F) CASE FRONT

$14^{3}/_{4}$

NOTE: GLUE REST CENTERED IN GROOVE IN FRONT

DOWEL CENTER

(G) FRONT REST (CUT TO FIT BETWEEN SIDES - $12^{1}/_{2}$" LONG)

a. (F) END VIEW

$^{1}/_{8}$

$^{3}/_{4}$

$^{3}/_{4}$

$^{3}/_{4}$

$^{3}/_{4}$

(G) REST

CASE FRONT. All that's left to complete the case is to add a $^{3}/_{4}$"-thick hardwood front *(Fig. 5)*. The front (F) covers the end of the case. And it will be used later to attach and support the adjustable table.

The width (height) of the front is the same as the sides ($6^{3}/_{4}$"). To provide the necessary clearance for the table ($^{3}/_{8}$" on each side), I cut the front so it ended up $^{3}/_{4}$" longer ($14^{3}/_{4}$") than the overall width of the case *(Fig. 5)*.

FRONT REST. To hold the front in place and support the weight of the table, I added a hardwood rest (G) *(Fig. 5)*. This rest fits into a shallow groove that's cut on the inside face of the front (F).

ASSEMBLY. With the rest glued in place, attach the front to the case *(Fig. 1)*. The first step is to transfer the locations of the holes in the sides to the front. To do this, I used dowel centers *(Fig. 5)*.

With the holes marked, drill oversize shank holes in the front. Then thread hanger bolts in the sides (see Shop Tip at right). Finally, slip on the front and secure it with washers and hex nuts.

TOP COVER

Once the case is complete, the next step is to make a top cover to fit between the sides *(Fig. 6)*. The top is barrel-shaped to fit over the motor and the sanding disc. To create this shape, I used a kerfing jig to bend a piece of plywood over two U-shaped pieces *(Fig. 6)*.

FACE AND BACK. These pieces, a face (H) and back (I), are cut from two iden-

SHOP TIP
Coupling Nut

To protect the full length of the threads on a hanger bolt, I use a coupling nut. A "jam" nut prevents the coupling nut from turning.

tical blanks of $^{3}/_{4}$" plywood. To determine the width of the blanks, measure the distance between the sides of the case and subtract $^{1}/_{4}$" for clearance. (This ended up at $12^{1}/_{4}$" on my case.)

SHOP JIG .... *Kerfing Jig*

The cover of the Disc Sander needs a lot of kerfs to allow it to wrap around the motor. Cutting this many kerfs in a sheet of plywood, using just a miter gauge on a table saw, would be an extremely tedious job. Not to mention the difficulty you'd have making sure the kerfs are evenly spaced.

So to make it a lot easier to cut all the kerfs in the top cover, I made this simple L-shaped jig (with an indexing pin), from a couple of pieces of $^{3}/_{4}$"-thick hardwood (see photo). It attaches to the miter gauge on my table saw.

The bottom portion of the "L" fits under the rabbet you cut on one edge of the cover, and it holds the indexing pin *(Fig. 1)*. The pin is just a No. 6 x 1" screw with the head cut off.

I positioned this pin on my jig to cut kerfs with a $^{1}/_{4}$" spacing. It automatically positions the cover to cut evenly-spaced kerfs with each pass *(Fig. 2)*.

The trick to using this jig is to start kerfing in the *center* and work your way out towards the ends *(Fig. 2)*. To do this, first cut a kerf in the center of the cover. Then place the cover on the jig so the kerf you just cut fits over the indexing pin. Now make another pass.

For the top cover, I continued kerfing like this to within $3^{1}/_{2}$" of the end (refer to *Fig. 7*). Then I flipped the cover and cut the rest of the kerfs in the other end.

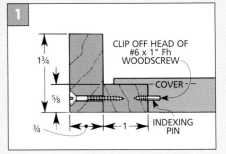

1

$1^{3}/_{4}$

$^{5}/_{8}$

$^{3}/_{4}$

CLIP OFF HEAD OF #6 x 1" Fh WOODSCREW

COVER

1

INDEXING PIN

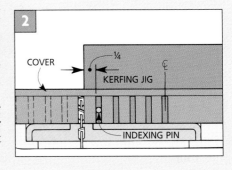

2

COVER

$^{1}/_{4}$

℄

KERFING JIG

INDEXING PIN

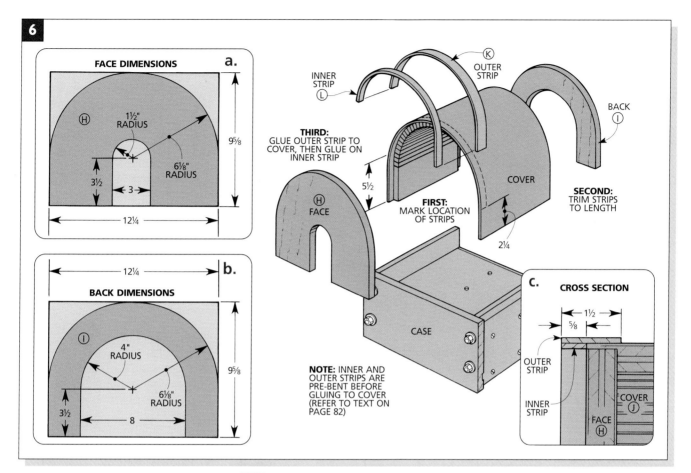

6

a. FACE DIMENSIONS

H
1½" RADIUS
6⅛" RADIUS
9⅝
3½
3
12¼

b. BACK DIMENSIONS

12¼
I
4" RADIUS
6⅛" RADIUS
9⅝
3½
8

INNER STRIP (L)
OUTER STRIP (K)
BACK (I)

THIRD: GLUE OUTER STRIP TO COVER, THEN GLUE ON INNER STRIP

SECOND: TRIM STRIPS TO LENGTH

COVER

H FACE

5½

FIRST: MARK LOCATION OF STRIPS

2¼

CASE

NOTE: INNER AND OUTER STRIPS ARE PRE-BENT BEFORE GLUING TO COVER (REFER TO TEXT ON PAGE 82)

c. CROSS SECTION

1½
⅝
OUTER STRIP
INNER STRIP
COVER (J)
FACE (H)

The next step is to lay out the top curve and cut these pieces to shape. To get a good fit when the top cover is glued on later, it's important that these top curves are cut identically.

To do this, I started by laying out and cutting the curve on one piece *(Figs. 6a and 6b)*. Then I used this as a template to shape the other piece.

This is just a matter of trimming the other blank to rough size, then using a flush trim bit in a router.

Once you've shaped both pieces, all that's left is to lay out and cut the curved opening in each piece. The face piece (H) has a small opening for the motor shaft. And the back piece (I) has a large opening to allow outside air to flow over the motor *(Figs. 6a and 6b)*.

COVER. With the back and face complete, the next step is to cut the top cover (J) from ¾" plywood *(Fig. 7)*. It's 11¼" wide and cut extra-long (27").

Now, cut ¾"-wide rabbets along the length of the cover. These rabbets allow the face and back to fit flush with the edges of the top cover.

KERFS. Next, to get the plywood to bend easily, I cut a series of uniformly-spaced saw kerfs *(Fig. 7)*. To cut the

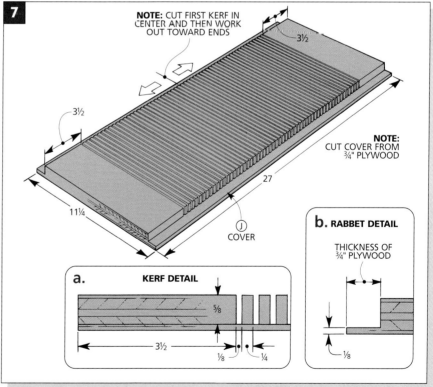

7

NOTE: CUT FIRST KERF IN CENTER AND THEN WORK OUT TOWARD ENDS

3½
3½
27
11¼

NOTE: CUT COVER FROM ¾" PLYWOOD

(J) COVER

a. KERF DETAIL
⅝
3½
⅛
¼

b. RABBET DETAIL
THICKNESS OF ¾" PLYWOOD
⅛

kerfs, I use a simple jig that attaches to the miter gauge on my table saw (see the Shop Jig on the facing page).

Note: Since the sides of the cover are straight near the bottom, you'll only need to kerf to within 3½" of each end *(Fig. 7)*.

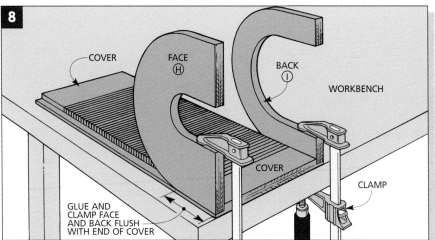

8

COVER

FACE
Ⓗ

BACK
Ⓘ

WORKBENCH

COVER

CLAMP

GLUE AND
CLAMP FACE
AND BACK FLUSH
WITH END OF COVER

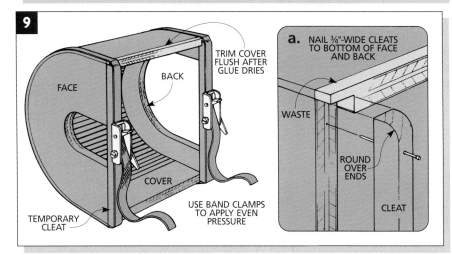

9

TRIM COVER
FLUSH AFTER
GLUE DRIES

FACE

BACK

COVER

TEMPORARY
CLEAT

USE BAND CLAMPS
TO APPLY EVEN
PRESSURE

a. NAIL ¾"-WIDE CLEATS
TO BOTTOM OF FACE
AND BACK

WASTE

ROUND
OVER
ENDS

CLEAT

ASSEMBLY. At this point the cover can be glued to the face and back. But instead of trying to glue, bend, and clamp these pieces together all at once, I used a two-step process that made assembly easier.

First, to keep the curved face and back aligned with the edges of the top, I glued the flat section of each piece flush with one end of the cover *(Fig. 8)*.

Then after the glue set up completely, I used band clamps to pull the cover tight over the face and back. But since the cover was cut extra-long, it extended past the ends of the face and back.

To prevent the band clamps from crushing the edge of the plywood, I temporarily tacked cleats to the bottom of the face and back *(Fig. 9a)*.

With the cleats in place, wrap the band clamps around the cover and cinch them down. Then when the glue is dry, trim the end of the cover flush with a hand saw.

TOP STRIPS. To complete the top, I added a pair of thin hardwood strips to the front edge of the cover (refer to *Figs. 6 and 6c* on page 81). The outer (K) and inner strips (L) cover the exposed plywood edge and help direct sawdust to the vacuum port.

These strips are cut extra-long (27") and then trimmed to exact length later. To get the strips to match the curve of the top, I pre-bent them. But don't worry.

DESIGNER'S NOTEBOOK

For a reliable way to sand consistent multiple pieces, add a series of pre-set stops to the adjustable table.

STOP SYSTEM

■ The adjustable table adds a lot of versatility to the Disc Sander. If you find you do a good amount of sanding with the table at an angle, you may want to add a simple stop system. It lets you set the angle of the table automatically for consistent and repeatable results.

■ This stop system uses an index pin that fits into a series of holes. The pin is just a ¼"-dia. bolt with the threads cut off. The holes are drilled through one tilt plate and into the sander case (see drawing).

To do this, start by adjusting the table to a 90° angle. (I used a try-square to position the table at true 90°.) Now, lock the table in place and drill the first hole.

■ You can drill additional holes for stops at the angles you use most, which for me were at 22½° and 45°.

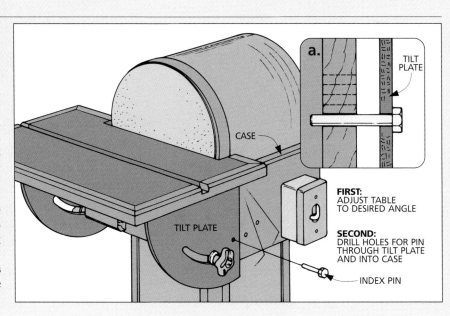

a.

TILT
PLATE

CASE

TILT PLATE

FIRST:
ADJUST TABLE
TO DESIRED ANGLE

SECOND:
DRILL HOLES FOR PIN
THROUGH TILT PLATE
AND INTO CASE

INDEX PIN

Bending these thin strips can be done easily, by soaking them in water for an hour or so first. Then clamp them around the top and let them dry.

While they dried, I marked the location of each end on the cover (refer again to *Fig. 6*). After the strips are dry, set them on the cover and transfer the marks.

Finally, cut the strips to length and glue them in place. Then you can set the cover aside. It's attached to the case later.

ADJUSTABLE TABLE

With the top cover finished, work can begin on the adjustable table *(Fig. 10)*. The table provides a large, flat work surface for sanding. And it can be tilted for sanding at an angle.

Note: If you plan on sanding a lot of workpieces at the same angle, you might want to add a stop system once the table is built. To learn more, see the Designer's Notebook on the previous page.

TABLE. The table is made up of a plywood and hardboard "sandwich" that's edged with hardwood *(Fig. 11)*. I started by cutting a ³⁄₄" plywood core (M) to size *(Fig. 11)*. Then, cut two ¹⁄₄" hardboard skins (N) slightly oversize and glue them to the core *(Fig. 11)*.

To get the edges flush, I used a flush trim bit in a router.

Now cut two grooves in the bottom of the table *(Fig. 11b)*. These grooves are ¹⁄₂" deep, and they're cut to match the thickness of the tilt plates added later.

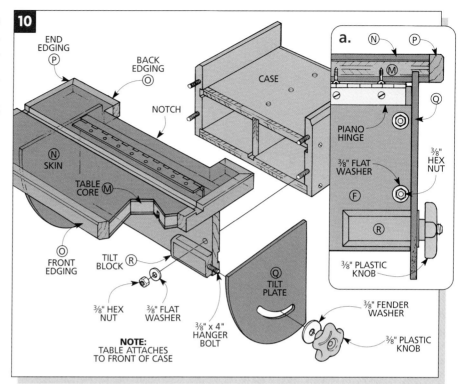

The distance between these grooves is the same as the length of the case front.

EDGING. To cover and protect the edges of the table, I cut front, back, and end edging (O, P) to fit and glued them in place *(Fig. 11)*. Then I routed ¹⁄₈"-wide chamfers on the top and bottom edges.

MITER GAUGE. Next, to provide better control when sanding miters and small pieces, I cut a groove in the tabletop for a miter gauge. Cut the groove centered on the width of the tabletop to fit your miter gauge *(Fig. 11a)*. (I used the miter gauge from my table saw.)

CUT NOTCH. Also, I wanted as much support as possible when sanding near the edge of the disc. So I cut a notch on the back edge. This way the table "wraps" around the case *(Figs. 10 and 11)*.

To do this, cut a notch centered between the grooves for the tilt plates (not on the length of the table) *(Fig. 11a)*.

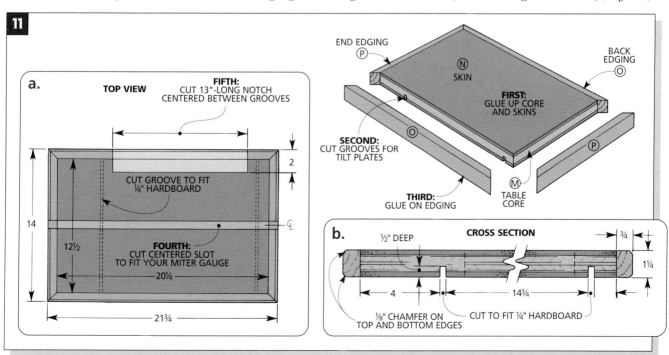

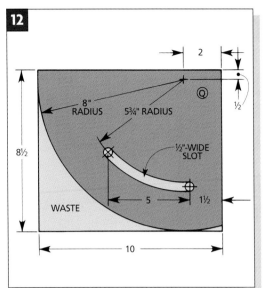

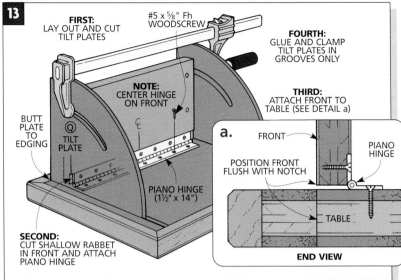

TILT PLATES. To allow the table to be angled for sanding, two tilt plates (Q) made from $1/4$" hardboard fit into the grooves cut earlier in the table.

To make identical plates, I stuck the two pieces of hardboard together with carpet tape and then laid out the curves *(Fig. 12)*. Next, I cut out the shape with a band saw (or you could use a jig saw) and sanded the edges smooth.

While the tilt plates are still fastened together, curved slots are cut in them *(Fig. 12)*. These are used later to lock the table at different angles. To cut the slots, I drilled a hole at each end of the slot and then removed the waste with a jig saw.

Once the slots are completed, the tilt plates can be separated and glued into the grooves in the table. But first, place the table face down on a bench. Then to keep the plates square to the table, attach the front of the case to the table with a piano

hinge *(Fig. 13)*. (You'll need to remove the front from the case to do this.)

To align the hinge, I use a simple trick (see the Shop Tip on the next page). Then, after screwing the hinge to the table, I glued and clamped the tilt plates in the grooves using the front (F) to square them up *(Fig. 13)*.

Note: I used No. 5 x $5/8$" screws to secure the hinge *(Fig. 13)*.

TILT BLOCKS. Finally, to help lock the table in place, I added a tilt block (R) to each end of the front (refer to *Fig. 10* on page 83 and *Fig. 14*). A hole drilled in each block accepts a $3/8$" hanger bolt that passes through the tilt plate *(Fig. 15)*.

The unusual thing here is that the hanger bolts are installed before the tilt blocks are attached. This allows you to position (and glue) the tilt blocks to the front (F) with the bolts centered in the slots *(Fig. 15a)*. This way the plates won't

bind on the bolts when the table is tilted. (If the bolts do bind, file the slots.)

Plastic knobs thread onto the ends of the hanger bolts and pinch the tilt plates against the blocks to lock them in place. Once the knobs are in place, re-attach the front (and table) to the case.

ASSEMBLY

The Disc Sander can be used on top of a workbench, or it can be mounted on an optional floor stand. (For more on the stand, see the Designer's Notebook starting on page 86.) If you're going to use the sander on your bench, you'll need to screw a pair of feet (S) to the case so you can clamp the sander in place *(Fig. 16)*.

MOUNT MOTOR. After attaching the feet, the next step is to locate the holes for mounting the motor. The size (horsepower) of the motor can vary. What's

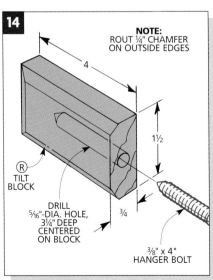

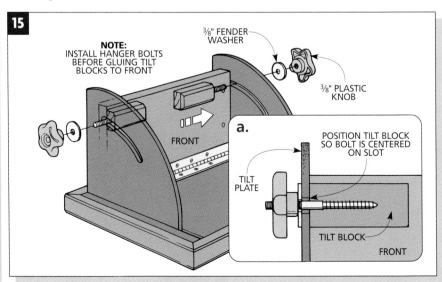

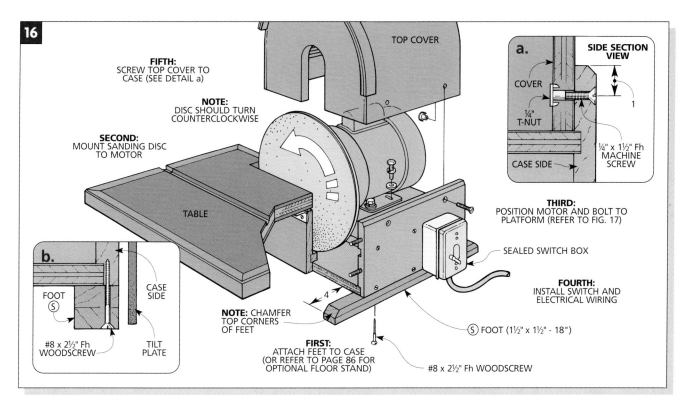

16

FIFTH:
SCREW TOP COVER TO
CASE (SEE DETAIL a)

TOP COVER

NOTE:
DISC SHOULD TURN
COUNTERCLOCKWISE

SECOND:
MOUNT SANDING DISC
TO MOTOR

TABLE

a.
SIDE SECTION
VIEW
COVER
¼"
T-NUT
CASE SIDE
¼" x 1½" Fh
MACHINE
SCREW
1

THIRD:
POSITION MOTOR AND BOLT TO
PLATFORM (REFER TO FIG. 17)

SEALED SWITCH BOX

FOURTH:
INSTALL SWITCH AND
ELECTRICAL WIRING

b.
FOOT
Ⓢ
CASE
SIDE
#8 x 2½" Fh
WOODSCREW
TILT
PLATE

NOTE: CHAMFER
TOP CORNERS
OF FEET

Ⓢ FOOT (1½" x 1½" - 18")

FIRST:
ATTACH FEET TO CASE
(OR REFER TO PAGE 86 FOR
OPTIONAL FLOOR STAND)

#8 x 2½" Fh WOODSCREW

important is to make sure that the direction and speed are correct.

The motor should turn counterclockwise so that dust is directed toward the dust port. And it should run at about 1725 RPM. This keeps the disc from spinning too fast and reduces the chance of burning a workpiece.

Before securing the motor on the platform, you'll first need to attach the sanding disc. It mounts directly to the ⅝" shaft of the motor and is locked in place with a set screw *(Fig. 17)*.

With the disc in place, center the motor on the platform (C) from side to side. Then slide it forward so there's about ⅛" of clearance between the front

face of the sanding disc and the notch in the adjustable table *(Fig. 17)*.

Now you can drill shank holes centered in the slots in the motor's base. Then secure the motor with hex bolts, washers, lock washers, and T-nuts. (The Shop Tip on page 24 shows an easy way to install the T-nuts.)

WIRING. Once the motor is in place, the next step is to wire it up. This could be as simple as wiring an electrical cord to it, but I added a switch so I could easily turn the sander on and off. I used a sealed switch box to keep out sawdust *(Fig. 16)*.

Safety Note: If you don't feel comfortable wiring the motor or switch, it's a good idea to consult a licensed electrician.

COVER. All that's left to complete the Disc Sander is to add the cover *(Fig. 16)*. It's held in place with machine screws and T-nuts *(Fig. 16a)*. Position the cover so the back edge is flush with the rear of the case *(Fig. 17)*. (The sanding disc should clear the face.) Then locate and drill four countersunk holes, insert the T-nuts, and screw on the cover. ■

SHOP TIP

Alignment Rabbet

To make it easier to install a piano hinge, cut a shallow "alignment" rabbet for it to sit in. This will keep the hinge parallel to the edge.

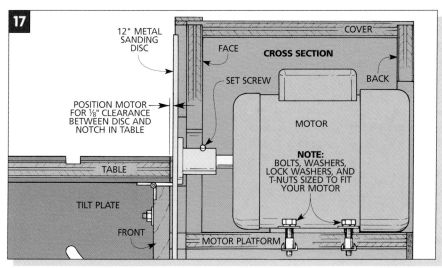

17

12" METAL
SANDING
DISC

FACE

CROSS SECTION

COVER

BACK

SET SCREW

POSITION MOTOR
FOR ⅛" CLEARANCE
BETWEEN DISC AND
NOTCH IN TABLE

MOTOR

TABLE

TILT PLATE

FRONT

NOTE:
BOLTS, WASHERS,
LOCK WASHERS, AND
T-NUTS SIZED TO FIT
YOUR MOTOR

MOTOR PLATFORM

DESIGNER'S NOTEBOOK

The stand turns the sander into a stationary power tool, making this shop-built tool more comfortable to work at. Its wide base adds stability. And a hollow column is filled with sand to deaden vibrations.

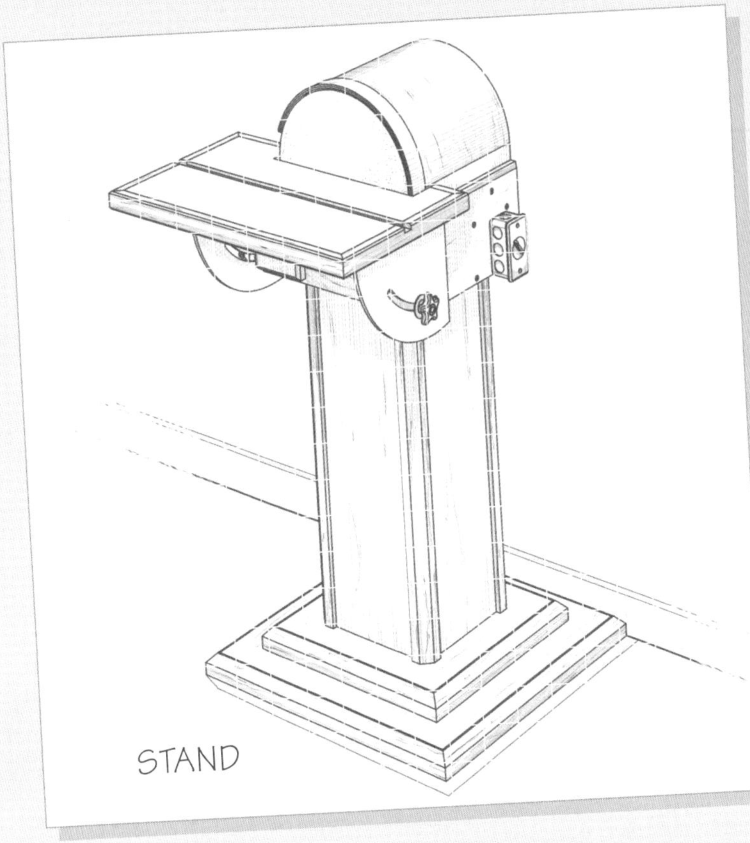
STAND

CONSTRUCTION NOTES:

■ As it is, the Disc Sander can be clamped directly to a bench in your workshop. Or you can build this stand to turn the sander into a stationary power tool. The stand consists of two main parts: a wide base to provide a stable foundation, and a hollow column that raises the sander up to a comfortable working height.

■ I started by making the base *(Fig. 1)*. It's made up of a lower and an upper section *(Fig. 1)*. The construction of each section is the same. They're just two plywood squares that are glued and screwed together. The only difference is their size. The lower base (T) is 20½" square. The upper base (U) is 14½" square.

■ To hide the edges of the plywood, I wrapped each section with some ¾"-thick hardwood edging. The lower (V) and upper (W) trim pieces are cut to match the height of each base (1½").

■ Next, cut a ⅝" chamfer on the top of each piece to relieve the sharp edges. Then miter them to length and glue the pieces in place *(Fig. 1)*.

■ To complete the base, center the upper base on the lower base and clamp them together. Then drive No. 8 x 2½" woodscrews up from the bottom *(Fig. 1)*.

■ At this point, work can begin on the column. It's just a hollow tube made up of hardwood corner posts and plywood panels *(Fig. 2)*. The advantage to building a hollow column is that you can fill it with sand to help anchor the stand and deaden vibration from the sander.

■ I started by making the four corner posts (X) *(Fig. 2)*. Each post is glued up from two pieces of ¾"-thick hardwood.

■ Then, to accept the plywood panels that are added later, ¼"-deep grooves are cut in each post *(Fig. 2a)*.

■ Next, rout a ¾"-wide chamfer on each outside corner *(Fig. 2a)*.

MATERIALS LIST

NEW PARTS

T	Lower Base (2)	¾ ply - 20½ x 20½
U	Upper Base (2)	¾ ply - 14½ x 14½
V	Lower Trim (4)	¾ x 1½ - 22
W	Upper Trim (4)	¾ x 1½ - 16
X	Corner Posts (4)	1½ x 1½ - 25
Y	Panels (4)	¾ ply - 7¾ x 25

HARDWARE SUPPLIES

- (28) No. 8 x 1¼" Fh woodscrews
- (4) No. 8 x 2½" Fh woodscrews
- (4) ⅜" x 4" hanger bolts
- (4) ⅜" hex nuts
- (8) ⅜" flat washers
- (4) ⅜" x 1" lag bolts
- (4) ⅜" x 5" lag bolts

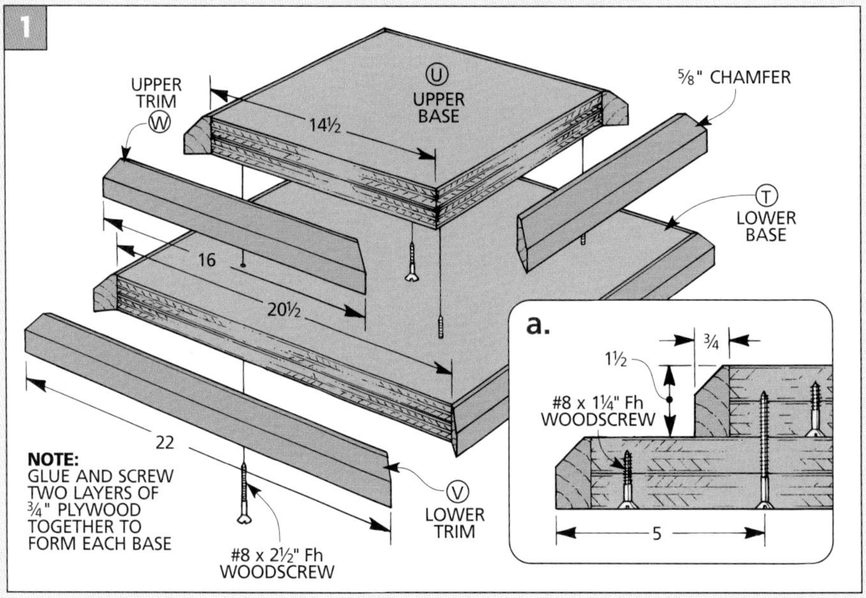
1
UPPER TRIM
W
U
UPPER BASE
⅝" CHAMFER
14½
T
LOWER BASE
16
20½
22
NOTE:
GLUE AND SCREW TWO LAYERS OF ¾" PLYWOOD TOGETHER TO FORM EACH BASE
#8 x 2½" Fh WOODSCREW
V
LOWER TRIM
a.
¾
1½
#8 x 1¼" Fh WOODSCREW
5

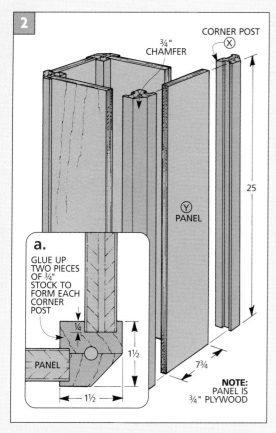

2

¾"
CHAMFER

CORNER POST
Ⓧ

25

Ⓨ
PANEL

a.
GLUE UP
TWO PIECES
OF ¾"
STOCK TO
FORM EACH
CORNER
POST

¼

1½

PANEL

1½

7¾

NOTE:
PANEL IS
¾" PLYWOOD

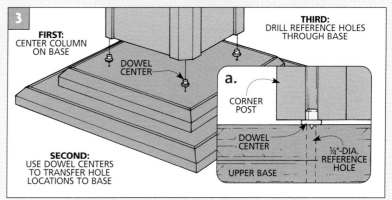

3

FIRST:
CENTER COLUMN
ON BASE

DOWEL
CENTER

THIRD:
DRILL REFERENCE HOLES
THROUGH BASE

a.

CORNER
POST

DOWEL
CENTER

UPPER BASE

¼"-DIA.
REFERENCE
HOLE

SECOND:
USE DOWEL CENTERS
TO TRANSFER HOLE
LOCATIONS TO BASE

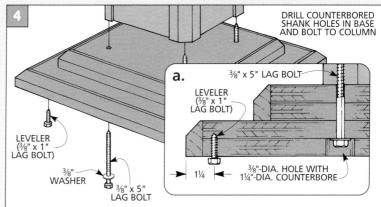

4

DRILL COUNTERBORED
SHANK HOLES IN BASE
AND BOLT TO COLUMN

a.

⅜" x 5" LAG BOLT

LEVELER
(⅜" x 1"
LAG BOLT)

LEVELER
(⅜" x 1"
LAG BOLT)

⅜"
WASHER

⅜" x 5"
LAG BOLT

1¼

⅜"-DIA. HOLE WITH
1¼"-DIA. COUNTERBORE

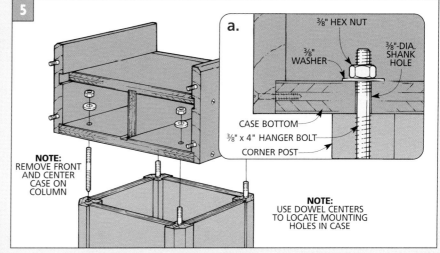

5

a.

⅜" HEX NUT

⅜"
WASHER

⅜"-DIA.
SHANK
HOLE

CASE BOTTOM

⅜" x 4" HANGER BOLT

CORNER POST

NOTE:
REMOVE FRONT
AND CENTER
CASE ON
COLUMN

NOTE:
USE DOWEL CENTERS
TO LOCATE MOUNTING
HOLES IN CASE

■ To complete the posts, I drilled ⁵⁄₁₆"-dia. pilot holes in each end *(Fig. 2a)*. These holes are for a set of bolts that are added later to attach the base and Disc Sander to the column *(Fig. 4a)*. (See the Shop Tip on page 79 for a shop-made jig that makes drilling these holes easier.)

■ After completing the corner posts, the next step is to cut four panels (Y) from ¾" plywood *(Fig. 2)*. These panels become the walls of the column and fit into the grooves you cut in the corner posts.

■ Once the panels are cut to size, you can begin assembling the column. Instead of trying to glue and clamp up everything at once, I did this in two steps.

First, I glued up corner posts and panels to form two sections. The important thing here is that the panels end up flush with the ends of the posts.

■ Then when these sections are dry, apply glue, assemble the column, and hold it all together with band clamps.

■ With the column complete, attach it to the base with lag bolts. The holes for the bolts are already drilled in the column corner posts. The tricky part is transferring the locations of the holes to the base.

My solution was to use dowel centers. To do this, insert a dowel center into each hole in the bottom of the column *(Fig. 3)*. Then center the column on the base and press down hard.

■ Once you've marked the hole locations on the base, the next step is to drill the holes for the lag bolts. The only problem is that these holes need to be counterbored — from the bottom *(Fig. 4a)*.

■ To transfer the hole locations to the bottom, I drilled a ¼"-dia. reference hole through all four layers of the base. Then it's just a matter of counterboring and enlarging each hole to ⅜".

■ Now, bolt the base to the column with ⅜" lag bolts and washers *(Fig. 4)*.

■ To complete the stand, I added four lag bolts to the bottom corners of the base *(Fig. 4a)*. These bolts serve as simple

levelers. This way you can adjust the bolts to compensate for any variations in your workshop floor.

■ Now all that's left is to attach the Disc Sander to the column. Start by removing the front (F) from the case. Then I used dowel centers to transfer the hole locations in the corner posts to the bottom of the case *(Fig. 5)*.

Note: The case is centered on the column side to side and front to back.

■ Finally, drill four ⅜"-dia. holes in the bottom of the case, and attach the case to the column with ⅜" hanger bolts, washers, and hex nuts.

Panel Saw

This shop-built Panel Saw allows precision crosscutting and ripping of large sheet goods. And it's only a fraction of the cost of professional saws. When not in use, it folds up flat and rolls for easy storage.

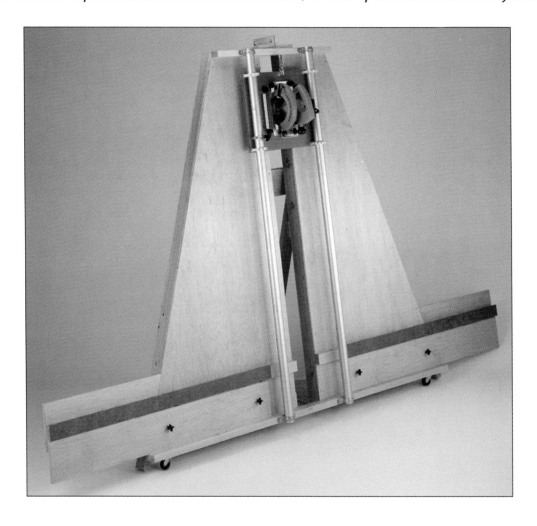

Panel saws are impressive. They make it easy for one person to accurately cut a plywood sheet.

The basic principle of these saws is simple. A sheet of plywood slides in and rests against a vertical bed. Then a circular saw is pulled down a couple of guide rails to cut the sheet.

A big drawback is the price of a store-bought saw. So I decided to build my own version with the features I like.

VERTICAL BED. First of all, there's a large A-shaped vertical bed that supports a sheet of plywood. So the bed won't twist or warp after assembly, it's made from ³⁄₄" birch plywood. For the rails that support the bed, I used Douglas fir for its strength and straight grain.

CARRIAGE ASSEMBLY. Another important feature is the carriage assembly. This assembly provides a way to slide a circular saw with a 7¹⁄₄"-dia. blade smoothly on a pair of guide tubes.

RIPPING. The Panel Saw can also be used for ripping. Just lock the carriage in place, rotate the saw 90°, and push the workpiece through the blade. To provide additional support when ripping a full

sheet of plywood, I added two removable "wings" to the sides of the saw.

MOBILE. Since the Panel Saw is about 10 feet long (with the wings), I attached casters to roll it around. When I'm done cutting, the Panel Saw folds up flat and rolls against the wall for storage. (Most of the hardware for this project is available from a hardware store, or see Sources on page 126 for other suppliers.)

DESIGN OPTION. I've also designed a router carriage for cutting grooves and dadoes in sheet goods. For more, see the Designer's Notebook on page 98.

EXPLODED VIEW

OVERALL DIMENSIONS:
116³/₈"W x 27¹/₄"D x 76⁷/₈"H

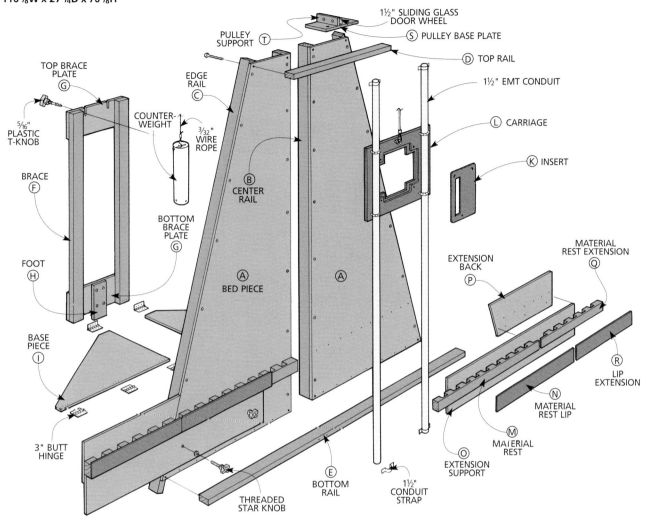

MATERIALS LIST

WOOD

A	Bed Pieces (2)	³/₄ ply - 36 x 72
B	Center Rails (2)	1¹/₂ x 3 - 72
C	Edge Rails (2)	1¹/₂ x 3 - 78
D	Top Rail (1)	1¹/₂ x 2³/₈ - 30⁵/₈
E	Bottom Rail (1)	1¹/₂ x 2³/₈ - 77⁷/₈
F	Braces (2)	1¹/₂ x 3 - 48
G	Top/Btm. Br. Plt. (1)	³/₄ ply - 6 x 15¹/₂
H	Foot (1)	³/₄ ply - 3 x 8
I	Base Pieces (2)	³/₄ ply - 19³/₄ x 32 rgh.
J	Turnbuttons (2)	³/₄ x 1¹/₂ - 3¹/₂
K	Insert (1)	¹/₄ hdbd. - 7³/₄ x 11³/₄
L	Carriage (2)	¹/₂ hdbd. - 15³/₄ x 19
M	Material Rest (2)	1¹/₄ x 2 - 33¹/₄
N	Matl. Rest Lips (2)	¹/₄ hdbd. - 2¹/₂ x 25³/₄
O	Ext. Supports (2)	³/₄ ply - 7 x 48
P	Ext. Back (2)	³/₄ ply - 7⁷/₈ x 24
Q	Matl. Rest Ext. (2)	1¹/₄ x 2 - 22
R	Lip Extensions (2)	¹/₄ hdbd. - 2¹/₂ x 22
S	Pulley Base Plate (1)	³/₄ ply - 6 x 9
T	Pulley Support (1)	³/₄ ply - 2 x 6
U	Pipe Cap (1)	³/₄ x 2¹/₂-dia. rough

HARDWARE SUPPLIES

(100) No. 8 x 1¹/₂" Fh woodscrews
(16) No. 8 x 1¹/₄" Fh woodscrews
(7) ¹/₄" x ³/₄" threaded round knobs
(7) ¹/₄" T-nuts w/ brad holes
(8) ¹/₄" x 1¹/₂" lag bolts
(18) ¹/₄" washers
(4) ¹/₄" x 1¹/₄" fender washers
(1) ¹/₄" x 4" hex bolt
(2) ¹/₄" x 1¹/₂" hex bolts
(3) ¹/₄" hex nuts
(2) ⁵/₁₆" x 3" hanger bolts
(3) ⁵/₁₆" plastic T-knobs
(4) ⁵/₁₆" x 2" - 3¹/₄" U-bolts
(18) ⁵/₁₆" hex nuts
(18) ⁵/₁₆" washers
(1) ⁵/₁₆" x 2" - 3¹/₄" square U-bolt

(1) ⁵/₁₆" lock nut w/ nylon insert
(4) ⁵/₁₆" x 2¹/₄" threaded star knobs
(4) ⁵/₁₆" T-nuts
(1) ⁵/₁₆" x 1¹/₂" eye bolt
(8) ³/₈" x 5" lag bolts
(8) ³/₈" washers
(34) ¹/₂" nylon spacers -.375 x .562
(5) ⁷/₈" nail-on plastic glides
(2) 1¹/₂" x 72" EMT conduit
(4) 1¹/₂" conduit straps
(2) 1¹/₂" sliding glass door wheels
(1) No. 6 x 1¹/₂" S-hook
(2) 2" swivel casters
(8) 3" butt hinges w/ screws
(1) 3" x 13" PVC pipe
(7 ft.) ³/₃₂" wire rope
(2) ³/₃₂" crimp-on clips
(16 lbs.) Lead weight (will vary with saw)

CUTTING DIAGRAM

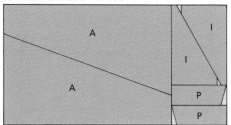

¾" BIRCH PLYWOOD - 48 x 96

NOTE: ALSO NEED FOUR
96" PIECES 2x8 DOUGLAS FIR

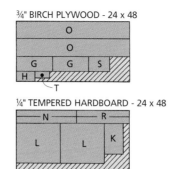

¾" BIRCH PLYWOOD - 24 x 48

¼" TEMPERED HARDBOARD - 24 x 48

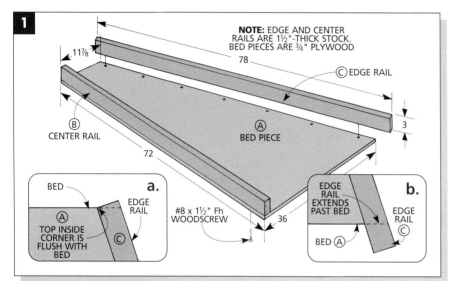

1

NOTE: EDGE AND CENTER
RAILS ARE 1½"-THICK STOCK.
BED PIECES ARE ¾" PLYWOOD

11⅞

78

Ⓒ EDGE RAIL

3

Ⓑ
CENTER RAIL

Ⓐ
BED PIECE

72

36

a.
BED
EDGE
RAIL
Ⓐ
TOP INSIDE
CORNER IS
FLUSH WITH
BED
Ⓒ

#8 x 1½" Fh
WOODSCREW

b.
EDGE
RAIL
EXTENDS
PAST BED
EDGE
RAIL
BED Ⓐ
Ⓒ

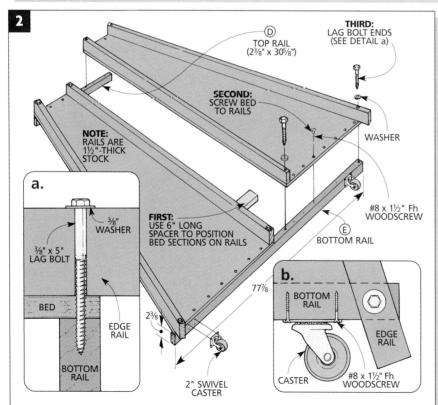

2

Ⓓ
TOP RAIL
(2⅜" x 30⅝")

THIRD:
LAG BOLT ENDS
(SEE DETAIL a)

SECOND:
SCREW BED
TO RAILS

WASHER

NOTE:
RAILS ARE
1½"-THICK
STOCK

a.
⅜"
WASHER
⅜" x 5"
LAG BOLT

BED

EDGE
RAIL

BOTTOM
RAIL

FIRST:
USE 6" LONG
SPACER TO POSITION
BED SECTIONS ON RAILS

#8 x 1½" Fh
WOODSCREW

Ⓔ
BOTTOM RAIL

77⅞

2⅜

2" SWIVEL
CASTER

b.
BOTTOM
RAIL

EDGE
RAIL

CASTER

#8 x 1½" Fh
WOODSCREW

I started on the Panel Saw by making the bed. The bed is built in two sections. Each section consists of a triangular piece of plywood with one edge rail and one center rail screwed to the long edges of each bed piece *(Fig. 1)*.

CUT PIECES. To make the bed sections, start by cutting two bed pieces (A) from a blank of ¾" plywood *(Fig. 1)*. To do this, I first raised the plywood off the floor with some scrap 2x4s. Then I clamped another 2x4 diagonally across the workpiece to act as a straightedge for the saw.

Next, cut the center and edge rails (B, C) to length *(Fig. 1)*.

Note: The edge rails are cut 6" longer than the center rails *(Fig. 1)*. I used straight-grained 2x8s for both the center and edge rails. I ripped them to a finished width of 3".

ATTACH RAILS. With all of the rails cut to size, they are ready to be clamped and screwed to the bed pieces. The edge rails (C) need to extend past the bottom edge of the bed. They will become two of the "feet" for the panel saw *(Fig. 1b)*. To ensure that both feet extend an equal distance on both sides, just position the top inside corner of each edge rail flush with the top of the bed *(Fig. 1a)*. The center rails (B) are left flush with the bottom edge of the bed.

CONNECT SECTIONS. After the two sections are complete, they're connected with a top and bottom rail (D, E) *(Fig. 2)*. I used the remainders of the 2x8s to make the rails, but this time the rails are ripped to a finished width of 2⅜".

CUTTING TROUGH. To prevent the circular saw from cutting into the bed, a space (cutting trough) is left between the two sections *(Fig. 2)*. I used a piece of 6"-long scrap 2x4 as the spacer to get both sections into place before screwing the bed pieces to the rails *(Fig. 2)*.

Note: This scrap spacer will be used later to position the guide tubes.

For added strength, I secured the ends of the edge and center rails to the top and bottom rails with lag bolts *(Fig. 2a)*.

CASTERS. Finally, to roll the saw around the shop, I screwed a pair of 2" swivel casters under the bottom rail *(Fig. 2b)*.

BACK SUPPORT

Once the bed is complete, the next step is to make the folding back support. In the "down" position, it holds the bed upright.

To move the Panel Saw, the back support folds up, and the saw can be rolled around on the casters.

The back support consists of two main parts: a brace assembly and two plywood base pieces *(Fig. 3)*.

BRACE ASSEMBLY. The brace assembly is a simple wood frame *(Fig. 4)*. The braces (F) are $1\frac{1}{2}$"-thick stock cut to a finished length of 48". Complete the frame by screwing a $\frac{3}{4}$" plywood top and bottom plate (G) to the braces *(Fig. 4)*.

To secure the brace assembly to the vertical bed, cut slots in the top plate *(Fig. 4a)*. The slots fit over hanger bolts installed in the center rails *(Fig. 3a)*. Tightening a plastic T-knob (or wing nut) locks the bed in place.

Note: A counterbore at the end of the slot prevents the knob from sliding as it's tightened *(Figs. 3a and 4a)*.

FOOT. Now all that needs to be done to complete the brace assembly is to screw a plywood foot (H) to the bottom plate *(Fig. 4)*. With the ends of the two edge rails, this foot creates a "tripod" that stabilizes the Panel Saw.

BASE. The last step is to build the base. The base is just two triangular-shaped pieces of plywood that keep the Panel Saw from racking *(Fig. 5)*.

The base pieces (I) are hinged to the bed and braces *(Fig. 5)*. Start by screwing the brace assembly to the base pieces. But to allow the back support to easily fold up, I left $\frac{1}{4}$" clearance between the base pieces and the center rails.

Note: To keep everything straight, screw the hinges to the bases first. Attach the back support with screws to the bed.

TURNBUTTON. Finally, screw a turnbutton (J) to each center rail to secure the back support in the "up" position *(Fig. 3)*.

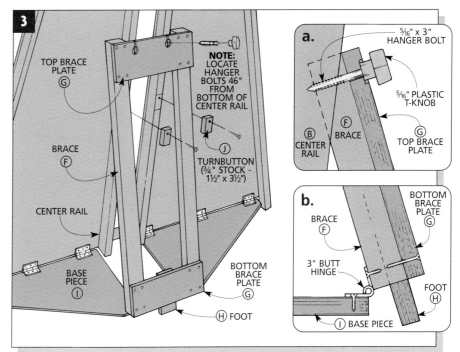

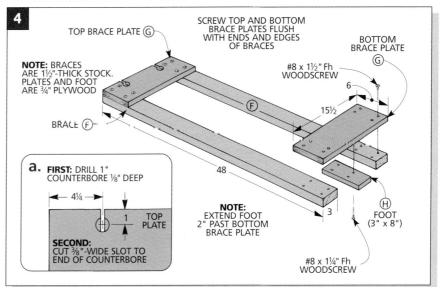

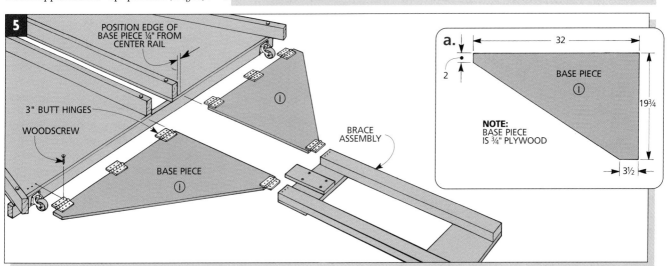

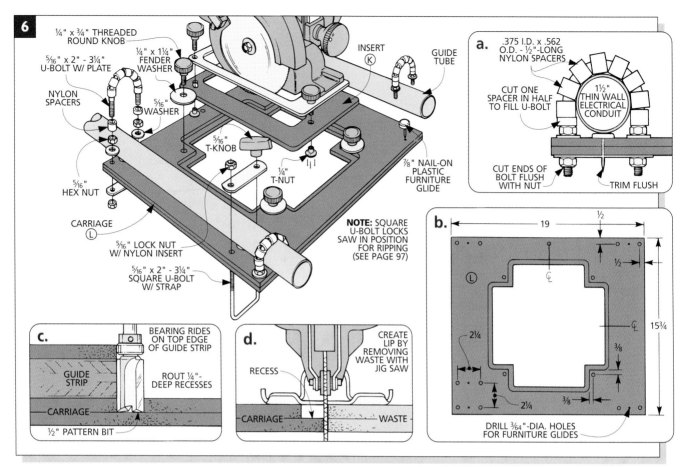

6

¼" x ¾" THREADED ROUND KNOB

⁵⁄₁₆" x 2" - 3¼" U-BOLT W/ PLATE

¼" x 1¼" FENDER WASHER

NYLON SPACERS

⁵⁄₁₆" WASHER

⁵⁄₁₆" T-KNOB

INSERT (K)

GUIDE TUBE

¼" T-NUT

⁵⁄₁₆" HEX NUT

CARRIAGE (L)

⁵⁄₁₆" LOCK NUT W/ NYLON INSERT

⁵⁄₁₆" x 2" - 3¼" SQUARE U-BOLT W/ STRAP

⅞" NAIL-ON PLASTIC FURNITURE GLIDE

NOTE: SQUARE U-BOLT LOCKS SAW IN POSITION FOR RIPPING (SEE PAGE 97)

a. .375 I.D. x .562 O.D. - ½"-LONG NYLON SPACERS

CUT ONE SPACER IN HALF TO FILL U-BOLT

1½" THIN WALL ELECTRICAL CONDUIT

CUT ENDS OF BOLT FLUSH WITH NUT

TRIM FLUSH

b. 19 — ½

(L)

2¼

½

15¾

⅜

2¼

⅜

DRILL ³⁄₆₄"-DIA. HOLES FOR FURNITURE GLIDES

c. BEARING RIDES ON TOP EDGE OF GUIDE STRIP

GUIDE STRIP

ROUT ¼"-DEEP RECESSES

CARRIAGE

½" PATTERN BIT

d. CREATE LIP BY REMOVING WASTE WITH JIG SAW

RECESS

CARRIAGE

WASTE

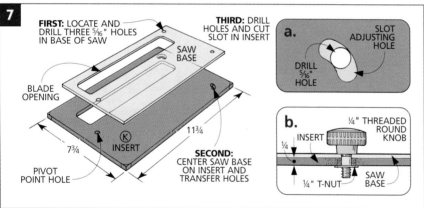

7

FIRST: LOCATE AND DRILL THREE ⁵⁄₁₆" HOLES IN BASE OF SAW

THIRD: DRILL HOLES AND CUT SLOT IN INSERT

SAW BASE

BLADE OPENING

(K) INSERT

11¾

7¾

PIVOT POINT HOLE

SECOND: CENTER SAW BASE ON INSERT AND TRANSFER HOLES

a. SLOT ADJUSTING HOLE

DRILL ⁵⁄₁₆" HOLE

b. ¼" THREADED ROUND KNOB

INSERT

¼

¼" T-NUT

SAW BASE

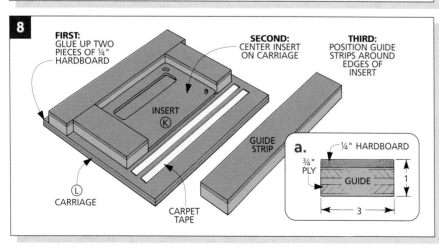

8

FIRST: GLUE UP TWO PIECES OF ¼" HARDBOARD

SECOND: CENTER INSERT ON CARRIAGE

THIRD: POSITION GUIDE STRIPS AROUND EDGES OF INSERT

INSERT (K)

GUIDE STRIP

(L) CARRIAGE

CARPET TAPE

a. ¼" HARDBOARD

¾" PLY

GUIDE

1

3

CARRIAGE ASSEMBLY

The heart of this Panel Saw is the carriage assembly. This versatile assembly provides an easy way to mount the saw. Plus, it allows you to easily rotate the saw for accurate crosscutting or ripping. The carriage assembly is built from three main parts: an insert attached to the base of the circular saw, a sliding carriage to hold the insert, and a pair of metal guide tubes that the carriage slides on.

INSERT. The base of the circular saw is attached to an insert (K) made of ¼" hardboard that fits into a recessed opening in the carriage (*Fig. 6*).

MOUNTING HOLES. The saw is then mounted to the hardboard insert with ¼" threaded knobs and T-nuts. This means you'll first have to drill three holes in the saw base (*Fig. 7*).

After drilling the holes, center the saw base on the insert, and transfer the location of the holes and the blade opening onto the insert. Now you can drill the holes and cut the slot in the insert.

ADJUSTMENT. Next, to provide a way to adjust the saw, enlarge the two holes at the end of the insert (*Fig. 7a*). The single hole at the other end of the insert will be used later as a "pivot point" to help position the saw blade.

CARRIAGE

Just as its name implies, the carriage "carries" the saw up and down the guide tubes on the Panel Saw. Depending on whether you're ripping or crosscutting a panel, the insert fits into one of the two recessed openings. To make the carriage (L), start by gluing together two pieces of $1/4$" hardboard *(Figs. 6 and 6b)*.

Creating the recessed openings is a simple two-step process. First, a $1/4$"-deep recess is routed in the carriage to match the shape of the insert *(Fig. 6c)*. Then a lip is created by removing the waste with a jig saw (or coping saw) *(Fig. 6d)*.

The trick to making the recess is to use the insert as a template and rout the recess with a pattern bit. First, center the insert on the carriage *(Fig. 8)*. Then, to guide the router, tape strips around the edges of the insert with carpet tape.

ROUT RECESS. Now you can remove the insert and rout one recess *(Fig. 6c)*. Then repeat the process, and rout a second recess 90° to the first *(Fig. 6b)*.

LIP. To complete the openings and form the lip for the insert, remove the waste with a jig saw *(Fig. 6d)*.

HARDWARE. All that's left is to drill holes and install hardware onto the carriage. To help the carriage slide smoothly without a lot of "play," I slipped nylon spacers over the four U-bolts. Just slide them over the bolts like you would when lacing beads on a necklace.

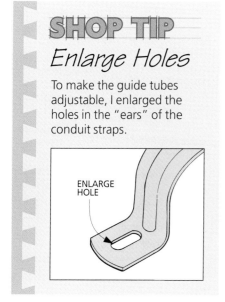

SHOP TIP
Enlarge Holes

To make the guide tubes adjustable, I enlarged the holes in the "ears" of the conduit straps.

ENLARGE HOLE

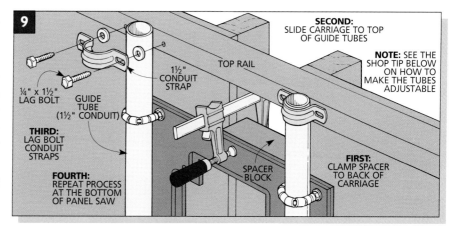

Note: You may need to cut one of the spacers in half to completely cover the U-bolt and surround the tube *(Fig. 6a)*.

Finally, to reduce the friction between the guide tubes and the carriage, I added nail-on plastic furniture glides between the ends of each U-bolt.

GUIDE TUBES

The next step in assembling the carriage is to use conduit straps to attach the carriage guide tubes to the top and bottom rails. (The tubes are just 6-foot long pieces of $1\frac{1}{2}$" "thin wall" electrical conduit.)

MOUNT CARRIAGE. Before attaching the guide tubes, slide the ends of the tubes through the carriage U-bolts. Now the carriage assembly can be slid over the top and bottom rails.

The key is to center the carriage on the cutting trough and position the guide tubes parallel with each other. An easy way to do this is to use the same spacer that was used earlier to form the cutting trough. Just clamp the spacer so it's centered on the back of the carriage and extends into the cutting trough *(Fig. 9)*.

As you slide the carriage to the top and bottom of the tubes, the spacer centers

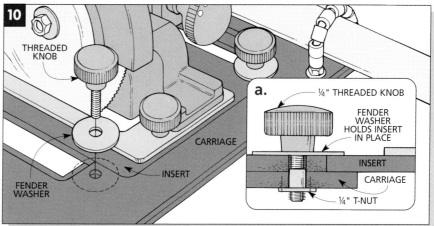

the carriage on the cutting trough, positioning the tubes parallel to each other.

INSTALL TUBES. Now the top and bottom ends of the guide tubes can be secured with the straps and lag bolts *(Fig. 9)*. But first, slot the holes in the "ears" of the conduit straps (see the Shop Tip at left). Next, place a square U-bolt and a locking knob on the carriage. This U-bolt is used to lock the carriage in place (see the Technique on page 97).

ATTACH INSERT. Finally, attach the insert to the carriage with knobs and T-nuts *(Fig. 10a)*. The knobs tighten against fender washers, holding the insert in place.

Thanks to a pair of recesses placed perpendicular to each other, the insert can be rotated 90° for crosscutting or ripping.

The Panel Saw is designed with a material rest to support sheet goods during a cut. Why not just use the bottom rail as a rest? Because the carriage would "bottom out" on the rail before the saw could cut all the way through a workpiece.

The material rest (M) is made of two 1¼"-thick blanks (one for each half of the bed) *(Fig. 11)*. A number of deep dadoes create openings in the rest that allow sawdust to fall through.

CHAMFER EDGES. To prevent sheet goods from "catching" on the material rest, the top edge of each opening is chamfered (see Shop Tip on this page). I also chamfered the edges of the bed next to the cutting trough.

LIP. Before attaching the material rest to the bed piece, glue a ¼" hardboard lip (N) flush with the ends of the material rest. This will help to "track" workpieces along the material rest *(Fig. 11)*.

Note: Cut the lip shorter than the rest to allow clearance for the carriage.

ATTACH REST. The last step is to clamp and screw the material rest to the bed *(Fig. 11a)*. The key here is to position the pieces so the top edges are level and are 90° to the cutting trough.

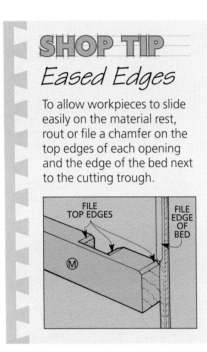

SHOP TIP

Eased Edges

To allow workpieces to slide easily on the material rest, rout or file a chamfer on the top edges of each opening and the edge of the bed next to the cutting trough.

FILE TOP EDGES

FILE EDGE OF BED

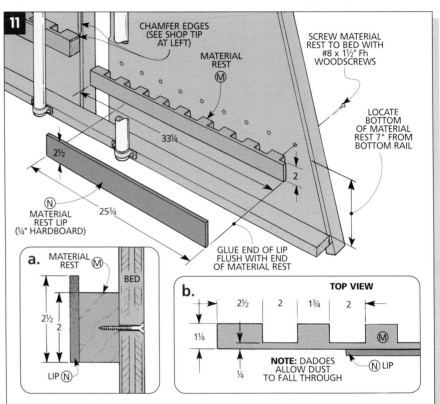

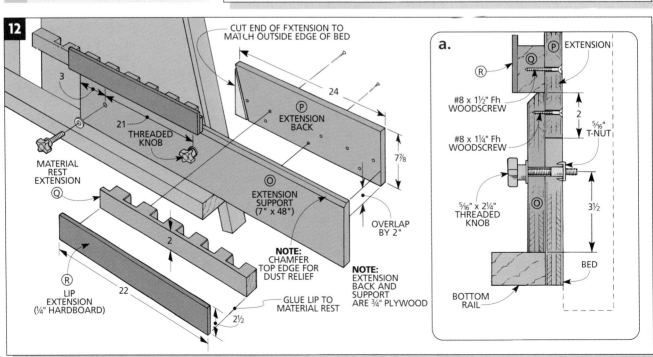

WINGS

To provide extra support when ripping, I built two "wings." Each wing consists of an extension support (O) and an extension back (P) *(Fig. 12)*.

The support is ripped to width from a 48"-long piece of plywood to fit between the material rest and the bottom rail.

Next, I cut the extension back to match the diagonal edges of the vertical bed, and screwed the pieces together *(Fig. 12a)*. To make the wings removable for storage, I drilled two holes for threaded knobs, T-nuts, and washers in each of the extension supports.

MATERIAL REST. Finally, build a material rest extension from $1\frac{1}{2}$" stock (Q) and a hardboard lip extension (R) for each wing *(Fig. 12)*.

PULLEY SYSTEM

All that's left to complete the Panel Saw is to add a pulley system and counterweight. The idea here is for the carriage to return easily to the top of the guide tubes when you finish a cut.

The pulley system consists of three parts: a pulley base plate (S), a pulley support (T), and a couple of $1\frac{1}{2}$" wheels used for sliding glass doors *(Fig. 13)*.

The base plate and pulley support are both made from $\frac{3}{4}$" plywood *(Fig. 13)*. After drilling holes and bolting the wheels to the pulley support, the two pieces can then be screwed together to form an upside-down T-shape *(Fig. 13a)*.

Note: Locate the pulley support so the pulleys (not the support) are centered on the length of the base plate.

The final step in completing the pulley system is to screw the base plate to the top rail so the pulleys are centered on the width of the cutting trough.

COUNTERWEIGHT

With the pulley system in place, the last step is to add a counterweight. The secret is to make the counterweight roughly equal to the combined weight of your circular saw and carriage. (In my case, this was sixteen pounds.)

This lets you control the saw as it cuts a panel. And it allows the saw to travel easily back to the top of the tubes.

LEAD SHOT. To make the counterweight, I filled a length of 3" PVC pipe with lead shot *(Fig. 15)*. But concrete, sand, or any other weight will work fine,

just as long as it clears the back support. To hold the shot in the pipe, I cut a $\frac{3}{4}$" hardwood pipe cap (U) to fit snugly inside the end of the pipe *(Fig. 15b)*.

WIRE CABLE. After the counterweight was done, I ran a 7-foot length of wire cable over the pulleys to connect the pipe to the carriage. Each end of the cable has a loop made with a crimp-on clip.

An S-hook in one loop hooks into an eye bolt that is installed on the carriage *(Fig. 14)*. (I cut off the exposed, threaded end of the eye bolt for clearance.) The other end slips over a bolt which passes through the top of the pipe *(Fig. 15a)*.

Note: To keep the loop from slipping to one side of the bolt, I filed a small notch in the middle of the bolt *(Fig. 15a)*. ∎

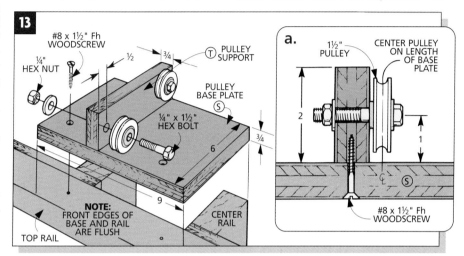

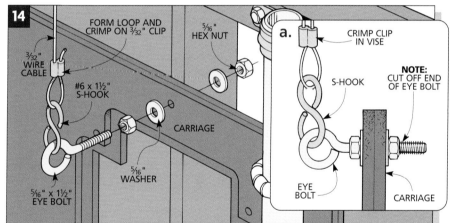

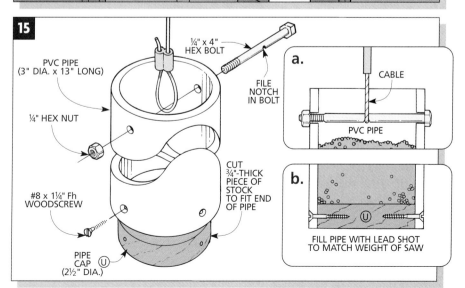

Taking a few minutes to tune up the Panel Saw is the secret to making perfect cuts. The idea is to adjust the guide tubes so they're 90° to the material rest.

First, you need to clamp a block of scrap to the carriage *(Step 1)*. Next, place a sheet of plywood (with a "factory" square corner) on the material rest so one edge extends into the cutting trough. Now slide the carriage along the guides, checking carefully for gaps.

If there are gaps, you'll need to adjust the guide tubes *(Step 2)*. This is done easily by first loosening the conduit straps. Then place a 6"-long scrap block between them to keep them parallel.

Next you'll check the saw blade for alignment. This is simple. Just mark a tooth on the blade's back side, then rotate the saw blade forward until the same tooth aligns with the plywood edge again *(Step 3)*. If there is a gap between the plywood edge and the marked tooth, the saw requires further adjustment.

To make this adjustment, loosen the threaded knobs on each side of the insert and pivot the saw. Test the adjustment by rotating the blade and watching the marked tooth again *(Step 4)*. Repeat until the marked tooth aligns with the plywood edge. Just be sure to tighten the knobs once the saw is aligned.

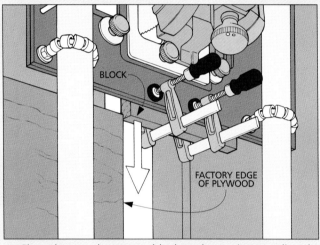

BLOCK

FACTORY EDGE OF PLYWOOD

1 First, clamp a short scrap block to the carriage to align the guide tubes. (This is the same scrap block you used earlier.) Then push a sheet of plywood against the edge of the block, and slide the carriage up and down to check for a gap.

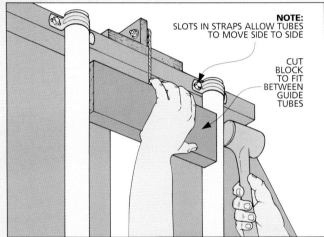

NOTE: SLOTS IN STRAPS ALLOW TUBES TO MOVE SIDE TO SIDE

CUT BLOCK TO FIT BETWEEN GUIDE TUBES

2 Then, to adjust the guide tubes, first loosen the top or bottom conduit straps. Then tap the tubes into position. The slots in the conduit straps make this easy. Cut a block to fit between the tubes to keep them parallel while they're adjusted.

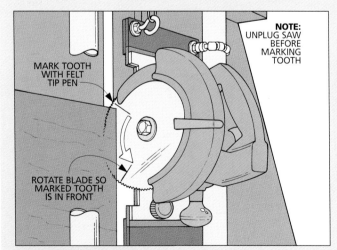

MARK TOOTH WITH FELT TIP PEN

NOTE: UNPLUG SAW BEFORE MARKING TOOTH

ROTATE BLADE SO MARKED TOOTH IS IN FRONT

3 The next step is to check the alignment of the saw blade. This is a rather simple process. Just mark a tooth on the blade's back side. Then rotate the blade forward until the marked tooth aligns with the plywood edge again.

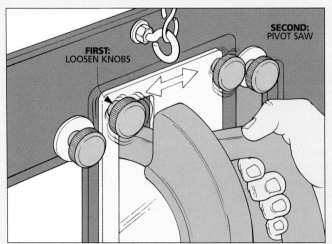

FIRST: LOOSEN KNOBS

SECOND: PIVOT SAW

4 If the distance between the marked tooth and the plywood edge varies, the saw needs to be adjusted. First you need to loosen the knobs that hold the saw to the insert. Then pivot the saw to align the blade.

TECHNIQUE . . . . *Using the Panel Saw*

The Panel Saw is not only capable of crosscutting, it's great at ripping large sheet goods as well. To do this, the carriage needs to be locked in place, then the workpiece is pushed through the blade (see photo at right). Setting up the saw for ripping from crosscutting only requires a few simple steps.

First, mount the saw in the carriage so the blade is perpendicular to the guide tubes (refer to *Fig. 2*).

Note: For a straight cut, it's important that the blade is perfectly aligned. If you're unsure of the alignment of the carriage, guide tubes, or saw blade, see the Setup article on the previous page.

Then slide the carriage to the desired position and lock it in place. (You should be able to line the cut up by positioning the plywood next to the saw blade.) Then, just tighten the T-knob against the strap on the square U-bolt (*Fig. 1*).

Some older circular saws aren't equipped with lock switches. If your saw doesn't have a lock switch, just use a spring clamp to hold down the trigger switch during a cut (*Fig. 2*).

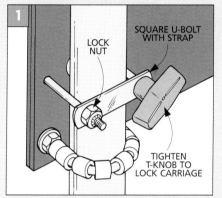

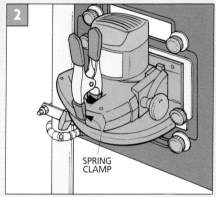

Once you have the saw in position, it needs to be locked into place. This is done by tightening the T-knob on the U-bolt.

You will need to push the panel through, so use the saw's lock switch. If there's no lock, place a clamp on the trigger switch.

STORAGE

Even though the Panel Saw is a large shop-built tool, I designed it so it's easy to move and store. To do this, the back support can be folded up flat into the back of the bed when you're finished cutting (see photo at right).

When it's folded up, the saw lifts off the rear foot and the two edge rails and rests on the casters (*Fig. 1*). Then you can roll the saw to another place in the shop, push it out to the driveway, or store it flat against a wall and out of the way.

The 3/4"-thick hardwood turnbuttons are the key to moving and storing the Panel Saw. To hold the back support in an upright position when moving or storing

the saw, lock the braces in place by rotating the turnbuttons that are located on the center rails (*Fig. 2*).

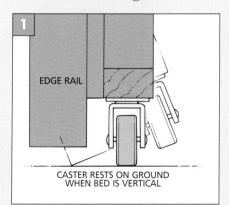

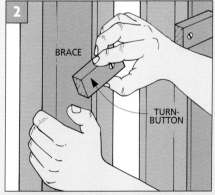

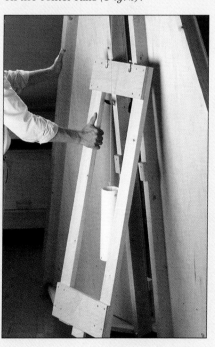

The casters on the bottom rails support the bed when the back support is folded up and the Panel Saw is placed in a vertical position. This helps to move the saw.

The turnbuttons on the center rails make it easy to lock the back support in an upright position for storage. Just twist them to lock the support in place.

PANEL SAW 97

DESIGNER'S NOTEBOOK

Add a base for a router and you can rout grooves and dadoes exactly where you want in either sheet goods or large glued-up panels. A bracket locks tight to the guide tube for stopped cuts.

CONSTRUCTION NOTES:

■ The router base consists of a hardboard insert with a pair of cleats that allow the base to be locked into the carriage (L). Hardwood spacers position the router and the insert in the carriage so the bit can reach the workpiece.

■ To build it, start by cutting the router insert (V) from ¼" hardboard. It's sized to fit down through the inside edge of the rabbet in the carriage base *(Fig. 1)*.

■ Next, drill a centered hole in the insert for the router bit. Use the manufacturer's base to lay out and add countersunk shank holes for mounting the router.

■ Now cut the insert cleats (W) to size from ¼" hardboard. The cleats become the lip that fits into the recess in the carriage (L). (Be sure to sand a small radius on the corners of the cleats so they fit snug in the carriage base.)

■ To complete the base, cut a pair of ¾"-thick hardwood spacers (X). Then the cleat and insert are glued and screwed to the spacers *(Figs. 1a and 1b)*.

■ So that I could rout stopped grooves and dadoes, I also made an adjustable stop. The stop is just a couple of hardwood brackets (Y) with openings that fit around the 1½"-dia. guide tube *(Fig. 2)*.

■ These brackets are small pieces, so start by ripping an extra-long blank to rough width (2⅛") from a piece of ¾"-thick stock. Now take the blank and lay

out and drill a 1½"-dia. hole centered on the width of the blank, and two shank holes on each side of the center hole *(Fig. 2)*. These shank holes are for the carriage bolts used to clamp the brackets around the guide tube.

■ Finally, rip the blank in half lengthwise and cut the brackets to finished length.

Note: To create a tight grip, the gap that's cut away by the blade kerf leaves a half-circle that will be slightly smaller than the outside of the guide tube.

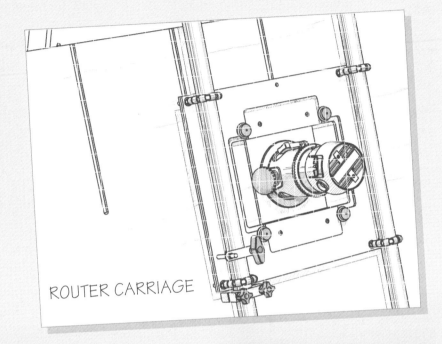

ROUTER CARRIAGE

MATERIALS LIST

NEW PARTS

V	Router Insert (1)	¼ hdbd. - 7 x 10
W	Insert Cleats (2)	¼ hdbd. - 2⅜ x 7¾
X	Insert Spacers (2)	¾ x 1½ - 7
Y	Stop Brackets (2)	¾ x 1 - 3

HARDWARE SUPPLIES

(8) No. 8 x ¾" Fh woodscrews
(2) 5/16" x 2½" carriage bolts
(2) 5/16" I.D. star knobs w/ washers

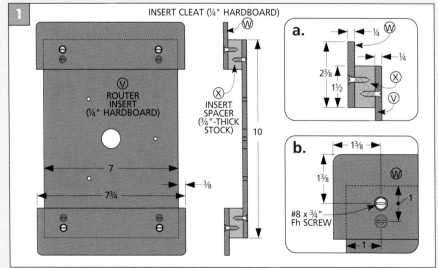

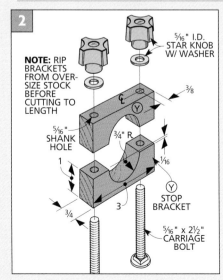

Low-Speed Grinder

Sharpen a chisel on the table saw? It might sound a bit crazy, but you'll love the results — a perfect hollow ground edge. This easy-to-build jig uses the motor on your table saw to turn the grinding wheel.

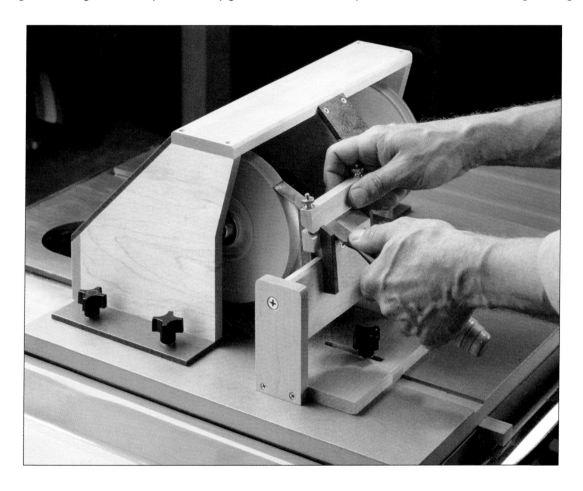

Woodworking catalogs are full of grinders that do a great job of sharpening chisels. The only drawback for a woodworker on a budget is the price. The good ones aren't cheap. That's why I decided to build my own low-speed grinding jig.

It's something I've been wanting to build for a long time. Like any grinder, it puts a hollow ground bevel on a chisel or plane iron, making the sharpening process much quicker. But unlike grinders that turn at a high speed, it works quickly without burning the metal and ruining the tool. The trick was coming up with a way to do it economically.

TABLE SAW MOTOR. Recently, a friend suggested that the jig could work on the table saw powered by its motor. I was intrigued by the idea, because right off the bat, I'm saving money since I don't have to buy a motor. And since the jig mounts to the saw's table, it doesn't take up any shop space.

PULLEYS. To get the power from the motor to the jig, you use the saw's arbor. Simply remove the blade and replace it with a small pulley. A larger pulley in the jig slows down the speed of the grinding wheel to about 1700 RPM.

And as an added bonus, there's also a tool rest and carriage that hold and guide

the blade. The tool rest lifts off easily so you can check your progress. And the carriage includes a micro-adjust feature so you don't remove the metal too quickly.

Note: Because this grinder requires some out-of-the-ordinary hardware (like pulleys and an arbor assembly), it's a good idea to have it on hand before beginning construction. This way, you'll avoid any surprises. See Sources on page 126 for help locating the hardware.

BASE. If you prefer for your grinder to have its own power source, you're in luck. The Designer's Notebook starting on page 108 has detailed plans for a stand-alone base with space for a motor.

EXPLODED VIEW

OVERALL DIMENSIONS:
20W x 19¾D x 8⅞H

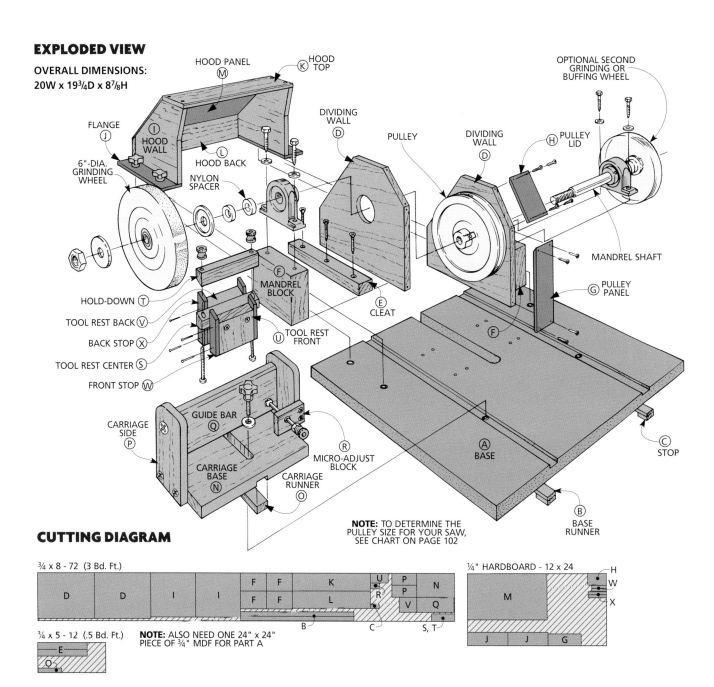

CUTTING DIAGRAM

¾ x 8 - 72 (3 Bd. Ft.)

¾ x 5 - 12 (.5 Bd. Ft.)

NOTE: ALSO NEED ONE 24" x 24"
PIECE OF ¾" MDF FOR PART A

¼" HARDBOARD - 12 x 24

NOTE: TO DETERMINE THE
PULLEY SIZE FOR YOUR SAW,
SEE CHART ON PAGE 102

MATERIALS LIST

WOOD

A	Base (1)	¾ MDF - 19 x 20
B	Base Runners (2)	¼ x ¾ - 19¾
C	Stops (2)	¼ x ¾ - ¾
D	Dividing Walls (2)	½ x 9¾ - 7⅝
E	Cleats (2)	¾ x 1⅛ - 8½
F	Mandrel Blocks (2)	1½ x 3 - 4½
G	Pulley Panel (1)	¼ hdbd. - 2 x 5²³⁄₃₂
H	Pulley Lid (1)	¼ hdbd. - 2 x 3³⁄₁₆
I	Hood Walls (2)	½ x 7⅜ - 7¾
J	Flanges (2)	¼ hdbd. - 2¼ x 6⅞
K	Hood Top (1)	½ x 3 - 13⅝
L	Hood Back (1)	½ x 2⅞ - 13⅝
M	Hood Panel (1)	¼ hdbd. - 7¹¹⁄₁₆ x 13⅝
N	Carriage Base (1)	½ x 4 - 6½

O	Carriage Runner (1)	⅜ x ¾ - 4
P	Carriage Sides (2)	½ x 2 - 4¼
Q	Guide Bar (1)	½ x 2½ - 6⅜
R	Micro-adjust Block (1)	½ x 1 - 1½
S	Tool Rest Center (1)	½ x 1¼ - 4
T	Hold-down (1)	½ x ⅞ - 4
U	Tool Rest Front (1)	½ x 1⅝ - 3 rough
V	Tool Rest Back (1)	½ x 2½ - 3 rough
W	Front Stops (2)	¼ hdbd. - ½ x 2½
X	Back Stops (2)	¼ hdbd. - ½ x 3⅛

HARDWARE SUPPLIES

(30) No. 6 x ¾" Fh woodscrews
(14) No. 6 x 1" Fh woodscrews
(6) No. 8 x 1¼" Fh woodscrews
(8) No. 8 x 2½" Fh woodscrews

(2) No. 14 x 1½" Fh woodscrews
(1) 10-32 x 2" Rh machine screw
(2) 10-32 x 2" Fh machine screws
(6) ¼"-20 threaded inserts
(1) Mandrel assembly w/ ⅝" drive shaft
(1) 2"-dia. hubless pulley
(1) 4"-6"-dia. pulley
(4) ¼" x 1½" lag screws
(4) ½" I.D. x 1" O.D. x ⅜" nylon spacers
(2) Grinding or buffing wheels
(5) ¼"-20 plastic star knobs w/ 1" stud
(9) ¼" flat washers
(1) 10-32 threaded insert
(3) 10-32 brass knurled knobs
(1) 10-32 hex nut
(8) ¾" brads

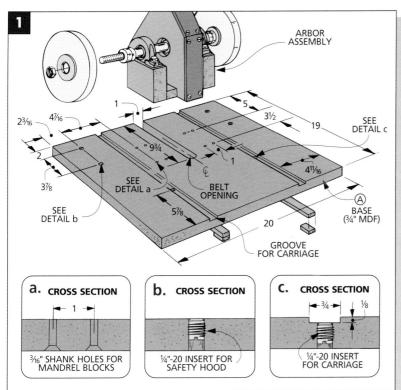

1

ARBOR ASSEMBLY

2³⁄₁₆
4⁷⁄₁₆
1
5
3½
19
SEE DETAIL c

9¾

2
3⁷⁄₈
SEE DETAIL a
SEE DETAIL b
BELT OPENING
5⁷⁄₈
4¹¹⁄₁₆
20
GROOVE FOR CARRIAGE
(A) BASE (¾" MDF)

a. CROSS SECTION
1
³⁄₁₆" SHANK HOLES FOR MANDREL BLOCKS

b. CROSS SECTION
¼"-20 INSERT FOR SAFETY HOOD

c. CROSS SECTION
¾
⅛
¼"-20 INSERT FOR CARRIAGE

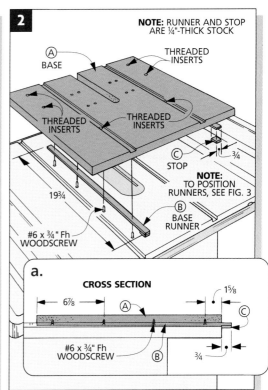

2

NOTE: RUNNER AND STOP ARE ¼"-THICK STOCK

(A) BASE
THREADED INSERTS
THREADED INSERTS
THREADED INSERTS
(C) STOP
¾
NOTE: TO POSITION RUNNERS, SEE FIG. 3
19¾
#6 x ¾" Fh WOODSCREW
(B) BASE RUNNER

a.
CROSS SECTION
6⁷⁄₈
(A)
1⁵⁄₈
(C)
#6 x ¾" Fh WOODSCREW
(B)
¾

BASE

The Low-Speed Grinder starts out as a simple base *(Fig. 1)*. It aligns the grinder on the table saw and serves as a platform for the arbor assembly and the tool rest.

BASE. To begin building the base (A), I started by cutting it to finished size (19" x 20") from ¾"-thick medium-density fiberboard (MDF) *(Fig. 1)*.

Next, an opening can be cut in back of the base to provide clearance for the belt. This 1"-wide opening is centered on the width of the base and is 9¾" long *(Fig. 1)*.

With the belt opening complete, I cut a couple of grooves on top of the base *(Figs. 1 and 1c)*. These will hold the tool carriage, allowing it to slide back and forth to adjust the position of the tool.

Next, I added six threaded inserts *(Fig. 1)*. Two are located in the grooves and will help to secure the carriage with a plastic knob *(Fig. 1c)*. The other four help to secure the safety hood *(Fig. 1b)*.

Note: I used my drill press to install the threaded inserts. To do this, start by cutting the head off a bolt that fits the insert. Next, thread a nut part way up and screw the insert onto the bolt so it "jams" against the nut. Then with the bolt gripped by the drill press chuck, you can hand-twist the insert straight down into the base while exerting downward pressure on the drill press quill.

There's one more set of holes to drill. These are countersunk shank holes for the screws that will secure the mandrel blocks to the base *(Figs. 1 and 1a)*.

RUNNERS. Now the base is ready for the runners that position it on the table saw *(Fig. 2)*. These ¼"-thick hardwood runners (B) are cut to fit the miter gauge slots in the table saw, but they're ¾" longer than the base. (They extend ¾" in front to allow room for stops added later.)

The goal here is to center the belt opening over the 2" pulley that's mounted to the saw's arbor *(Fig. 3b)*. (Temporarily install the pulley to position the base.)

When the base is in position, slide the saw's rip fence up against it *(Fig. 3)*. Now you can remove the base without worrying about changing its position.

To install the runners, I applied a little glue and set them in the miter gauge slots, using washers to shim them above the table *(Fig. 3a)*. Then I set the base in place and pressed down until the glue had plenty of time to set up.

STOPS. Next, add screws to secure the runners *(Fig. 2a)*. Then to hold the base flush with the front of the saw's table, I glued a ¼"-thick stop (C) to the bottom of each runner *(Figs. 2 and 2a)*.

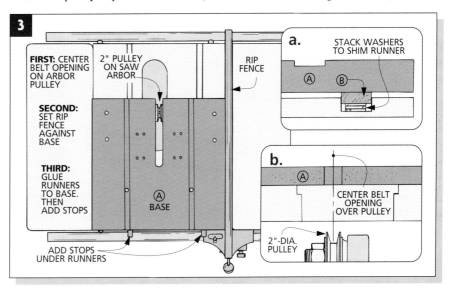

3

FIRST: CENTER BELT OPENING ON ARBOR PULLEY
2" PULLEY ON SAW ARBOR
RIP FENCE

SECOND: SET RIP FENCE AGAINST BASE

THIRD: GLUE RUNNERS TO BASE. THEN ADD STOPS
(A) BASE

ADD STOPS UNDER RUNNERS

a.
STACK WASHERS TO SHIM RUNNER
(A) (B)

b.
(A)
CENTER BELT OPENING OVER PULLEY
2"-DIA. PULLEY

With the base complete, now you can work on the arbor assembly that's added to the top of the base (refer to *Fig. 1* on page 101). The arbor assembly is made up of a small housing with a mandrel shaft for the pulley and grinding wheels.

DIVIDING WALLS. The arbor assembly starts out as a couple of identical 1/2"-thick hardwood dividing walls (D) *(Figs. 4 and 4a)*. Once these two pieces are cut to size and shape, you can drill a pair of clearance holes for the hub extensions on the large pulley. Note that each wall will require a different size hole. (See the Shop Info below for more on arbor speeds and pulley sizes.)

CLEATS. Next, to attach the dividing walls to the base, I added a small cleat (E) to each wall *(Fig. 4)*. Before gluing the cleats in place, drill countersunk shank holes for screwing the cleat (and dividing wall) to the base *(Figs. 4a and 5a)*.

When attaching the dividing walls to the base, the pulley and drive shaft will need to be sandwiched between the walls *(Figs. 5 and 5a)*. If you're using a solid V-belt, you'll want to position it over the pulley at this time. Since I chose a link belt, it can be added after the jig is completed. (For more on link belts, see the Shop Tip on the next page).

MANDREL SUPPORTS. Two pillow blocks support the mandrel shaft, and these require wood supports to lift them to the proper height *(Fig. 6)*. I cut the mandrel blocks (F) to size. Then I spot glued and screwed them to the base. (The shank holes have already been drilled, but you'll need to drill pilot holes for the 2 1/2"-long screws.)

With the mandrel blocks in place, slide the pillow blocks onto the shaft and then secure them to the mandrel blocks with lag screws and washers *(Fig. 6)*.

Now the grinding wheels can be added to the shaft. To position them over the grooves in the base, I used a couple of 3/8"-long nylon spacers *(Fig. 6a)* and locked them in place with a wheel nut.

PANEL AND LID. At this point, the grinder part of this jig is functional. But before adding the carriage and tool rest,

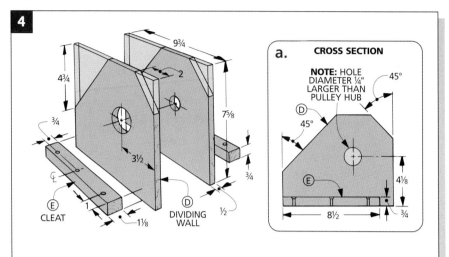

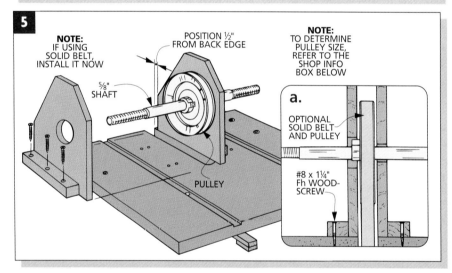

SHOP INFO . . . . *Pulley Size*

Besides the usual variety of hardware, you'll need to buy an arbor, a grinding wheel (or two), plus two pulleys and a link belt for the Low-Speed Grinder.

ARBOR ASSEMBLY. The arbor assembly is available locally or through the Sources listed on page 126. But wherever you get it, make sure it uses ball bearings (and not bronze bearings).

PULLEYS. For the pulleys, you need to make sure you order the right size. The pulley attached to the arbor of the table saw is a 2" outside diameter, hubless pulley. The important thing here is that its inside bore matches the diameter of the arbor on your saw. (Mine was 5/8".)

The size of the larger pulley (the one between the dividing walls) depends on the speed of your table saw's arbor.

Note: To determine the arbor speed, you will need to check the manufacturer's name plate on the saw's motor. This is easy to do on most contractor's saws, but if you have a cabinet saw, you may need to check the manual.

Most arbor speeds fall somewhere between 3000 and 4500 RPM, so I've included a chart with the appropriate pulley size (see box). Pulleys sized between 4" and 6" will turn the wheel within acceptable speed ranges.

ARBOR SPEED	PULLEY SIZE	WHEEL SPEED
3000 RPM	4"-DIA.	1500 RPM
3500 RPM	4"-DIA.	1750 RPM
4000 RPM	5"-DIA.	1600 RPM
4500 RPM	6"-DIA.	1500 RPM

SHOP TIP

Link Belts

This belt is made up of removable links, so you can easily adjust it to the size you need. They cost more than regular belts, but the interlocking links reduce vibration to run smoothly and quietly.

I decided to cover the exposed pulley and belt. So the last two items to add to the arbor assembly are a pulley panel (G) and pulley lid (H) *(Fig. 6)*.

These pieces are cut to fit over the front two edges of the dividing walls, and the edges where they meet are beveled at $22\frac{1}{2}°$. The exposed edge of the pulley lid (H) is cut at $45°$ *(Fig. 6)*.

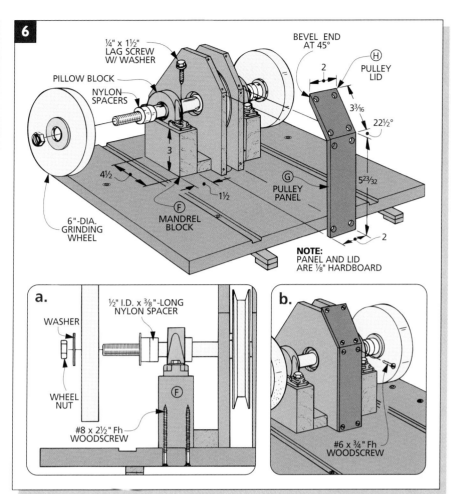

SHOP INFO .... *Choosing a Grinding Wheel*

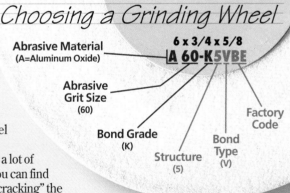

Using a grinder to sharpen a chisel or plane iron can be a frustrating experience. It's just as easy to burn the tip of the tool as to get a sharp edge. Building the Low-Speed Grinder is the first step to solving this problem. The second (and maybe just as important) step is using the right grinding wheel.

ALUMINUM-OXIDE WHEEL. What I use most for grinding is a white or pink aluminum-oxide wheel. (I have both 60-grit and 120-grit wheels.) It cuts fast. But just as important, the binder or "glue" used on this type allows the abrasive particles to break away faster than on an all-purpose one. This is good for two reasons.

First, the cutting surface doesn't get clogged up with bits of cut-off metal. Since the wheel isn't clogged up, the tool doesn't get as hot while grinding.

Plus, these "fresh," sharp cutting edges are continuously being exposed, so the wheel cuts quicker and cooler.

CODE. So how do you know if the wheel is a 60-grit aluminum-oxide wheel? One way is to look at a code printed on a paper washer on the wheel itself (see photo).

The code on the label has a lot of technical information. But you can find out all you need to know by "cracking" the code in the first three parts.

ABRASIVE TYPE AND GRIT. For example, the letter "A" indicates that this wheel has abrasive particles made of aluminum oxide. And the "60" next to the "A" refers to the grit (see photo).

BOND GRADE. Another thing the code will tell you is the grade of the bond. Basically, this is the measurement of how easily the abrasive particles will break away from the grinding wheel.

With a soft bond grade, the particles separate relatively easy (as with white and pink wheels). But on a wheel with a hard bond (like a gray, all-purpose wheel), the particles are a little more stubborn.

To distinguish the bond grade of one wheel from another, most manufacturers use a lettering system that ranges from "A" to "Z" (with "A" being the softest and "Z" the hardest).

Note: The white wheel I prefer using has a bond grade of "K," which is about average but still fairly soft.

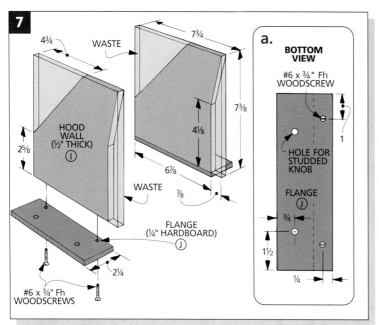

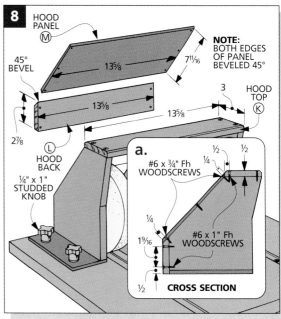

SAFETY HOOD

Any time a chisel or a plane iron is hollow ground, you'll produce lots of sparks — and a lot of fine, black grinding dust. To contain both of these by-products, I added a safety hood to the grinding jig *(Fig. 9)*. Besides keeping the dust from spreading out and covering your saw, the hood also covers the opening in back of the divider walls, so the sparks and dust can't get down inside the saw.

SAFETY HOOD WALLS. To make the hood, I started with the walls (I) *(Fig. 7)*. After cutting the $\frac{1}{2}$"-thick blanks to size, I beveled the back corner at 45° to match the shape of the dividing walls on the arbor assembly.

Now lay out and cut the front edges of the hood walls using a band saw *(Fig. 7)*. This simply provides clearance so more of the grinding wheel is exposed.

FLANGES. To secure the hood to the table, I glued and screwed $\frac{1}{4}$"-thick hardboard flanges (J) to the bottom edge of the walls *(Fig. 7)*. Then I set the wall assemblies over the threaded inserts in the base and marked the positions of the shank holes on the flanges *(Fig. 7a)*.

After these holes were drilled, I mounted the flanges and walls to the base with studded plastic knobs *(Fig. 8)*. Now the openings between these two walls can be covered by a top, back, and panel.

TOP AND BACK. To enclose the safety hood, I simply connected the walls with two hardwood pieces and a hardboard panel. First, I measured from the outside edge of one wall to the outside edge of the other. Then I cut a hood top (K) and back (L) from $\frac{1}{2}$"-thick hardwood *(Fig. 8)*. (I used hardwood since the hood gets lifted by the top piece.) These pieces are cut to match the edges of the walls (I), and the back has its top edge beveled 45° to accept the hood panel *(Fig. 8a)*.

Also, I relieved the sharp edges of the top piece *(Fig. 8a)*. Then I glued and screwed the top and back pieces to the walls of the hood.

PANEL. Finally, the hood panel (M) can be added between the hood top and back. This piece is $\frac{1}{4}$" hardboard and has both edges beveled 45°. This way, when the hood panel is glued and screwed in place, it fits tight against the top and flush with the back *(Fig. 8a)*.

With the grinding part of the jig complete, I began work on the carriage *(Fig. 10)*. This part of the jig does three things. First, it positions the blade forward or backward on the base. It also allows the tool to tip into and away from the grinding wheel. Finally, it guides the blade side-to-side across the wheel.

BASE. To build the carriage, start with the carriage base (N) which is a $1/2$"-thick hardwood blank *(Fig. 10)*. The first thing to do to this blank is cut a centered, $1/4$"-deep dado that's $3/4$" wide.

RUNNER. With this dado cut, next I made a $3/8$"-thick runner (O) and glued it in the dado. Then a $1/4$"-wide slot can be cut in both the base and runner *(Figs. 11 and 11a)*. This allows you to adjust the position of the carriage when you secure it to the base of the grinder *(Fig. 10)*.

SIDES. Next, I cut two $1/2$"-thick carriage sides (P) that will be added to the base. After these pieces were cut to size, I rounded over the top corners *(Fig. 10b)*. Then I drilled countersunk shank holes for the screws that attach the sides to the base *(Figs. 10a and 10b)*.

I used woodscrews to hold a tilting guide bar between the sides *(Fig. 10a)*. Since these screws act as pivot pins for the guide bar, they need to be lined up with each other. One way to do this is to tape the sides together while drilling the countersunk shank holes. Then separate the sides and glue and screw them to the base *(Figs. 10a and 10b)*.

GUIDE. Next, I added the guide bar (Q) that supports the tool rest *(Figs. 10 and 10b)*. This is simply a $1/2$"-thick piece. I chamfered the top edges to reduce friction and prevent binding.

After drilling the pilot holes in the ends of the guide, it can be screwed between the two sides.

Note: To get the guide centered, you may have to back one screw off and tighten the other until it's just right.

ADJUSTMENT BLOCK. The last piece to screw to the carriage is a micro-adjust block (R) *(Figs. 10 and 12)*. This $1/2$"-thick block has a threaded insert for a machine screw. The screw acts as a stop for the tool rest guide, and a knurled knob makes it easy to turn the machine bolt.

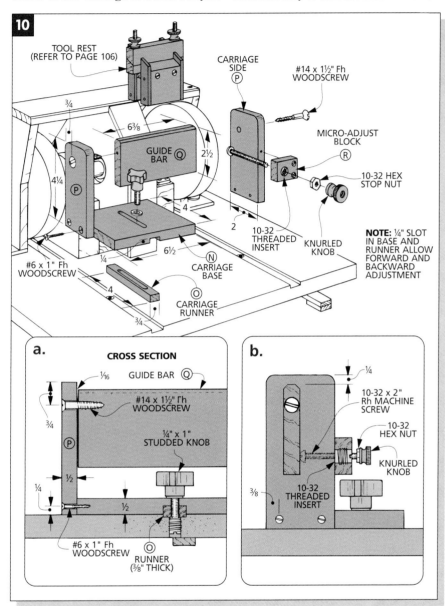

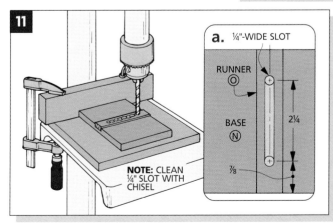

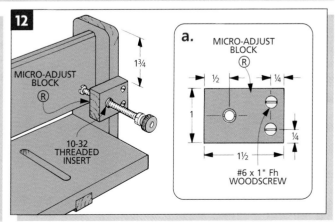

The grinder has a tool rest with a hold down to clamp a blade securely while the tool rest slides back and forth across the grinding wheel *(Fig. 13)*. But what I like is when the tool is clamped in place, the rest still simply lifts off the carriage. This way, it's easy to check your progress.

CENTER PIECE. The tool rest is made of three pieces. I started with the tool rest center (S) and the hold-down (T) that applies clamping pressure *(Fig. 14)*. These start out as a single, oversize blank. This way, it's easy to line up the pilot holes for the machine screws and knurled knobs that apply the pressure.

But first you need to cut a notch on the bottom corners of the blank *(Fig. 14a)*. Then the countersunk pilot holes can be drilled through the blank *(Fig. 14b)*.

HOLD-DOWN. Now, the hold-down (T) can be ripped from the center piece (S) *(Fig. 14)*. To do this, I tilted the saw blade to cut a 30° bevel and ripped the $\frac{7}{8}$"-wide hold-down from the blank.

FRONT AND BACK. Next, I cut the tool rest front (U) and back (V) pieces to size *(Fig. 15)*. These pieces are taller (wider) than the center piece so the tool rest will fit over the guide bar on the carriage. After the three pieces are glued and screwed together, bevel the top edge 30° just like the hold-down *(Fig. 16)*.

FRONT AND BACK STOPS. Now add the front (W) and back stops (X) to both sides of the tool rest *(Figs. 13 and 17)*. These pieces also have a 30° bevel on top, and they're glued and nailed to the front and back pieces.

To attach the hold-down, epoxy the screws into the pilot holes. Then the hold-down and knurled knobs can be added.

If you find your tool rest doesn't slide as smoothly across the guide bar as you like, a little sanding will solve the problem. Just don't sand the guide bar — it should stay perfectly straight. ■

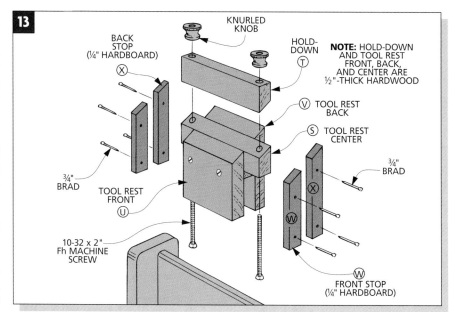

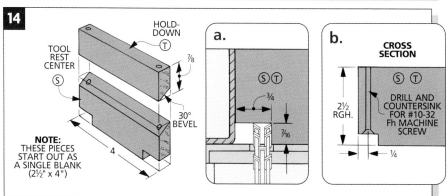

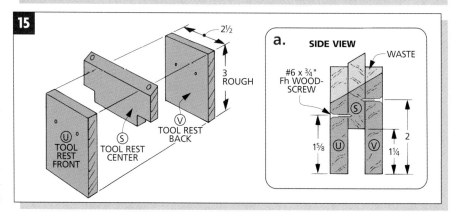

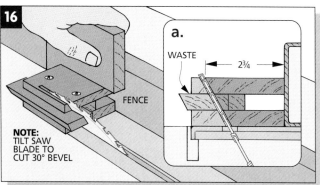

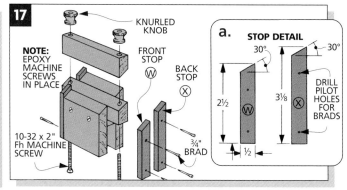

With the jig complete, it can be set up on the table saw. This will take a few minutes the first time, but after that, it shouldn't take much longer than changing a saw blade.

The first thing to do is remove the rip fence, insert plate, and saw blade. Then the hubless pulley can be added to the saw's arbor (detail 'a' in drawing). The pulley's outside diameter is 2". And the bore should match the diameter of the arbor.

Note: Remove the pulley's set screw before installing it. Then it's held in place with the arbor nut.

Next, raise the saw's arbor to get the belt around the pulley. Then set the jig in place and slip the belt over the pulley. Now lower the arbor until the belt is tight (detail 'b').

With the jig in place, you're ready to start sharpening. But before you adjust the carriage and tool rest (*Steps 1 through 3 below*), place the safety hood over the inserts and tighten it down.

FIRST: REMOVE RIP FENCE, THROAT PLATE, AND SAW BLADE

SECOND: SLIDE JIG INTO POSITION

THIRD: RAISE ARBOR TO HIGHEST POSITION AND INSTALL BELT ON PULLEY

a. BLADE WASHER — 2"-DIA. HUBLESS PULLEY — SAW ARBOR NUT — **NOTE:** REMOVE SET SCREW FROM PULLEY

b. TIGHTEN BELT SO IT DEFLECTS ¼" - ½" — LARGE PULLEY — BELT — 2" PULLEY — RAISE ARBOR TO INSTALL BELT — LOWER ARBOR TO TIGHTEN BELT

ADJUSTING THE JIG

Placing the chisel or plane iron in the jig and getting it adjusted is a simple three-step process (see photos).

After the carriage is set in the groove in the base, the first thing to do is secure the blade in the tool rest (*Step 1*). Then, with the blade projecting out a few inches, I push the tool against the stops on one side of the tool rest. Then I tighten the knurled nuts on the hold-down.

Now the position of the blade can be fine-tuned. But this time, I move the carriage slightly until the blade touches the wheel at the center of the bevel (*Step 2*). Then I "lock" the carriage down.

Keep in mind that by following this procedure, you're simply copying the angle of the bevel that's already on the blade. In most cases, this isn't much of a problem — most blades are "factory ground" to the right angle anyway (about 25°). But if you want to change the angle of the bevel, then cut this angle on a small scrap and use it to set the position of the carriage and holder.

With the carriage tightened down, next I set the micro-adjust screw (*Step 3*).

To do this, adjust the screw so it allows the blade to just touch the wheel. Then tip the chisel back, turn the power on, and gently feed the blade into the wheel. And when grinding, I found it works best to focus on sliding the tool rest smoothly from side to side.

Note: It may be necessary to make a few adjustments once you start grinding. If the edge of the blade is straight, but not square to the sides, just cock the tool slightly in the tool holder. If you have a convex edge, you'll need to grind down the center until it's straight.

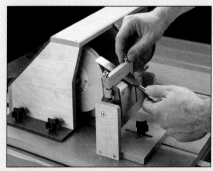

1 First, slide the tool under the hold-down so it protrudes a few inches and is butted against one of the stops. Then tighten down the knurled knobs on top.

2 Next, to fine-tune the position of the tool, simply slide the carriage in or out until the blade is touching the grinding wheel right at the center of its bevel.

3 Finally, to set the depth of the grind, turn the micro-adjust screw until it just touches the guide bar on the carriage. Now you're ready to test the setup.

DESIGNER'S NOTEBOOK

Converting the Low-Speed Grinder from one that's powered by a table saw motor into one that has its own power source is easy. All that's needed is a stand with four sturdy legs and a place to mount a motor.

CONSTRUCTION NOTES:

■ Everything about the construction of the Low-Speed Grinder is the same, except that you'll want to leave off the base runners (B) and stops (C) from the original base (A).

■ Start by building the legs (Y). They're ripped to width and cut to length from 3/4" plywood *(Fig. 1)*. All eight leg pieces are identical, except for one small thing. There's a cutout for an electrical box on one of the leg pieces *(Fig. 1a)*. Later when the stand is assembled, be sure that the leg piece with the cutout is facing to the front of the table.

Note: You could also simply purchase a motor that's hard-wired with a plug. Then all you do is just plug it into a wall outlet to turn it on. But, as always when tackling a job with electrical wiring, if you're not comfortable doing it yourself, be sure to contact a local electrical contractor to do this job for you.

■ Now cut a taper on one edge of each leg *(Fig. 1)*. I cut the tapers on the band saw

and then sanded the edges smooth.

■ Then the leg assemblies are simply butted together, and attached with glue and screws.

■ Next, I made the side (Z), front (AA), and back (AA) stretchers. They're all cut to size from 3/4" plywood. (You'll need to make a total of five front and back stretchers. Four of them are used as stretchers, but one will get used as the back side of a storage tray that gets added later.)

■ Before you go any further, cut a 1/4" wide, 1/4"-deep groove in two of the front stretchers for the tray bottom *(Fig. 2)*.

■ Now you can begin to put the stand together. To do this, first add a pair of side stretchers to two of the leg assemblies with glue and screws *(Fig. 2)*.

■ Then, build a second side assembly and connect the two together with the four front and back stretchers *(Fig. 3)*.

Note: Make sure the groove you've cut in the stretcher that you're placing in the lower front is facing "in" to accept the tray bottom.

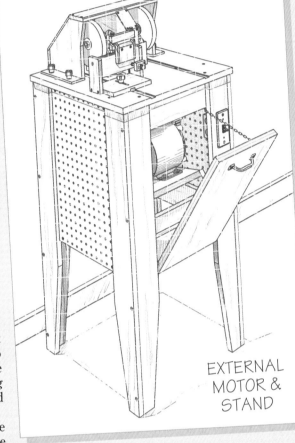

EXTERNAL MOTOR & STAND

■ You can add a small tray to the front of the stand next. This tray comes in handy for a couple of reasons. First, it's a good place to store a wheel dresser and grinding supplies. And later, when the

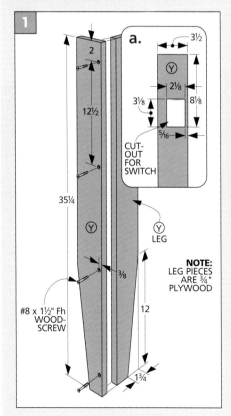

MATERIALS LIST

CHANGED PART

A	Base (1)	3/4 MDF - 19 x 20

NEW PARTS

Y	Legs (8)	3/4 ply - 3 1/2 x 35 1/4
Z	Side Stretchers (4)	3/4 ply - 3 1/2 x 17
AA	Fr./Bk. Stretchers (5)	3/4 ply - 3 1/2 x 16 1/2
BB	Tray Bottom (1)	1/4 pgbd. - 3 1/2 x 16 1/2
CC	Motor Mount (1)	3/4 ply - 10 x 12
DD	Pegboard Sides (2)	1/4 pgbd. - 11 1/2 x 20
EE	Pegboard Back (1)	1/4 pgbd. - 11 x 20
FF	Door (1)	3/4 ply - 10 3/4 x 19 7/8
GG	Hangers (2)	1/2 dowel - 3

Note: Do not need parts B, C.

HARDWARE SUPPLIES

(24) No. 8 x 1 1/2" Fh woodscrews
(48) No. 8 x 1 1/4" Fh woodscrews
(12) No. 8 x 3/4" Fh woodscrews
(4) 5/16" x 1 1/2" carriage bolts
(4) 5/16" washers
(4) 5/16" hex nuts
(1) 1 1/2" x 10" piano hinge
(1) 1 1/2" x 10 1/2" piano hinge
(1) Motor, 1500-1750 RPM
(1) Magnetic catch
(1) Sash pull
(1) 12"-long chain w/ screws

motor is set in place, it supports the motor mount until you get the hinge installed.

■ To build the tray, cut the tray bottom (BB) to size and place it in the groove in the front stretcher, then slide in the last stretcher and screw it in place *(Fig. 4)*.

■ At this point, the stand is ready for the grinder base. But before adding it you'll need to construct a place to put the motor. The motor mount (CC) is just a piece of ³/₄" plywood that's attached to the lower back rail with a piano hinge *(Fig. 5)*.

■ After cutting the motor mount to size, it is mounted to the back rail. To do this, first screw the piano hinge to the mount. Then hold the mount so there's a small space between it and the inside edge of the side stretcher and screw the hinge to the back stretcher.

■ Now set the base (A) on the stand, centering it front to back and side to side, and attach it with screws *(Fig. 3)*. Place the arbor assembly (with the belt looped over the large pulley) on the base and drop the belt through the slot.

■ Position the motor on the mount, then lift the mount up so you can loop the belt over the motor pulley. (You may need a helper to do this.) Then, with the motor positioned so the belt is taut and the pulleys aligned (you can use a shop rule to align them), mark and drill four over-sized shank holes. Finally, attach the motor to the motor mount with the carriage bolts, hex nuts, and washers.

■ Next, I cut the sides (DD) and back (EE) from ¹/₄" pegboard and screwed them in place between the legs *(Fig. 6)*.

Note: I used pegboard here to allow adequate ventilation for the motor.

■ Finally, I added a door. It's just a piece of plywood that's hinged at the bottom. Start by cutting the door (FF) to size from ³/₄" plywood *(Fig. 7)*.

■ Once again, I used a piano hinge on the bottom edge of the door. For the best appearance, rout or cut a shallow ³/₁₆" deep rabbet along the bottom, inside edge of the door *(Fig. 7)*. This way the hinge is inset slightly when it's installed, allowing the door to sit flush with the legs. Then I added a handle at the top.

■ Before mounting the door, drill a pair of holes on its inside edge and glue the ¹/₂" dowel hangers (GG) for storing an extra grinding stone or two *(Fig. 7)*. (The dowel holes are angled upwards at 15° so the grinder wheels won't fall off when the door is closed.)

■ Finally, a chain keeps the door from opening too far. A magnetic catch and strike plate keep the door closed *(Fig. 7)*.

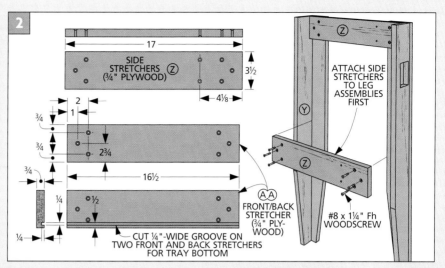

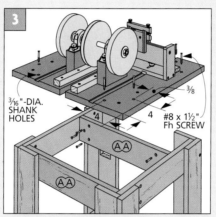

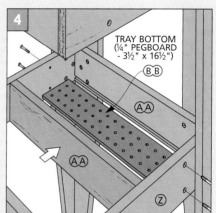

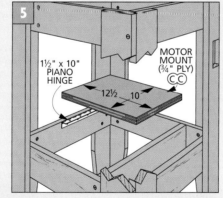

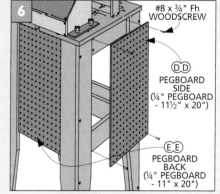

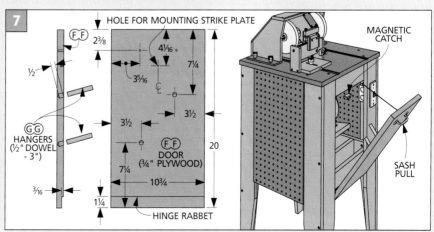

LOW-SPEED GRINDER **109**

Edge Sander

This shop-built tool is loaded with great features. The large front table provides solid support for large workpieces and an end table wraps around the belt so you can sand curved pieces as well.

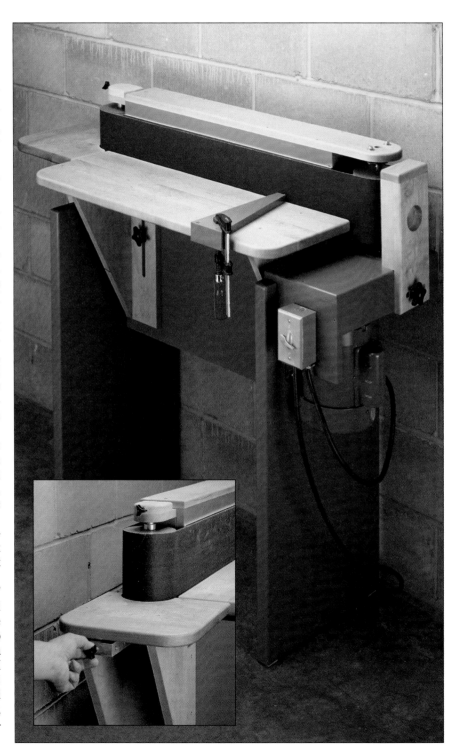

Some years back, I bought an inexpensive edge sander for my shop. It sounded like a great way to take the drudgery out of sanding.

The basic principle of an edge sander is simple — it's like a huge portable belt sander lying on its side. With a long, wide sanding belt running around a pair of rollers, it removes stock in a hurry. And since the rotation of the belt is in line with the workpiece, it doesn't leave any cross-grain scratches.

In spite of that, I was disappointed with my store-bought sander. It vibrated and shook like an old washing machine. And it was a pain trying to keep the tracking on the sanding belt adjusted properly. So when the bearings on the rollers finally seized up and died, all I could say was "good riddance."

SHOP-BUILT SANDER. That's when I came up with the idea of building my own Edge Sander. It may sound crazy, but after it was complete and I had used it for a while, I knew I had a winner. This big, green sanding machine is an impressive tool. In fact, it put my old, inexpensive edge sander to shame.

FEATURES. The sander runs smooth and strong — just like you'd expect from an "industrial quality" tool. And when you adjust the tracking (see inset photo), the belt not only shifts up or down on the rollers instantly — it stays put.

If you combine that with the other features incorporated into this unit, I think you'll be convinced — this shop-built Edge Sander really is better.

For instance, the end table "wraps" around an idler roller so you can sand curved pieces. And an adjustable mounting plate guides the end table up and down, allowing you to always have a fresh portion of the belt to sand on. (I made the front table adjustable as well.) Or clamp a stop on the front table to sand the ends of a workpiece square. Finally, changing belts is easy, thanks to a quick-release tension assembly.

EXPLODED VIEW

OVERALL DIMENSIONS:
54W x 18½D x 45¼H

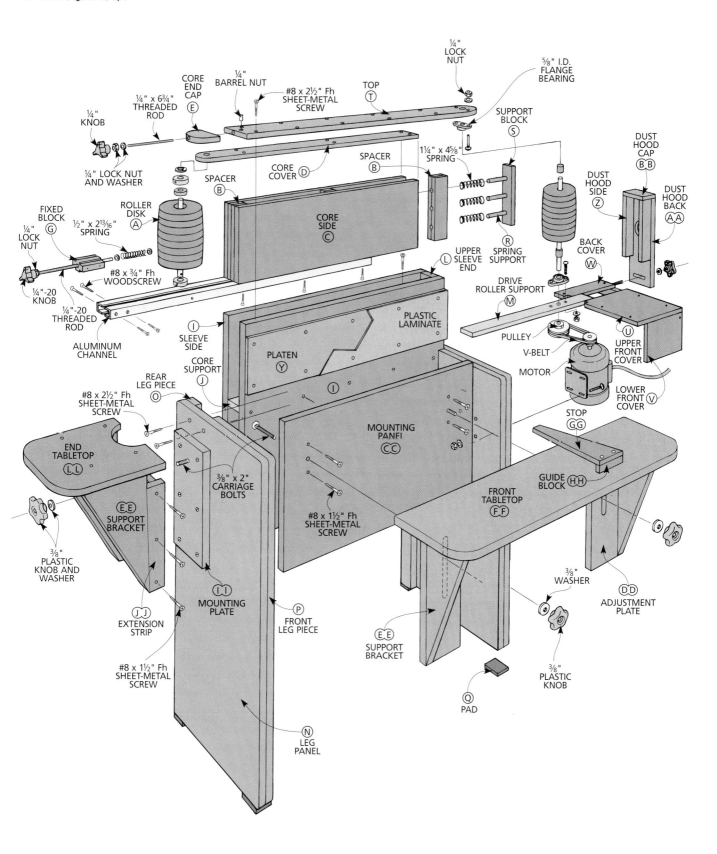

¼" KNOB

¼" x 6¾" THREADED ROD

¼" LOCK NUT AND WASHER

CORE END CAP
E

¼" BARREL NUT

#8 x 2½" Fh SHEET-METAL SCREW

TOP
T

¼" LOCK NUT

⅝" I.D. FLANGE BEARING

SUPPORT BLOCK
S

DUST HOOD CAP
BB

DUST HOOD SIDE
Z

DUST HOOD BACK
AA

FIXED BLOCK
G

ROLLER DISK
A

½" x 2¹³⁄₁₆" SPRING

SPACER
B

CORE COVER
D

SPACER
B

1¼" x 4⅝" SPRING

CORE SIDE
C

SPRING SUPPORT
R

BACK COVER
W

¼" LOCK NUT

#8 x ¾" Fh WOODSCREW

¼"-20 KNOB

¼"-20 THREADED ROD

ALUMINUM CHANNEL

SLEEVE SIDE
I

UPPER SLEEVE END
L

DRIVE ROLLER SUPPORT
M

PLASTIC LAMINATE

PLATEN
Y

PULLEY

V-BELT

MOTOR

UPPER FRONT COVER
U

LOWER FRONT COVER
V

CORE SUPPORT
J

REAR LEG PIECE
O

#8 x 2½" Fh SHEET-METAL SCREW

END TABLETOP
LL

EE SUPPORT BRACKET

⅜" PLASTIC KNOB AND WASHER

JJ EXTENSION STRIP

II MOUNTING PLATE

⅜" x 2" CARRIAGE BOLTS

MOUNTING PANEL
CC

#8 x 1½" Fh SHEET-METAL SCREW

STOP
GG

GUIDE BLOCK
HH

FRONT TABLETOP
FF

⅜" WASHER

⅜" PLASTIC KNOB

ADJUSTMENT PLATE
DD

P FRONT LEG PIECE

EE SUPPORT BRACKET

Q PAD

#8 x 1½" Fh SHEET-METAL SCREW

LEG PANEL
N

CUTTING DIAGRAM

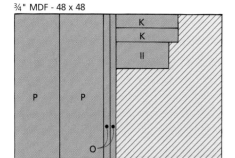

¾" MDF - 48 x 48
K
K
II
P
P
O
U
W
V
S

NOTE: ALSO NEED ONE 12" x 36" PIECE OF PLASTIC LAMINATE, THREE ¾"-DIA. - 6" HARDWOOD DOWELS, AND ONE 12" x 36" PIECE OF ¼" PLYWOOD

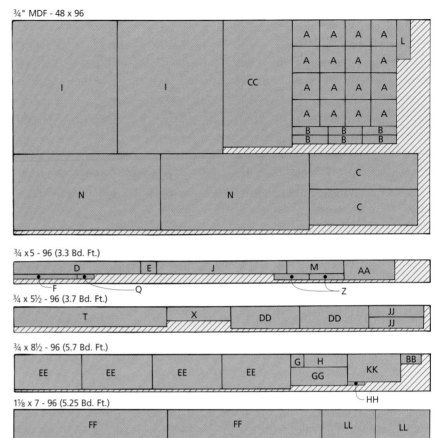

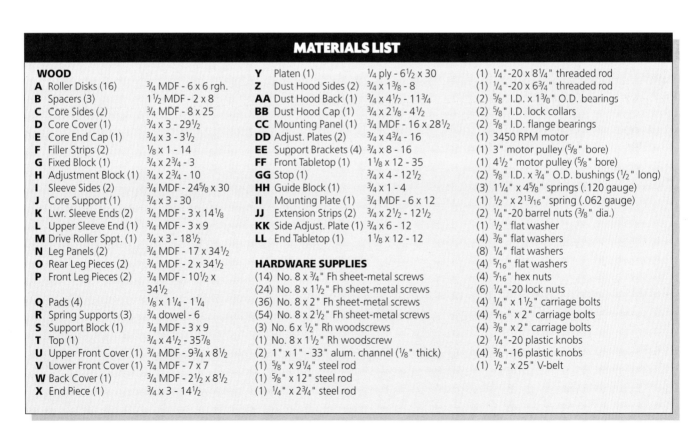

¾" MDF - 48 x 96
I
I
CC
A
L
B
N
N
C
C
¾ x5 - 96 (3.3 Bd. Ft.)
D
E
J
M
AA
F
Q
Z
¾ x 5½ - 96 (3.7 Bd. Ft.)
T
X
DD
DD
JJ
JJ
¾ x 8½ - 96 (5.7 Bd. Ft.)
EE
EE
EE
EE
G
H
GG
KK
BB
HH
1⅛ x 7 - 96 (5.25 Bd. Ft.)
FF
FF
LL
LL

MATERIALS LIST

WOOD

- **A** Roller Disks (16) — ¾ MDF - 6 x 6 rgh.
- **B** Spacers (3) — 1½ MDF - 2 x 8
- **C** Core Sides (2) — ¾ MDF - 8 x 25
- **D** Core Cover (1) — ¾ x 3 - 29½
- **E** Core End Cap (1) — ¾ x 3 - 3½
- **F** Filler Strips (2) — ⅛ x 1 - 14
- **G** Fixed Block (1) — ¾ x 2¾ - 3
- **H** Adjustment Block (1) — ¾ x 2¾ - 10
- **I** Sleeve Sides (2) — ¾ MDF - 24⅝ x 30
- **J** Core Support (1) — ¾ x 3 - 30
- **K** Lwr. Sleeve Ends (2) — ¾ MDF - 3 x 14⅛
- **L** Upper Sleeve End (1) — ¾ MDF - 3 x 9
- **M** Drive Roller Sppt. (1) — ¾ x 3 - 18½
- **N** Leg Panels (2) — ¾ MDF - 17 x 34½
- **O** Rear Leg Pieces (2) — ¾ MDF - 2 x 34½
- **P** Front Leg Pieces (2) — ¾ MDF - 10½ x 34½
- **Q** Pads (4) — ⅛ x 1¼ - 1¼
- **R** Spring Supports (3) — ¾ dowel - 6
- **S** Support Block (1) — ¾ MDF - 3 x 9
- **T** Top (1) — ¾ x 4½ - 35⅞
- **U** Upper Front Cover (1) — ¾ MDF - 9¾ x 8½
- **V** Lower Front Cover (1) — ¾ MDF - 7 x 7
- **W** Back Cover (1) — ¾ MDF - 2½ x 8½
- **X** End Piece (1) — ¾ x 3 - 14½
- **Y** Platen (1) — ¼ ply - 6½ x 30
- **Z** Dust Hood Sides (2) — ¾ x 1⅜ - 8
- **AA** Dust Hood Back (1) — ¾ x 4½ - 11¾
- **BB** Dust Hood Cap (1) — ¾ x 2⅛ - 4½
- **CC** Mounting Panel (1) — ¾ MDF - 16 x 28½
- **DD** Adjust. Plates (2) — ¾ x 4¾ - 16
- **EE** Support Brackets (4) — ¾ x 8 - 16
- **FF** Front Tabletop (1) — 1⅛ x 12 - 35
- **GG** Stop (1) — ¾ x 4 - 12½
- **HH** Guide Block (1) — ¾ x 1 - 4
- **II** Mounting Plate (1) — ¾ MDF - 6 x 12
- **JJ** Extension Strips (2) — ¾ x 2½ - 12½
- **KK** Side Adjust. Plate (1) — ¾ x 6 - 12
- **LL** End Tabletop (1) — 1⅛ x 12 - 12

HARDWARE SUPPLIES

- (14) No. 8 x ¾" Fh sheet-metal screws
- (24) No. 8 x 1½" Fh sheet-metal screws
- (36) No. 8 x 2" Fh sheet-metal screws
- (54) No. 8 x 2½" Fh sheet-metal screws
- (3) No. 6 x ½" Rh woodscrews
- (1) No. 8 x 1½" Rh woodscrew
- (2) 1" x 1" - 33" alum. channel (⅛" thick)
- (1) ⅝" x 9¼" steel rod
- (1) ⅝" x 12" steel rod
- (1) ¼" x 2¾" steel rod
- (1) ¼"-20 x 8¼" threaded rod
- (1) ¼"-20 x 6¾" threaded rod
- (2) ⅝" I.D. x 1⅜" O.D. bearings
- (2) ⅝" I.D. lock collars
- (2) ⅝" I.D. flange bearings
- (1) 3450 RPM motor
- (1) 3" motor pulley (⅝" bore)
- (1) 4½" motor pulley (⅝" bore)
- (2) ⅝" I.D. x ¾" O.D. bushings (½" long)
- (3) 1¼" x 4⅝" springs (.120 gauge)
- (1) ½" x 2 13/16" spring (.062 gauge)
- (2) ¼"-20 barrel nuts (⅜" dia.)
- (1) ½" flat washer
- (4) ⅜" flat washers
- (8) ¼" flat washers
- (4) 5/16" flat washers
- (4) 5/16" hex nuts
- (6) ¼"-20 lock nuts
- (4) ¼" x 1½" carriage bolts
- (4) 5/16" x 2" carriage bolts
- (4) ⅜" x 2" carriage bolts
- (2) ¼"-20 plastic knobs
- (4) ⅜"-16 plastic knobs
- (1) ½" x 25" V-belt

Just like a portable belt sander, this shop-built Edge Sander has two rollers that guide the sanding belt: a drive roller and an idler roller *(Figs. 2 and 3)*. The biggest difference is in the size of these rollers. Since the sanding belt you'll be using with the Edge Sander is 6" wide and 89" long, the rollers are quite a bit larger than those found on a belt sander.

DISKS. Each roller consists of a stack of eight disks made from ³⁄₄" medium-density fiberboard (MDF) *(Fig. 1)*. They start out as 6"-square blanks *(Step 1 in Fig. 1a)*. (You'll need 16 altogether.)

To form pockets for a pair of bearings that are added later, I drilled a counterbore in two of the blanks *(Step 2)*. And there's a ³⁄₄"-dia. hole in each blank to accept the shaft of the roller *(Step 3)*.

After drilling all the holes, the disks (A) can be cut to shape. To ensure that each one is uniform in size, I used a wing cutter in the drill press *(Step 4)*.

GLUE-UP. Now you're ready to glue the disks together to form the two rollers. The disks are quite smooth, so the rollers will want to move around during glue up. An easy way to keep the edges aligned is to slip the disks onto a ³⁄₄"-dia. steel rod.

Note: The two counterbores on the idler roller face the outside.

CROWN. When the glue dries, you'll need to rout a slight (¹⁄₈") crown across each roller. This crown centers the belt on the roller and keeps it from slipping off. A hand-held router and "turning jig" make quick work of this. (For more on building the turning jig, see page 115.)

SHAFTS. The next step is to add a metal shaft to each roller *(Figs. 2 and 3)*. (You'll have to remove the ³⁄₄" rod first.) Each shaft is cut from a length of ⁵⁄₈"-dia. steel rod. But the shafts are not identical.

IDLER SHAFT. One thing to note about the shaft for the idler roller is there's a hole near the bottom end *(Fig. 2)*. Later, this hole will accept a pin that's used to fasten the shaft to the tracking system.

To center the shaft inside the idler roller, a bearing is slipped over each end and pressed into the counterbore drilled earlier. The purpose of these bearings is to allow the idler roller (not the shaft) to spin freely during operation.

With the bearings installed, it's just a matter of positioning the roller on the shaft. It's held in place by slipping a lock collar onto each end of the shaft and tightening a set screw *(Fig. 2)*.

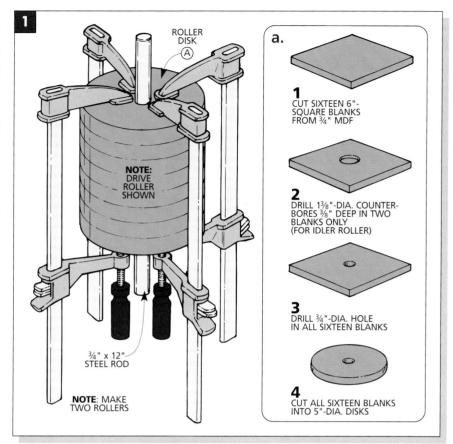

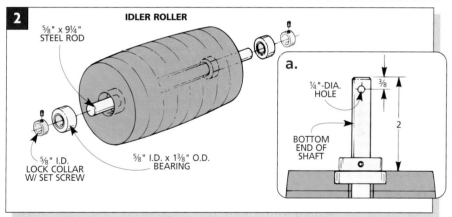

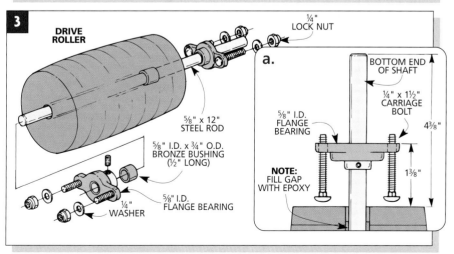

A slow-setting epoxy fills the gap between the shaft and the drive roller. Before it "welds" them together, press a bushing into the opening.

DRIVE SHAFT. Now add the shaft for the drive roller (refer to *Fig. 3* on page 113). This shaft is longer than the one for the idler roller, allowing for a pulley that's attached later. And it isn't fixed. Instead, the shaft is glued to the roller so they spin together as a unit (see photo at left).

BUSHINGS. Before the epoxy cures, you'll need to press a bushing into the opening at each end of the roller. These bushings center the shaft inside the roller.

FLANGE BEARINGS. To allow the shaft to spin without overheating, it's supported by a flange bearing (a bearing inside a metal flange) that slips over each end.

Later, the flange is secured with carriage bolts. It's easiest to install the bolts now, then tighten a set screw that holds each flange bearing on the shaft (refer to *Fig. 3a* on page 113).

CORE

Now turn your attention to the core. It's part of a system that applies tension to the sanding belt and is made up of a simple, rectangular assembly that consists of three narrow spacers (B) sandwiched between two MDF sides *(Fig. 4)*.

Each spacer is made by gluing up two pieces of ³⁄₄" MDF *(Fig. 5)*. Before gluing on the core sides (C), it's easiest to drill three holes in one of the spacers for a tension assembly that's added later.

COVER. The core is enclosed on the top by a long, narrow cover (D) *(Fig. 6)*. An oversize hole near one end of the cover accepts the shaft on the idler roller. To keep the shaft from denting the cover, I drilled holes in a washer and screwed it over the hole *(Fig. 4a)*.

Note: You'll need to enlarge the hole in the washer first (see photo below).

END CAP. To complete the core, I added a short, hardwood end cap (E) *(Fig. 6)*. It has a hole for a mechanism that releases tension on the sanding belt. After gluing the end cap to the cover and cutting a curve on the end, round over the top edge and screw the cover in place.

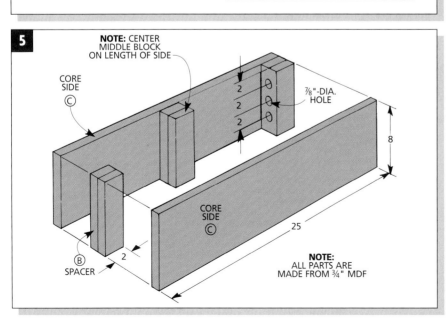

4

CORE COVER (D)

CORE END CAP (E)

SPACER (B)

CORE SIDE (C)

#6 x ½" Rh WOODSCREW

½" WASHER (SEE DETAIL a AND PHOTO AT RIGHT)

NOTE: COVER AND END CAP ARE MADE FROM ³⁄₄"-THICK HARDWOOD

a.

END CAP

#8 x 2½" Fh SHEET-METAL SCREW

(D)

(C)

NOTE: ENLARGE HOLE IN ½" WASHER TO ⁵⁄₈" I.D.

5

NOTE: CENTER MIDDLE BLOCK ON LENGTH OF SIDE

CORE SIDE (C)

⁷⁄₈"-DIA. HOLE

8

CORE SIDE (C)

25

(B) SPACER

2

NOTE: ALL PARTS ARE MADE FROM ³⁄₄" MDF

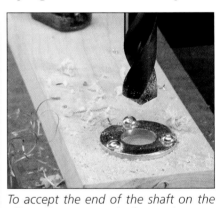

To accept the end of the shaft on the idler roller, I screwed a ¹⁄₂" washer to a piece of scrap and enlarged the hole by boring it out with a ⁵⁄₈" twist bit.

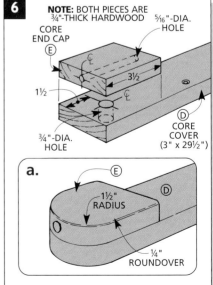

6

NOTE: BOTH PIECES ARE ³⁄₄"-THICK HARDWOOD

⁵⁄₁₆"-DIA. HOLE

CORE END CAP (E)

3½

1½

³⁄₄"-DIA. HOLE

(D) CORE COVER (3" x 29½")

a.

(E)

1½" RADIUS

(D)

¼" ROUNDOVER

The sander's rollers are barrel-shaped with a slight "crown" in the middle. This keeps the sanding belt centered on the rollers and prevents it from slipping off.

To form the slight crown on the rollers, I used a hand-held router with a straight bit and a simple "turning" jig (see photo at right).

TURNING JIG. The jig is just an open box with two sides and two ends *(Fig. 1)*. What makes it work is a curved "track" along the top edge of the sides that guides the base of the router. As the router follows the track, an identical crown is routed on the roller.

To lay out the curve for the track, I used an old, but simple, trick. With a helper bending a scrap of hardboard to the desired shape, carefully mark the curve along the top edge of the side *(Fig. 1a)*.

After sanding the sides to shape, you can complete the track by routing a rabbet along the top edge *(Fig. 1b)*.

In addition to the rabbets, you'll need to cut a pair of dadoes in each side to accept the end pieces. The length of the space between these dadoes should allow

the roller to fit between the end pieces with ¹⁄₁₆" of clearance.

ENDS. With the sides complete, you can turn your attention to the ends. They're cut to length so the base of the router fits between the rabbets in the sides. Also, you'll need to drill a centered hole in each end to accept the metal rod that runs through the roller. (It's the ³⁄₄"-dia. rod used when gluing up the roller.)

CRANK. Once the holes are drilled, you can add the hand crank that's used to turn the metal rod. The crank consists of a hardwood arm and a handle made from a short dowel *(Fig. 1)*.

The handle is screwed into a counterbore drilled in one end of the arm. At the other end, there's a hole with an intersecting kerf. A screw squeezes the kerf together and pinches the arm on the shaft.

SETUP. Now it's just a matter of setting up the router turning jig. Start by placing a roller inside the box and sliding the rod all the way through. Then set the base of the router in the track so the bit is centered on the length of the roller *(Fig. 2a)*. When determining the depth of cut, you want to adjust the bit so it just grazes the top edge of the roller.

ROUT CROWN. Now you'll need a helper again to turn the roller while you rout the crown. The idea is to turn the roller counterclockwise while you slowly rout from one end of the roller to the other (starting near the crank) *(Fig. 2)*.

Note: You'll need to make several passes to clean up the roller.

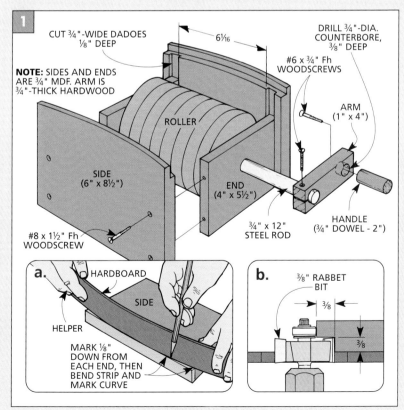

1

CUT ¾"-WIDE DADOES ⅛" DEEP

6¹⁄₁₆

DRILL ¾"-DIA. COUNTERBORE, ⅜" DEEP

#6 x ¾" Fh WOODSCREWS

NOTE: SIDES AND ENDS ARE ¾" MDF. ARM IS ¾"-THICK HARDWOOD

ROLLER

ARM (1" x 4")

SIDE (6" x 8½")

END (4" x 5½")

#8 x 1½" Fh WOODSCREW

¾" x 12" STEEL ROD

HANDLE (¾" DOWEL - 2")

a. HARDBOARD

SIDE

HELPER

MARK ⅛" DOWN FROM EACH END, THEN BEND STRIP AND MARK CURVE

b. ⅜" RABBET BIT

⅜

⅜

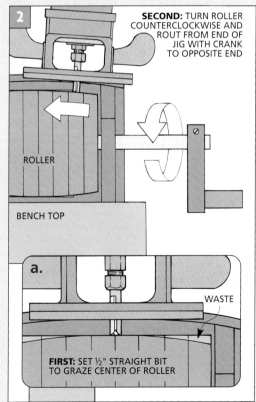

2 **SECOND:** TURN ROLLER COUNTERCLOCKWISE AND ROUT FROM END OF JIG WITH CRANK TO OPPOSITE END

ROLLER

BENCH TOP

a.

WASTE

FIRST: SET ½" STRAIGHT BIT TO GRAZE CENTER OF ROLLER

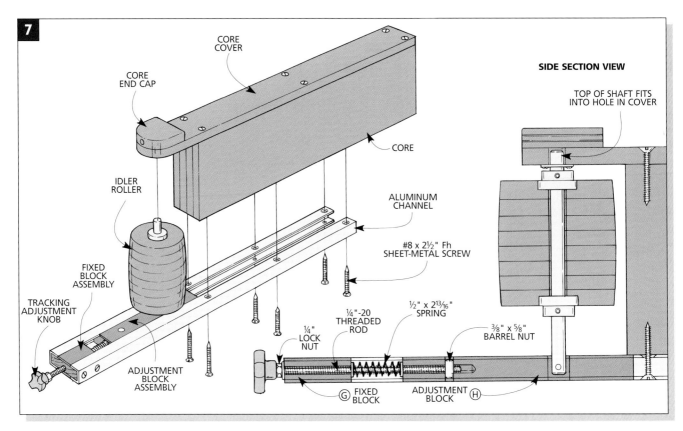

7

CORE
COVER

CORE
END CAP

IDLER
ROLLER

FIXED
BLOCK
ASSEMBLY

TRACKING
ADJUSTMENT
KNOB

ADJUSTMENT
BLOCK
ASSEMBLY

CORE

ALUMINUM
CHANNEL

#8 x 2½" Fh
SHEET-METAL SCREW

¼"-20
THREADED
ROD

½" x 2¹³⁄₁₆"
SPRING

¼"
LOCK
NUT

⅜" x ⅝"
BARREL NUT

FIXED
BLOCK
(G)

ADJUSTMENT
BLOCK
(H)

SIDE SECTION VIEW

TOP OF SHAFT FITS
INTO HOLE IN COVER

TRACKING SYSTEM

The heart of the Edge Sander is a tracking system that lets you quickly adjust the position of the sanding belt on the rollers.

This system consists of a pair of U-shaped pieces of aluminum channel that fit around two wood blocks *(Fig. 7)*. A short, fixed block is permanently attached to the channel. And a long adjustment block slides back and forth inside.

The significant thing about the sliding block is that it captures the bottom end of the shaft on the idler roller *(Fig. 7)*. This means that the shaft tilts to one side or the other as you adjust the block in or out. It's this tilting action that causes the sanding belt to travel up or down on the rollers.

ALUMINUM CHANNEL. I began by cutting the two pieces of aluminum channel to length *(Fig. 8)*. Drilling a pair of countersunk holes in the side of each piece will make it easy to attach the fixed block later. Also, it's best to drill countersunk holes in the top and bottom so the core can be attached (refer to *Fig. 11a*

and photo on the next page). The countersink on the bottom of the channel recesses the screw head. And the one on the top forms a pocket for any wood fibers that pull out as you drive in a screw.

BLOCKS. After drilling the holes, you can concentrate on the two blocks. They start out as a single oversize blank of hardwood *(Fig. 8)*. It's thicknessed to fit snug inside the channel, yet it still needs to slide back and forth.

Once you're satisfied with the fit, the blank can be ripped to width. The idea

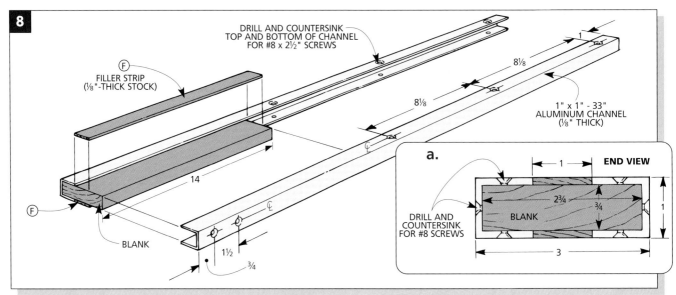

8

DRILL AND COUNTERSINK
TOP AND BOTTOM OF CHANNEL
FOR #8 x 2½" SCREWS

FILLER STRIP
(⅛"-THICK STOCK)

(F)

(F)

BLANK

14

8⅛

8⅛

1

1" x 1" - 33"
ALUMINUM CHANNEL
(⅛" THICK)

1½

¾

a.

DRILL AND
COUNTERSINK
FOR #8 SCREWS

BLANK

1

2¾

¾

3

1

END VIEW

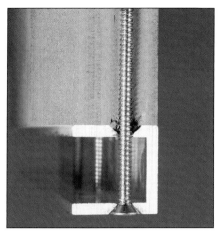

To make sure the aluminum channel seats tight against the MDF, drill countersinks on top of the channel. This creates pockets for fibers that pull out as you drive the screw.

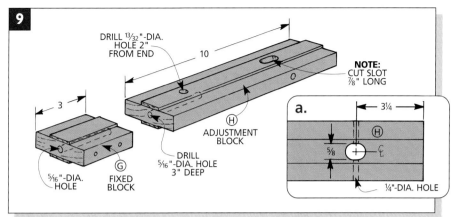

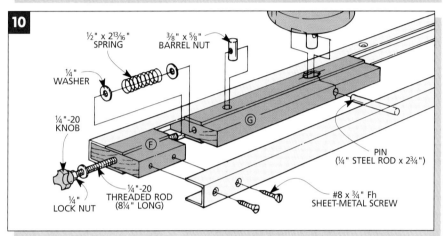

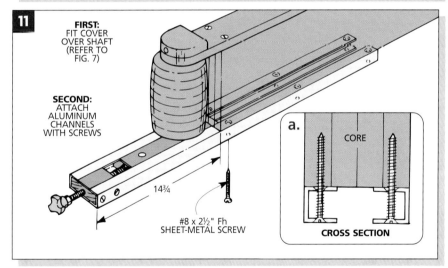

here is to make the combined width of the blank (with the aluminum channel attached) equal to the thickness of the core assembly. This way, you'll be able to slide the entire assembly smoothly into a sleeve which is added later. (To accomplish this, I ripped my blank $2^3/4$" wide.)

FILLER STRIPS. After slipping both pieces of aluminum channel onto the blank, I added the two filler strips (F) *(Fig. 8)*. These are thin ($1/8$") strips of hardwood that are ripped to width to fit between the channel, then glued in place.

CUT BLOCKS TO LENGTH. When the glue dries, it's just a matter of removing the channel and cutting the fixed (G) and adjustment blocks (H) to length *(Fig. 9)*.

With blocks in hand, I drilled a hole in the end of each one for a threaded rod that's part of the adjustment mechanism.

Note: I used a simple jig for my drill press to hold the long adjustment block steady (see the Shop Tip on page 79).

Before assembling the tracking system, you'll need to drill a few more holes in the adjustment block. A hole that intersects the hole for the threaded rod will hold a barrel nut (added later).

Also, drilling two more holes will allow you to secure the shaft of the idler roller. A slot provides clearance for the shaft as it tilts from side to side *(Fig. 9a)*. And an intersecting hole in the edge will accept a metal pin that holds the shaft in place.

ASSEMBLY. Now you're ready to assemble the tracking system. Start by screwing the fixed block (G) to one piece only of the aluminum channel *(Fig. 10)*. Then, after fitting the adjustment block into the same channel, you can add the adjustment mechanism.

The key here is a threaded rod that passes through the hole in the fixed block *(Fig. 7)*. There's a knob tightened against a lock nut on one end of the rod. And a spring and two washers slip over the other end to prevent any vibration from affecting the adjustment. Now simply thread the rod into the barrel nut that fits in the hole in the adjustment block.

IDLER ROLLER. Next, secure the bottom end of the shaft on the idler roller. It fits in the slot in the adjustment block.

To hold the shaft in place, tap a pin into the hole in the edge and through the hole in the shaft drilled earlier. Screwing the second piece of channel in place over the blocks traps the pin *(Fig. 10)*.

ATTACH CORE. All that's left is to attach the core to the channel. After setting the cover (D) over the shaft of the idler roller, the channel assembly is simply screwed to the sides (C) *(Figs. 11 and 11a)*.

Note: To avoid kinking the channel, don't overtighten the screws.

BASE

The Edge Sander is supported by a heavy-duty base. The base consists of four parts: a sleeve that houses the core built earlier; two legs made from large, layered pieces of MDF; a tension assembly that uses heavy-duty springs to keep the belt from slipping; and a top that covers the rollers, core, and tracking system *(Fig. 12)*.

SLEEVE

Besides connecting the legs, the sleeve forms an opening that allows the core assembly to fit inside.

SIDES. The sleeve is made up of two large, 3/4" MDF sides (I) with narrow strips sandwiched in between *(Figs. 12 and 13)*. This creates an opening at the top for the core assembly and the drive roller support. The important thing is the size of this opening.

To ensure the correct amount of tension on the large sanding belt, the sides need to be wide enough (and tall enough) so the core slides smoothly without binding. At the same time, you want a snug fit so the tension won't pull the rollers out of alignment.

To create just the right "friction fit," I ripped a 3/4"-thick hardwood core support (J) to width so it's just a hair wider than the thickness of the core assembly. (Mine was 3".) It's positioned so the core assembly (which sits on top of it) will end up just below the top of the sides.

The ends of the sleeve are enclosed by two lower sleeve ends (K) and an upper sleeve end (L). The thing to be aware of is that the upper sleeve end doesn't extend all the way down to the core support. Instead, a 3/4"-tall opening allows a support for the drive roller to slide inside.

DRIVE ROLLER SUPPORT. After gluing and screwing the sleeve together, add the drive roller support (M). It's an extra-long strip of hardwood that cantilevers past the end of the sleeve *(Fig. 13)*.

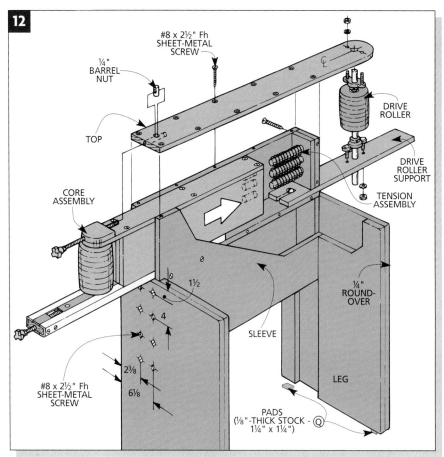

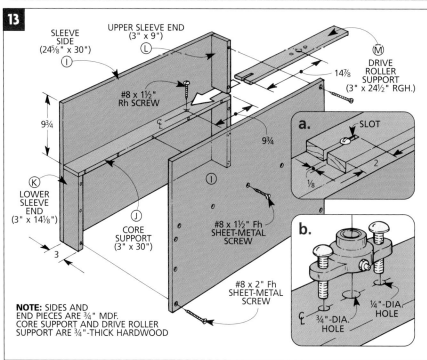

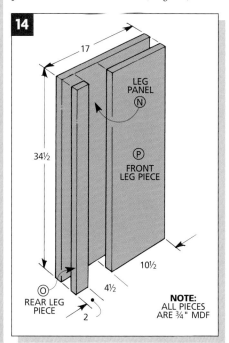

The end of the drive roller support that sticks out acts as a mounting platform for the lower flange bearing on the drive roller *(Fig. 16c)*. So it's best to drill holes now for the shaft of the roller and the bolts that secure the flange *(Fig. 13b)*.

The end inside the sleeve has a short slot cut in it *(Fig. 13a)*. Later, this allows you to make the initial adjustment on the drive roller. But for now, just "snug" the support down with a screw.

LEGS

Once the sleeve assembly is complete, you're ready to add the legs.

SLAB. Each leg is a slab made of three pieces of MDF. A large, full-width leg panel (N) is on the outside *(Fig. 14)*. On the inside is a narrow rear leg (O) and a wider front leg (P) that form a groove to accept the sleeve. And a pad (Q) is glued to the bottom corner of each leg *(Fig. 12)*.

ATTACH SLEEVE. To make sure the sleeve stays put, I used glue and sheet-metal screws to attach it to the legs. (See the Shop Tip on page 11 for more on using sheet-metal screws in MDF.)

Note: To position the sleeve, place the drive roller support and core assembly on top of the legs.

TENSION ASSEMBLY

At this point, you can add the tension assembly. It prevents the sanding belt from slipping on the rollers.

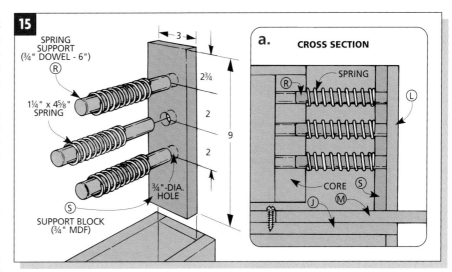

SPRINGS. The secret is a set of three heavy-duty springs (see the Shop Info on page 58) that fit loosely over the spring supports (R) *(Fig. 15)*. By pushing against the core, they exert outward pressure on the idler roller. It's this pressure that applies tension to the sanding belt.

To make this work, the dowels are glued into holes in a support block (S). Once the support block is glued to the upper sleeve end (L), the opposite ends of the dowels fit into the holes in the core as you slide it into the sleeve *(Fig. 15a)*.

TOP

Now all that's left is to add the top. In addition to enclosing the upper part of the sleeve, the top has two other jobs.

ANCHOR. First, one end of the 3/4"-thick hardwood top (T) anchors the upper flange bearing on the drive roller *(Figs. 16a and 16b)*. So here again, you'll need to drill three holes, one for the shaft of the roller and two for the bolts that secure the flange bearing.

TENSION RELEASE. To make it easy to change sanding belts, the opposite end of the top has a mechanism that releases tension on the belt. This requires drilling two holes — one in the end, and an intersecting hole in the top.

When the top is screwed in place, the rod passes through the end cap (E) and threads into the barrel nut. Tightening a knob on the end of the rod moves the core assembly farther into the sleeve so you can slip a belt on or off.

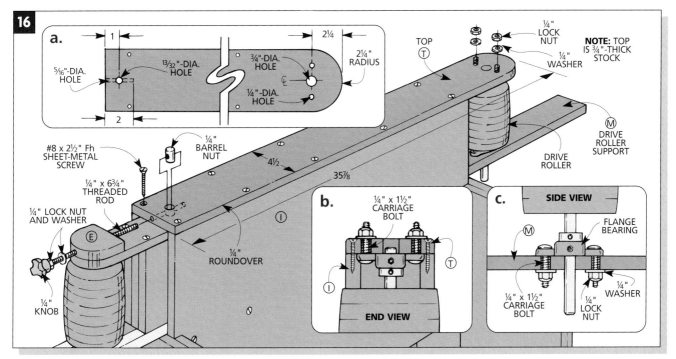

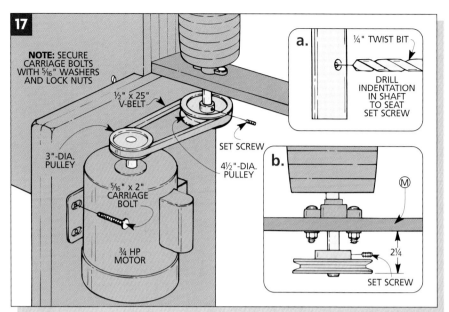

17

NOTE: SECURE
CARRIAGE BOLTS
WITH ⁵⁄₁₆" WASHERS
AND LOCK NUTS

½" x 25"
V-BELT

3"-DIA.
PULLEY

⁵⁄₁₆" x 2"
CARRIAGE
BOLT

¾ HP
MOTOR

SET SCREW

4½"-DIA.
PULLEY

a. ¼" TWIST BIT

DRILL
INDENTATION
IN SHAFT
TO SEAT
SET SCREW

b. Ⓜ

2¼

SET SCREW

MOTOR & PULLEY GUARD

At this point, the sander is starting to look like a piece of industrial machinery. Once the base is complete, the next step is to mount the motor and add a pulley guard. (To find a motor, pulleys, and all the hardware needed to power the Edge Sander, see Sources on page 126.)

MOTOR. Because of the dust produced when sanding, I used a totally enclosed, fan-cooled (TEFC) motor. It's a ¾ horsepower motor with a ⁵⁄₈" arbor *(Fig. 17)*.

This motor spins at 3450 RPM. But I didn't want the sanding belt to turn that fast. At that speed, it's likely to burn the surface of the workpiece.

PULLEYS. So I reduced the speed of the belt considerably by using two different size pulleys. A 3"-dia. pulley on the motor is secured with a key that fits a groove in the arbor.

And a second 4½"-dia. pulley on the drive roller is held in place by a set screw. The set screw tightens into an indentation drilled in the drive roller shaft. To locate the pulley on the shaft, you'll first need to position the pulley with about 2¼" clearance between the bottom edge of the

drive roller support and the bottom of the pulley *(Fig. 17b)*. Then mark the location of the set screw on the shaft. Now you can use a ¼" twist bit to drill the shallow indentation *(Fig. 17a)*.

MOUNT MOTOR. To mount the motor, start by slipping a V-belt onto the pulleys. Then, with the motor positioned so the belt is taut and the pulleys are aligned (you can use a 12" shop rule to align them), mark and drill holes for the bolts that hold the motor in place *(Fig. 17)*.

Once the holes are drilled, you can mount the motor. The mounting bracket should have elongated slots, making it easy to mount the motor first. Then slip the V-belt on the pulleys, before sliding the motor out and tightening the bolts.

PULLEY GUARD. The next step is to add a guard to cover the pulleys and V-belt *(Fig. 18)*. The pulley guard is "pieced" together around the drive roller support.

The area above the pulleys and in front of the motor is enclosed by three cover pieces (U, V, W) that are made from ¾" MDF. Start by cutting the pieces to size. Then screw these three cover pieces to the slab legs *(Fig. 18)*.

Finally, an end piece (X) completes the guard. It's made from ¾"-thick hardwood and is cut to fit below the upper front and back cover and butt up against the lower front cover.

Be sure to keep the flange bearings greased on a regular basis to prevent them from overheating.

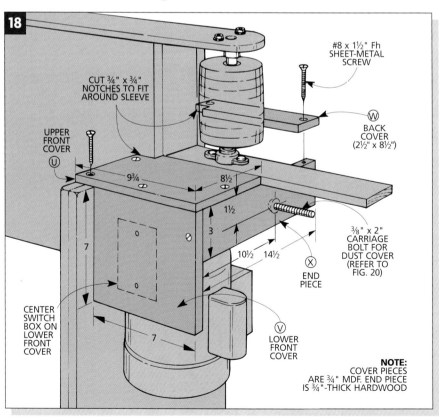

18

CUT ¾" x ¾"
NOTCHES TO FIT
AROUND SLEEVE

#8 x 1½" Fh
SHEET-METAL
SCREW

Ⓦ BACK
COVER
(2½" x 8½")

UPPER
FRONT
COVER
Ⓤ

9¾

8½

1½

3

7

10½   14½

Ⓧ END
PIECE

⅜" x 2"
CARRIAGE
BOLT FOR
DUST COVER
(REFER TO
FIG. 20)

CENTER
SWITCH
BOX ON
LOWER
FRONT
COVER

7

Ⓥ LOWER
FRONT
COVER

NOTE:
COVER PIECES
ARE ¾" MDF. END PIECE
IS ¾"-THICK HARDWOOD

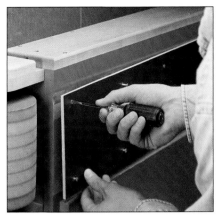

To make the platen easy to replace if it gets worn, plastic laminate is glued to ¹/₄" plywood, then simply screwed to the sleeve.

A dust hood will be added later, so to support it I slipped a bolt through a hole in the end piece before attaching the pieces of the pulley guard with screws.

SWITCH. All that's left is to add an on/off switch. After mounting it to the lower front cover, just run a power cord between the motor and the switch.

PLATEN

To produce a smooth, even surface when sanding, the sanding belt runs across a platen attached to the sleeve.

The platen (Y) is just a piece of plywood with plastic laminate glued to the front *(Fig. 19)*. (I used contact cement.)

Then, to ensure that the platen supports the entire width of the sanding belt, the top and bottom edges extend ¹/₄" above and below the rollers.

By attaching the platen with screws only (no glue), it's easy to replace if the laminate gets worn.

At this point, you can install the sanding belt and check the operation of the sander. This is covered in the Setup article beginning on page 124.

DUST HOOD

Once the belt is installed, add a dust hood that hooks up to your shop vacuum.

The dust hood is quite simple. Two sides (Z) and a back (AA) form a U-shaped assembly that corrals the dust *(Fig. 20)*. And a cap (BB) encloses the top.

Before gluing up the dust hood, you'll need to cut a hole in the back to fit the hose on your shop vacuum. Also, there's a slot that fits over the bolt in the pulley guard. This lets you slide the dust hood back and forth (see photos).

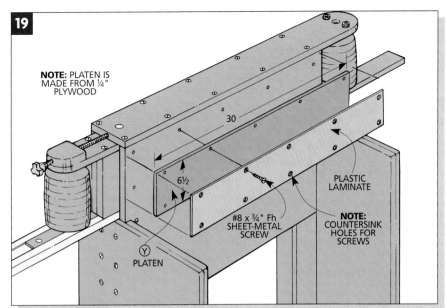

19

NOTE: PLATEN IS MADE FROM ¼" PLYWOOD

30

6½

#8 x ¾" Fh SHEET-METAL SCREW

PLASTIC LAMINATE

NOTE: COUNTERSINK HOLES FOR SCREWS

Y PLATEN

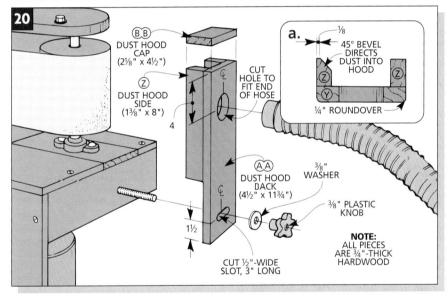

20

B B
DUST HOOD CAP
(2⅛" x 4½")

Z
DUST HOOD SIDE
(1⅜" x 8")

4

CUT HOLE TO FIT END OF HOSE

a.

⅛

45° BEVEL DIRECTS DUST INTO HOOD

Z

Z

Y

¼" ROUNDOVER

A A
DUST HOOD BACK
(4½" x 11¾")

⅜" WASHER

⅜" PLASTIC KNOB

NOTE: ALL PIECES ARE ¾"-THICK HARDWOOD

1½

CUT ½"-WIDE SLOT, 3" LONG

Most of the fine dust can be collected by sliding the dust hood all the way forward. This offers the most efficient dust collection.

Or you can move it back to allow long pieces to extend past the dust hood. Just loosen the plastic knob to adjust it.

FRONT TABLE

The sander has two sanding tables: a large front table that provides solid support for a workpiece, and a smaller end table. To take advantage of the full width of the belt, you can raise both of them up and down. This way, when you're sanding a workpiece, the thickness of the piece is centered on the length of the roller.

MOUNTING PANEL. The front table is held in place by a mounting panel (CC) *(Fig. 21)*. It's attached to the sleeve so the top edge is $1\frac{1}{8}$" above the legs *(Fig. 21b)*. This way, the mounting panel acts as a stop that keeps the tabletop from dropping below the belt *(Fig. 21a)*.

Before screwing the panel in place, I slipped two bolts into counterbored shank holes in the back. They're used as "hangers" to hold the table in place.

TABLE SUPPORTS. The next step is to add two $\frac{3}{4}$"-thick hardwood table supports. Each one consists of a slotted adjustment plate (DD) and a triangular support bracket (EE) that are glued and screwed together *(Fig. 22)*.

TABLETOP. Now you're ready to add the front tabletop (FF). It's a $1\frac{1}{8}$"-thick slab that I glued up out of hardwood *(Fig. 22)*. To "soften" its look and feel, I shaped the outside corners in a curve and rounded over all the edges except the one closest to the sanding belt.

To provide support right up next to the belt, the tabletop is attached to the supports so there's a slight overhang.

Note: To make it easy to position the tabletop, you may want to fit the table supports on the bolts first.

STOP. Finally, in order to sand the ends of a workpiece square, I added a stop (GG) with a guide block (HH) that can be clamped to the table *(Fig. 23)*.

END TABLE

This Edge Sander can also be used to sand a curved workpiece. Just push the workpiece against the curved sanding surface created by the idler roller.

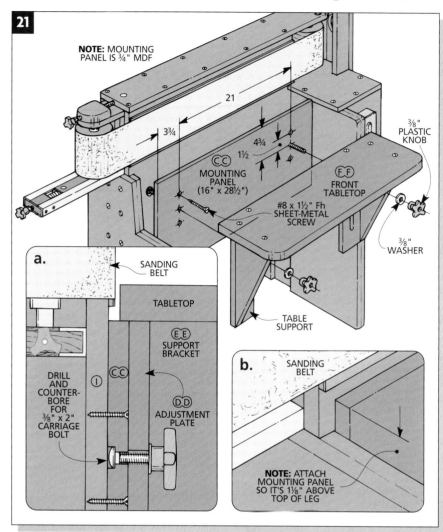

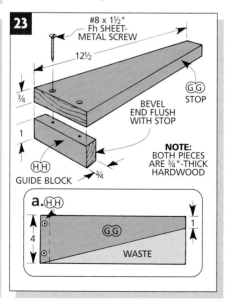

To provide support for the workpiece, I added a sturdy end table that "wraps" around the idler roller. It adjusts up and down, so you can set both tables at the same height to increase the overall size of the worksurface.

MOUNTING PLATE. The end table is held in place by a mounting plate (II). Once again, a bolt slipped through from the back serves as a hanger *(Figs. 24 and 24a)*. Screwing the mounting plate to the leg traps the head of the bolt.

TABLE SUPPORTS. The next step is to add two table supports. As before, each one starts out as a triangular support bracket (EE) *(Fig. 25)*. But here, I glued an extension strip (JJ) to each one. These strips do two things.

First, the strips are attached to a slotted adjustment plate (KK) to form a wide, U-shaped opening. This opening fits snug over the mounting plate (II) which keeps the end table aligned as you slide it up and down.

The second purpose of the extension strips has to do with the front table. Since it overhangs the leg, the strips act as spacers to provide clearance between the two tables *(Fig. 24a)*.

TABLETOP. Once the table supports are complete, you can add the end tabletop (LL). Like the front tabletop, it's made of 1⅛"-thick hardwood. But to provide support for the workpiece all the way around the idler roller, there's a curved notch on the inside edge.

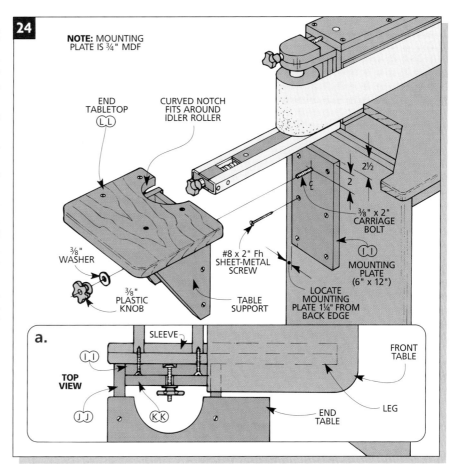

In addition, I cut and sanded a curve on the outside corners to protect the user from knocking against it. Then I eased the sharp edges by routing a roundover on all the edges except around the notch.

ATTACH TABLETOP. Now attach the tabletop so it overhangs the support by ¼". Also, you'll want to check that there's a consistent amount of clearance between the notch and the idler roller. ∎

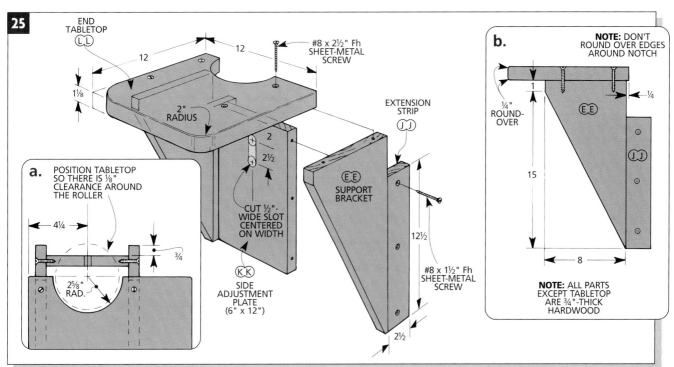

With the construction of the Edge Sander complete and the platen in place, you're almost ready to start putting it to use sanding your projects. Before you do any sanding of course, you'll have to install and adjust the sanding belt.

SANDING BELT. This Edge Sander is designed to use a 6"-wide sanding belt that's 89" long (see photo at bottom right of the next page).

Of course, a sanding belt that size isn't something you just pick up at your local hardware store or lumber yard. At one time you actually had to order these long, wide sanding belts specially made from a sanding supplies manufacturer. And you can still choose this option if you're ordering larger quantities, but we managed to find a couple of woodworking specialties suppliers that stock them. (A list of these sanding suppliers can be found in Sources on page 126.)

GRITS. Okay, so now you've found a place to get a sanding belt. The next question is, which grit should you choose? For most work, I've found that a 100-grit belt works just fine. But occasionally, if I need to "hog off" a lot of material, I'll switch to an 80-grit belt. And you may want to consider getting a finer grit belt (like 120-grit) for more delicate work.

RELEASE TENSION. Once you have the sanding belt in hand, the next step is to release the spring-loaded tension that's pushing the two rollers apart. To do this, just tighten the tension adjustment knob *(Fig. 1)*. This pushes the entire assembly (the idler roller, tracking system, and core) into the sleeve.

Changing Belts. *Tightening a quick-release tension device makes it easy to install or change a sanding belt.*

INSTALL BELT

Now it's just a matter of slipping the sanding belt over each of the rollers. To put tension back on the belt, loosen the adjustment knob *(Fig. 2)*. There's no need to "back" the adjustment mechanism all the way out. A half turn or so is all it takes to "pop" the core back out of the sleeve and apply tension to the belt.

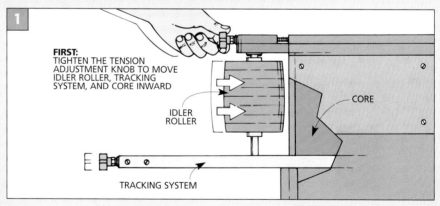

1

FIRST:
TIGHTEN THE TENSION ADJUSTMENT KNOB TO MOVE IDLER ROLLER, TRACKING SYSTEM, AND CORE INWARD

IDLER ROLLER

CORE

TRACKING SYSTEM

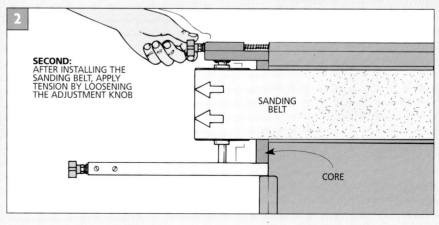

2

SECOND:
AFTER INSTALLING THE SANDING BELT, APPLY TENSION BY LOOSENING THE ADJUSTMENT KNOB

SANDING BELT

CORE

ADJUSTING THE BELT

Making the initial tracking adjustment on the Edge Sander not only keeps the sanding belt centered on the rollers, it also establishes the final position of the drive roller and its support.

To adjust the tracking, start by rotating the sanding belt by hand as you turn the tracking adjustment knob, raising or lowering the belt until it's centered (*Step 1*). Then tap the drive roller support in or out to position the belt on the drive roller (*Step 2*). Now flip the power switch quickly on and off to check the tracking.

Once you get the belt to track accurately, screw the drive roller support in place and cut off the waste at the end with a hand saw (*Step 3*).

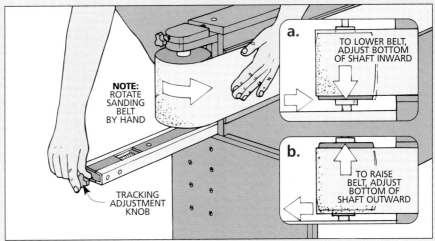

1 *To adjust the tracking, slide the sanding belt across the platen by hand. If the belt rides too high (detail 'a') or too low (detail 'b'), turn the adjustment knob to move the roller in the direction shown.*

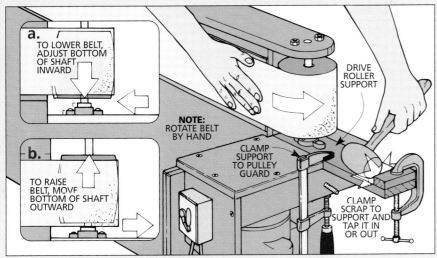

2 *Still turning the belt by hand, tap the support in or out to position the belt on the drive roller. Clamping the support snug (not tight) keeps the tension on the belt from shifting it out of position as you make the adjustment.*

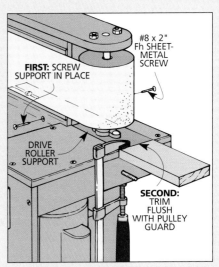

3 *Finally, secure the drive roller support with screws and cut the end flush with the pulley guard.*

Adjust Table. *The large front table on the shop-built Edge Sander provides rock-solid support when sanding a workpiece. To take advantage of the full width of the sanding belt, you can quickly adjust the height of the table. Just raise one end and lock it in place. Then repeat the process at the opposite end of the table.*

This 6" wide, 89"-long sanding belt is made for industrial sanders similar to the Edge Sander. Belts like this are available in a variety of grits and make quick work of the toughest sanding jobs. You'll likely have to order them from one of the Sources on page 126.

One of the first things we take into consideration when designing projects at *Woodsmith* is whether the hardware is affordable and easy to find. Does it complement the project? Is it appropriate? But, most important, is the hardware commonly available?

You'll probably be able to find most of the hardware and supplies for the projects in this book at your local hardware store or home center. Another source for some of the unusual items (like wooden wheels, plastic canisters, and springs) is hobby shops. Sometimes, though, you may have to order the hardware through the mail. If that's the case, we've tried to find reputable mail order sources with toll-free phone numbers and web sites (see Mail Order Sources box at right).

Note: We *strongly* recommend that you have all of your hardware and supplies in hand before you begin building any project in this book. There's nothing more discouraging than beginning a project and finding out that the hardware you ordered for it doesn't fit or is no longer available.

MAIL ORDER SOURCES

Some of the most important "tools" you can have are mail order catalogs. The ones listed below are filled with special hardware, tools, finishes, lumber, and supplies that can't be found at a hardware store or home center. You should be able to find many of the supplies for the projects in this book in one or more of these catalogs.

It's amazing what you can learn about woodworking by looking through these catalogs. If they're not currently in your shop, you may want to have them sent to you. You can order your catalog by phone or online.

Note: The information below was current when this book was printed. August Home Publishing does not guarantee these products will be available nor endorse any specific mail order company, catalog, or product.

THE WOODSMITH STORE

10320 Hickman Road
Clive, IA 50325
800-835-5084
www.woodsmithstore.com
Our own retail store filled with tools, hardware, books, finishing supplies. Though we don't have a catalog, we do send out items mail order. Call for information.

LEE VALLEY TOOLS

P.O. Box 1780
Ogdensburg, NY 13669-6780
800-871-8158
www.leevalley.com
Several catalogs actually, with hardware, tools, and finishes. A good source of hinges, catches, knobs, pulls, link belts, and sanding supplies.

ROCKLER WOODWORKING AND HARDWARE

4365 Willow Drive
Medina, MN 55340
800-279-4451
A very good hardware catalog, with a full line of hardware and tool supplies including knobs, inserts, glides, router bit guards, steel rules, and a nice variety of finishing supplies.

MCMASTER-CARR

P.O. Box 4355
Chicago, IL 60680-4355
www.mcmaster.com
For motors and mechanical items, this is the place. Springs, pulleys, mandrels, bearings, and pillow blocks are just a few of the items featured in their expansive catalog.

WOODCRAFT

560 Airport Industrial Park
Parkersburg, WV 26102-1686
800-225-1153
www.woodcraft.com
Just about everything for the woodworker, including all knds of knobs, threaded inserts, swivel casters, butt hinges, T-nuts, and wing nuts. They also stock mandrel assemblies, and grinding and buffing wheels.

GRAINGER

455 Knightsbridge Parkway
Lincolnshire, IL 60069-3639
877-503-2363
www.grainger.com
A definitive source of mechanical items such as motors, springs, belts, pulleys, mandrels, pillow blocks, and bearings.

SHOPSMITH

6530 Poe Ave.
Dayton, OH 45414-2591
800-543-7586
www.shopsmith.com
The 12" metal sanding disc used on the Disc Sander (pages 76-87) is available through Shopsmith.

KLINGSPOR'S WOODWORKING SHOP

P.O. Box 3737
Hickory, NC 28603-3737
800-228-0000
www.woodworkingshop.com
The premier catalog for sanding supplies of all shapes and sizes—including belt sander, disc sander, and drum sander belts. They also stock mandrels and pulleys.

AUGUST HOME
PUBLISHING COMPANY

President & Publisher: Donald B. Peschke
Executive Editor: Douglas L. Hicks
Project Manager/Senior Editor: Craig L. Ruegsegger
Creative Director: Ted Kralicek
Art Director: Doug Flint
Senior Graphic Designers: Robin Friend, Chris Glowacki
Assistant Editor: Joel Hess
Editorial Intern: Cindy Thurmond
Graphic Designers: Jonathan Eike, Vu Nguyen

Designer's Notebook Illustrator: Chris Glowacki
Photographer: Crayola England
Electronic Production: Douglas M. Lidster
Production: Troy Clark, Minniette Johnson
Project Designers: Chris Fitch, Ryan Mimick, Ken Munkel, Kent Welsh
Project Builders: Steve Curtis, Steve Johnson
Magazine Editors: Tim Robertson, Terry Strohman
Contributing Editors: Vincent S. Ancona, Jon Garbison, Phil Huber,
Brian McCallum, Bryan Nelson, Ted Raife
Magazine Art Directors: Cary Christensen, Todd Lambirth
Contributing Illustrators: Harlan Clark, Mark Higdon, David Kreyling,
Erich Lage, Roger Reiland, Kurt Schultz, Cinda Shambaugh, Dirk Ver Steeg

Corporate V.P., Finance: Mary Scheve
Controller: Robin Hutchinson
Production Director: George Chmielarz
Project Supplies: Bob Baker
New Media Manager: Gordon Gaippe

For subscription information about
Woodsmith and *ShopNotes* magazines, please write:
August Home Publishing Co.
2200 Grand Ave.
Des Moines, IA 50312
800-333-5075
www.augusthome.com/customwoodworking

Woodsmith® and *ShopNotes*® are registered trademarks of August Home
Publishing Co.

©2003 August Home Publishing Co.
All rights reserved. No part of this book may be reproduced in any form or by
any electronic or mechanical means, including information storage and retrieval
devices or systems, without prior written permission from the publisher, except
that brief passages may be quoted for reviews.
First Printing. Printed in U.S.A.

Oxmoor House®

Oxmoor House, Inc.
Book Division of Southern Progress Corporation
P.O. Box 2463, Birmingham, Alabama 35201

ISBN: 0-8487-2691-X
Printed in the United States of America

To order additional publications, call 1-205-445-6560.
For more books to enrich your life, visit **oxmoorhouse.com**